CLEAR WRITING

CLEAR WRITING

Marilyn B. Gilbert
Praxis Corporation
New York, New York

John Wiley & Sons, Inc.
New York • London • Sydney • Toronto

Library of Congress Catalog Card Number: 70-38627

ISBN 0-471-29896-4

Printed in the United States of America.

10 9 8 7 6 5 4

Preface

When I first started to teach writing, I made a common mistake: I thought my task was to teach the set of rules I had learned in school. I thought that if I taught these rules well, my students could apply them easily and write good prose forever after.

But I've learned that a writer doesn't simply follow rules. He has a million options and can express his meaning in many different ways. Once he selects a route, he applies the rules that will best help him convey his meaning. He may also break a rule now and then to achieve a special effect. His goal is always a clear, effective message; the rules are merely the tools he uses.

Clear Writing is really two books in one. The main part of the text teaches the basic techniques of writing and provides practice in using them. Then, for permanent reference or quick review, the Appendix presents a summary of these techniques in a concise guide and a set of charts. The guide and charts should be more useful for most people than any of the available style books designed for the professional writer.

In preparing *Clear Writing*, I carefully analyzed the everyday writing needs of people who are *not* professional writers, to isolate the most important principles. (In doing so I left out many details—some of which most students already know and some they probably never need to know.) I then organized these principles into sections called frames, defined each principle, explained why it is important, and demonstrated how it is applied. Then I asked the student to apply the principle and practice it.

The authors of many textbooks, programmed or otherwise, promise the student that he'll be an expert after finishing the book. Unfortunately I can't make this promise—there are no absolute right or wrong ways to write and no one has yet determined the characteristics of a "perfect writer." Our hope is always for improvement, and the students who tried out this program in early drafts are witnesses that the promise of improvement can be made.

Many people have given me help—my family, my friends, some college English teachers who identified student writing levels, some college students who read and tested the materials, the composition teachers who critiqued the manuscript, and various members of the John Wiley editorial and production staffs. I want to thank all of these people. But I received special help from Irene Brownstone of Wiley, and I thank Irene particularly.

MARILYN B. GILBERT

New York, New York
November 1971

How to Use This Book

Whether you are using this book in class or on your own, you should follow these steps:

1. Take the Preview at the beginning of the chapter and check your answers. Then mark the Self-Evaluation Record to see what you need to concentrate on and what you can skim over lightly.
2. Study the chapter. Answers to each frame are given below the dashed lines; keep them covered until you have worked as much as you can on each writing exercise. Then compare your own work with the suggested answers. (If your answers are very different from those given, be sure you understand why before going on.)
3. Complete the Review at the end of the chapter and mark the Self-Evaluation Record, to check your progress.
4. If you feel you need extra practice, do the Practice Exercises for that chapter in the Appendix. (Other composition books are sources of additional exercises, if necessary.) When you are sure you know how to apply each principle in the chapter, go on to the next chapter.
5. For review or reference at any time, turn to the Concise Guide for Clear Writing and to the charts in the Appendix.

Contents

Two Main Clauses Joined: With a Colon, 63
Run-on Sentences, 66
Using Your Judgment, 67
To Introduce a Set of Unlinked Sentences: Link with Transitions, 68
A Set of Unlinked Sentences: Link with Pronoun Replacements, 71
A Set of Unlinked Sentences: Repetitions for Emphasis, 72
A Set of Unlinked Sentences: Variety of Sentence Patterns and Lengths, 73
Linking Main Ideas, 77

Chapter 4 IMPROVING EMPHASIS 85

Descriptions can make your writing much more informative and much more interesting—provided they are handled effectively. This chapter teaches you techniques of using descriptions for emphasis.

Descriptions, 88
A Special Description: Not a Sentence, 89
A Special Description: A Sentence, 93
A Special Description: Expresses Ownership, 98
A Special Description: Obvious Words Are Left Out, 100
Copyediting Descriptions, 105

Chapter 5 SIMPLIFYING DESCRIPTIONS 110

Making complex descriptions both clear and interesting is easier than you think if you follow a simple rule or two: Here you'll learn now to reduce long clauses and phrases to concise, two-word descriptions.

Two-Word Description, 112
Joining Two-Word Descriptions, 116
A Three-Word Description, 117

Chapter 6 MAKING A LIST AND CHECKING IT TWICE 128

Here, you'll learn to arrange a set of similar ideas as a list under one common heading. This arrangement tells your reader exactly how all the ideas included in the list are related.

An Introduction to Any Complete List, 131
A Regular, Complete List, 133
An Outline List, 141
An Incomplete List, 144
Copyediting Lists, 149

Chapter 7 AGREEING TO BE CONSISTENT 154

Most of the time, making verbs agree with their subjects is as natural in writing as it is in speech. But in some situations, agreement is not obvious. This chapter will teach you how to handle agreement in those less-obvious situations.

The Word **ONE** Is the Subject, 157
A Pronoun Like **EVERYONE** Is the Subject, 159
The Word **NUMBER** Is the Subject, 161
A Collective Noun Is the Subject, 162
Using Pronouns to Avoid **NOT**, 165
Collective Nouns, 166
Combining Sentences, 166

Chapter 8 SPEAKING DIRECTLY 170

Shifts in point of view, in time, or in word order are other examples of a lack of agreement which can be very confusing to the reader. This chapter will teach you how to correct some of these lapses in style.

A Shift in Viewpoint or in Time, 174
The Word **ONLY** or **JUST**, 180
A Passive Sentence, 184

Chapter 9 PARING THE WORDS TO SPARE THE PARAGRAPH 194

Here, you'll learn how to spot those extra words that clutter up your writing. You will also practice weeding out this "deadwood."

The Word THERE, 197
The Word IT As the Subject, 198
Avoiding Wordy Expressions, 203
Avoiding Repetitions, 206
Reducing Paragraphs, 210

Chapter 10 BEING SPECIFIC 216

This chapter won't teach you the right words to use in each situation: The only way to learn this is to read the work of good writers, and to practice writing yourself. But here you will learn some "do's" and "don'ts" in selecting words to make your writing more interesting and effective.

Using Specific Verbs, 219
Using Specific Nouns, 222

No book on writing would be complete without giving you some instruction on the mechanics of writing. This chapter will teach you a set of rules for dealing with some of the more important details in writing, and it will give you practice in applying them.

These exercises give additional practice in applying the principles covered in each chapter of the book.

This is a reference to the principles of style which you may use to refresh your memory after you have completed the exercises in Clear Writing.

These are a set of charts which will be a complete reference to you as you write. Each chart lists the various situations that may occur, and for each entry provides suggested responses with examples.

CLEAR WRITING

Introduction

Many people imagine that just as soon as a professional writer gets an idea for a story or an article, he sits right down at the typewriter and pounds out a perfect manuscript.... But it doesn't happen that way for anyone—not even the professional.

Norman Mailer is an example. Here is a manuscript page from something he wrote.* Notice all the corrections:

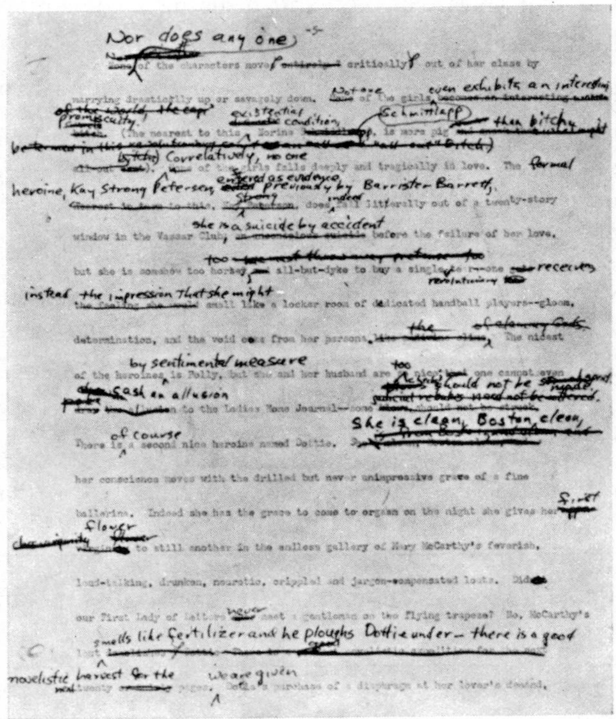
Nor does any one

[illegible] of the characters move [illegible] critically out of her class by

even exhibits an interesting

marrying drastically up or savagely down. Not one of the girls [illegible]

existential condition

Schmittlapp

then bitchy

promiscuity. (The nearest to this, Norine [illegible]pp, is more pig [illegible]

Correlatively, no one

[illegible]). [illegible] of the girls falls deeply and tragically in love. The formal

heroine, Kay Strong Petersen, entered as evidence previously by Barrister Barrett,

Strong

indeed

[illegible], does fall literally out of a twenty-story

she is a suicide by accident

window in the Vassar Club, [illegible] before the failure of her love,

too

but she is somehow too horsey, [illegible] all-but-dyke to buy a single [illegible] receives

instead the impression that she might

[illegible] smell like a locker room of dedicated handball players--gloom,

the

determination, and the void come from her person, [illegible] The nicest

by sentimental measure

too

of the heroines is Polly, but she and her husband are [illegible] one cannot even

cash an allusion

should not be [illegible]

[illegible] to the Ladies Home Journal--come [illegible]

She is clean, Boston clean,

of course

There is a second nice heroine named Dottie. [illegible]

her conscience moves with the drilled but never unimpressive grace of a fine

first

ballerina. Indeed she has the grace to come to orgasm on the night she gives her

flower

[illegible] to still another in the endless gallery of Mary McCarthy's feverish,

loud-talking, drunken, neurotic, crippled and jargon-compensated louts. Did

never

our First Lady of Letters [illegible] meet a gentleman on the flying trapeze? No, McCarthy's

smells like fertilizer and he ploughs Dottie under—there is a good

lout [illegible]

novelistic harvest for the

we are given

[illegible] twenty [illegible] pages. Dottie's purchase of a diaphragm at her lover's demand,

Manuscript page by Norman Mailer

*Note: He is writing about Mary McCarthy's novel <u>The Group.</u> From WRITERS AT WORK: The Paris Review Interviews, Third Series

Most good professional writers like Norman Mailer first jot down the main things they want to include so they can be sure they won't leave anything out. Then they fill in this skimpy outline with sentences and paragraphs. When they're all through, they have something very far from a finished product. But at least everything is there, and they have something to work from. As the famous short-story writer Guy de Maupassant put it, "Get black on white."

This book won't teach you what to write about or even how to get ideas. (Except occasionally in school, no one ever writes unless he already has something to write about.) But you should learn how to turn your very first attempt—writers call this a "first draft"—into clear, effective writing.

You can expect to make many changes between your first draft and your last. You'll also need to correct the common errors in punctuation, capitalization, and spelling that you're bound to make—especially if you type. These repairs could add up to a lot of rewriting. But you can save yourself most of it if you form the habit of using a convenient set of symbols—called copyediting symbols—that professional writers use.

Let's see what they are now, so you can use them throughout the book.

Printers and editors who deal with the printed page every day use a great number of these copyediting symbols. (Chart 1 on page 313 has fifteen of the most common ones.) But writers don't need to use nearly so many. In fact, they can get along nicely with just the four in the table below, plus two more you'll learn in Chapter 1.

Study this table carefully. In the examples note that the symbol shows exactly where the change belongs and what this change should be.

ERROR	SYMBOL	MEANS	EXAMPLE
A sentence, word, letter, or punctuation mark is left out.	∧	Add or insert.	Copyediting symbols ^are^ helpful.
A word, letter, or punctuation mark is wrong.	(delete mark)	Take out or delete.	Copyediting symbols are ~~are~~ helpful.
A lower-case (small) letter should be a capital.	≡	Capitalize.	copyediting symbols are helpful.
A capital letter should be a lower-case (small) letter.	/	Use a lower-case (small) letter.	Copyediting Symbols are helpful.

The two sentences below have several errors. Using the copyediting symbols, see if you can CORRECT them all.

(1) Her name is jane, and She is prety.

(2) copyediting marks Are helpful too the writer

CHECK YOUR ANSWERS

- - - - - - - - - - - - - - - - - - -

(1) Her name is jane, and She is prety.

Her name is jane, and She is prety. pretty.

(2) copyediting marks Are helpful too the writer.

Probably the main advantage of copyediting symbols is that they help you to keep track of all the changes you want to make in your work. But you don't actually have to make these changes until you're ready to retype a new draft.

Four errors in the letter below have already been detected, but there are still sixteen more. See how many you can find, and USE the copyediting marks to point out the changes that are needed.

Remember,

^ means "insert"

means "delete"

/ means "make a small letter"

≡ means "capitalize"

Dear Mr. Rogers,

you should begin to use copediting marks In your office becasue these symbols have exact the same meaning too the Typist as tHey have to the Writer First, the write can correct his manuscrip. Then, the typist types the pags, being sure to mak all the Changes that ar indicated by the copyediting marks. the advantag are clear.

Sincerely,

Mary Page

- - - - - - - - - - - - - - - - - - -

Suggestions

you should begin to use copediting marks In your office becasue these symbols have exact the same meaning too the Typist as tHey have to the Writer First, the write can correct his manuscrip Then, the typist types the pags, being sure to mak all the Changes that ar indicated the copyediting marks. the advantag are clear.

Samples (a) and (b) show two common kinds of errors and how they should be changed:

(a) Only a few schools are offer courses in black history this year.

(b) His pass record is good, for a politician.

With the missing -ing after the word offer, sample (a) didn't make any sense. Sample (b) didn't make sense before it was copyedited either because pass means "to go ahead." Errors like these are hard to spot because they are already words—just not the right words.

As you get more practice in criticizing your own writing, you'll be able to spot more of the errors. For now, pick up as many as you can, using the COPYEDITING marks to point out how to correct them. And ALWAYS keep your dictionary at your side, to use whenever you aren't sure about a spelling. It is NEVER cheating to look up a word in the dictionary!

Try COPYEDITING these sentences:

(1) Enviormental matters are now of grate concern.

(2) cigarette advertising is now ban from television.

(3) He pass all his coarses last Year.

(4) A football player don't dare miss his classes.

(5) Adolp hitler was a paintner—a house paintner.

(6) Most city schoo are overcrowd, and Teacher are underpayed.

(7) Southren colleges are begin to deal with things poeple said they wood never face.

(8) The station isnt televise the footbal game next weak.

(9) Wimen's libration groups have already picket some magazines.

(10) United states Citizens are get advantages When they travel.

Suggestions

(1) Enviormental matters are now of grate concern.

(2) cigarette advertising is now ban from television.

(3) He pass all his coarses last year.

(4) A football player don't dare miss his classes.

(5) Adolp hitler was a paintner—a house paintner.

(6) Most city schoo are overcrowd, and teacher are underpayed.

(7) Southren colleges are begin to deal with things poeple said they wod never face.

(8) The station isnt televise the footbal game next weak.

(9) Wimen's libration groups have already picket some magazines.

(10) United states citizens are get advantages when they travel.

Keeping your dictionary handy, COPYEDIT this paragraph for common errors.

(a) Some National sport is always claim our our attension. (b) But the season overlap so much that we can never watch one compleet season in one major sport without miss some of the exsitement in another. (c) for exampel, football begin when baseball really begin to get interesting. (d) Basketball and hosckey begin at the peek of the Football season. (e) then, just as basketball and hokcey are reach thier climacts, baseball start over again.

- - - - - - - - - - - - - - - - - - -

Suggestions

(a) Some National sport is always claim our our attension. (b) But the season overlap so much that we can never watch one compleet season in one major sport without miss some of the exsitement in another. (c) for exampel, football begin when baseball really begin to get interesting.

(d) Basketball and hoeckey begin at the peek of the Football season.

(e) then, just as basketball and hokeey are reach thier climaets, baseball start over again.

COPYEDIT this passage for common errors, and don't hesitate to use your dictionary.

(a) When the seventys open, the pollsters disclosed that Student taste in reading was not waht we had thought. (b) Ernest Hemingway was first, although we had thought his day had long since past. (c) George Orwell was second, and J. D. Salinger was thrid—two old standbys on college reading lists. (d) But The big supprise was Kurt Vonnegut, who rank just behind Jacqueline susann.

- -

Suggestions

(a) When the seventies opened, the pollsters disclosed that student taste in reading was not what we had thought. (b) Ernest Hemingway was first, although we had thought his day had long since passed. (c) George Orwell was second, and J.D. Salinger was third—two old standbys on college reading lists. (d) But the big surprise was Kurt Vonnegut, who ranked just behind Jacqueline Susann.

Now go on to Chapter 1.

CHAPTER ONE

Reading for Sense

Remember, everybody can write a first draft. This book teaches you how to turn that first draft—no matter how crude it may be—into clear, effective English. With the copyediting marks you have just learned (plus two more coming up), you can indicate all the repairs you need to make.

But, before worrying about whether all the commas and the periods are in the right places, you should always read through a first draft just to be sure it makes sense. Are the ideas divided into sensible units or paragraphs? Are the sentences within each paragraph arranged in some sensible order? Do any sentences merely repeat an idea you've expressed before? These are the questions you'll consider in this chapter.

Before you start, however, turn to the preview of Chapter 1, which follows. There will be a similar preview before each chapter that will help you find out what kinds of things you already know well enough to skim over lightly and what you will need to concentrate on.

PREVIEW

1. The passage below has not been paragraphed. Put a check (✓) beside each sentence that you think should begin a new paragraph.

(1) The air and water in Ticonderoga, New York, are now purer than they have been for years. (2) Residents claim that they are breathing more easily and having many fewer problems keeping their houses clean.

(3) What happened was that contamination from the town's main industry, a big paper mill, was checked. (4) This situation seems like a rare success story in pollution control. (5) However, just below the surface of closeby Lake Champlain is a 300-acre mound of sludge left over from the paper mill and other similar industries dating back 200 years. (6) Even though the black ooze has stopped coming from the mill, gas bubbles still rise from the decomposing sludge. (7) Bits of decaying material occasionally come to the surface. (8) Residents are certain that the sludge

is a continuing threat and must be removed. (9) But the paper company contends that it is not responsible for sludge that others also dumped.

(10) And, in any case, all of it was dumped when this sort of disposal was considered reasonable.

2. One of the sentences in this paragraph is probably out of order, Read the paragraph first and then answer the two questions following it:

(1) Italian Americans gathered for their second annual rally in New York City in a party mood, eager to celebrate Italian unity. (2) The rally opened with a prayer for the life of Joseph Colombo instead. (3) Their party mood was soon over, when Joseph Colombo, reputed head of the Mafia, was shot and wounded. (4) For the next three hours the crowd responded listlessly to politicians and entertainers. (5) Their minds were mostly on reports of Joseph Colombo's condition.

(a) Which sentence do you think is out of order? __________

(b) Where do you think it would fit in better? __________

3. One sentence in this paragraph contains information that is given in other sentences. Read the paragraph to decide which it is:

(1) Many colleges across the country now offer courses in women's studies. (2) These colleges are trying to correct their image of favoring male students. (3) These courses examine the role of women in history and discuss how women can affect current social problems such as drugs, pollution, and racism. (4) The main reason for women's studies, the colleges claim, is that women have been neglected in traditional disciplines. (5) The colleges are also trying to change the impression that women are "second-class citizens."

Which was the unnecessary sentence? __________

Suggested Answers

1. You might have paragraphed the passage in several ways. One possibility was to start a new paragraph with sentence 4. But you might have started with sentence 5 instead. You might have had just two paragraphs, or you might have started a third paragraph with sentence 8.

2. (a) Sentence 2.

   (b) Between sentence 3 and sentence 4.

3. Sentence 2.

   (It repeats information included in sentences 4 and 5.)

If you answered each question correctly, you can just lightly review the chapter. Otherwise, you should mark the Self-Evaluation Record for Chapter 1 appropriately. Under the column Preview put a check (✓) alongside any question that you answered satisfactorily. The blanks will then show you what you need to concentrate on.

SELF-EVALUATION RECORD FOR CHAPTER 1

	PREVIEW	FRAMES	REVIEW
Question 1		1 through 4, 6, 11	
Question 2		5 through 8, 11	
Question 3		9 through 11	

Continue to frame 1.

PARAGRAPHING

1. Writing and speaking are very similar. One major difference is that in writing we must group our ideas into paragraphs. There are no fixed rules about when to start a new paragraph; it can be any length, although the "average" paragraph has four to five sentences. Each sentence, however, must be related to a central thought.

In reading a first draft for sense alone, you may find that you have combined two thoughts that would be more effective if they were apart. To indicate this, you can insert a special paragraphing symbol (¶) right before the sentence that starts the new thought.

Notice that this paragraphing symbol looks something like a capital P for Paragraph. So ¶ is a shortcut way to indicate that a new idea, or approach, is about to begin.

As you read this passage, find the sentence that starts a new thought:

(1) In Manhattan few workers—if any—are able to earn their living directly from the environment. (2) Most Manhattanites must sit at desks and do paper-and-pencil work. (3) Or they can sell man-made goods or their own services to one another. (4) Yet close by, in Southern New Jersey, is a huge tract of wilderness, called the Pine Barrens, which offers many opportunities for earning a living directly from the soil. (5) In early spring the natives of the Pine Barrens can gather sphagnum moss from the lowland forests there. (6) In June and July they can pick blueberries. (7) In August and September they can pick cranberries. (8) In winter they can chop cordwood and burn charcoal. (9) And then soon it is spring, so they can start all over again.

Did you say that sentence 4 was the beginning of the paragraph? INSERT the paragraphing symbol right before sentence 4, and ANSWER these questions briefly in your own words.

(a) What would you say is the main thought of paragraph 1?

(b) What would you say is the main thought of paragraph 2?

- -

Suggestions

....one another. ¶ (4) Yet close by, in Southern New Jersey, is ...

(a) Manhattanites don't earn their living directly from the environment.
(b) Natives of the Pine Barrens may earn their living from the land if they choose to do so.

Another way to paragraph this passage might be to start the new paragraph with sentence 5. In that case the whole first paragraph would be an introduction to the second, which describes how natives of the Pine Barrens may earn their living directly from the land.

Still another possibility is to start one new paragraph with sentence 4 and another with sentence 5. Then sentence 4 would stand alone as a bridge from the first paragraph to the third.

2. Assume that the passage below is your first draft. As you read it through for sense, you find that there are really two thoughts and that they would make a better impression if they were separated. INSERT the paragraphing symbol where you think the second paragraph ought to begin:

(1) Communes have sprung up across the country, from East to West and from North to South. (2) Young people enjoy the communal, or "communistic," style of living, which lets them share similar ideas with their fellow "communists." (3) They also find that living in these communes is economical because they can divide expenses with other young people like themselves. (4) But communes are not new. (5) Historians believe that Jesus belonged to a commune, for example. (6) And there were communes throughout the history of Europe, and later in the United States. (7) Many of these earlier communes, however, were formed for the advantages of self-government.

Now ANSWER these questions briefly in your own words.

(a) What do you think is the central thought of paragraph 1?

(b) What do you think is the central thought of paragraph 2?

\- - - - - - - - - - - - - - - - - -

<u>Suggestions</u>

... like themselves. ¶ (4) But communes are not new. (5) Historians....

(a) The advantages of communes to young people nowadays.
(b) The historical meaning of communes.

3. Again, assume that this passage is a first draft. READ it through and then PARAGRAPH it by inserting the paragraphing symbol appropriately.

(1) In the nineteenth century, before women had the vote, Lucy Stone was an ardent suffrage leader. (2) But she wanted to demonstrate woman's equality with man in other ways too. (3) For example, she refused to take her husband's name. (4) Although she was legally "Mrs. Henry Brown Blackwell," she insisted on being called "Lucy Stone." (5) Many emancipated women of the early twentieth century followed Lucy Stone's example. (6) But perhaps none of these women had the cooperation of her husband as much as Betty Gram. (7) During the dozen years that she was married to the political commentator Raymond Swing, he was known as "Raymond Gram Swing." (8) He went back to "Raymond Swing" only after he married another woman in 1945.

In your own words DESCRIBE the main thought of each paragraph.

- - - - - - - - - - - - - - - - - - -

Suggestions

¶ (5).

(a) Lucy Stone showed her equality by refusing to take her husband's name.

(b) Other women later followed Lucy Stone's example.

Perhaps you thought sentence 3 could start a new paragraph as well as sentence 5. In that case the first paragraph would be an introduction to the views of Lucy Stone. The second paragraph, starting with sentence 3, would be an example of the way she showed equality with her husband. The third paragraph would explain how others followed Lucy's example.

MISPLACED SENTENCES

4. As you read over your work to see that it makes sense, you may notice that a sentence is out of place. But you don't necessarily have to write the paragraph over again. You can use another copyediting symbol—the shift—to show where the sentence belongs. The shift symbol looks like this: . The misplaced sentence is circled, and an arrow is drawn from the circled sentence to where it fits.

Read this paragraph and note how the sentences were rearranged.

(1) Commercial aviation has some colorful terms, or jargon. (2) Two interesting examples are no-show and go-show. (3) The no-show is a person who holds a reservation but doesn't cancel when he changes his plans. (4) As a result, the plane goes off with an empty seat. (5) A go-show goes to the airport with a ticket but without a reservation. (6) He hopes that some no-show will supply a seat for him at the last minute. (7) The no-show is a nuisance to airline officials.

Did you follow the directions and read sentence 7 before you read sentence 5? If not, the ideas bounced from no-show to go-show and back to no-show again. But the paragraph is clear if you read the sentences in their corrected order.

5. A good, informative paragraph usually has some details and examples to illustrate the central thought. Common sense generally suggests where these details and examples are most effective. For instance, in a paragraph explaining how the United States became involved in Vietnam, events could be described in a chronological order—that is, in order of time.

A chronological treatment is only one possibility. You might arrange your examples from most important to least important, from least important to most important, or in any other sensible way that you think would be effective.

READ this paragraph, and look for one sentence that doesn't seem to be in a sensible place. USE the shift symbol to put this sentence where it will fit in better:

(1) Marist College, a small liberal arts college in New York State, has an unusual recruitment program. (2) These recruiters get college credits, salaries, and the use of cars. (3) Instead of sending administrators to high schools to recruit freshmen for the following year, Marist sends some of its own juniors and seniors. (4) The college students give the high schoolers a view of what it is like to be a student at Marist. (5) The high school students find that what actual Marist students say is more meaningful than the usual information the Marist administrators give.

- -

Sentence 2 belongs just before sentence 4:

. . . State, has an unusual recruitment program. (2) These recruiters get college credits, salaries, and the use of cars. (3) Instead of sending administrators to high schools to recruit freshmen for the following year, Marist sends some of its own juniors and seniors. (4) The . . . .

6. This time MAKE any changes in the paragraphing and sentence order that you think would improve the passage:

(a) First, put the paragraphing symbol in front of any sentence that should begin a new paragraph.

(b) Second, transfer any sentence that is out of order.

(1) The word blooper, meaning "blunder" or "error," is fairly new in slang. (2) In a famous example before the days of television, a beloved entertainer called Uncle Don was reading the Sunday funnies over the air. (3) When he finished and said "goodbye" tenderly, he then assumed he was genuinely off the air; unfortunately, he wasn't. (4) Usually, the error is unintentional, like a slip of the tongue by some well-known personality that makes him appear ridiculous. (5) What the kids heard went something like this: "There! That ought to hold the damned little brats for awhile." (6) The word blooper is also used in baseball slang,

but in a different sense. (7) It means a lightly hit fly ball that drops just beyond the infield and goes for a base hit. (8) This kind of ball used to be called a "Texas leaguer."

- - - - - - - - - - - - - - - - - -

Suggestions

(a) [illegible] (6).

(b) Sentence 4 belongs in front of sentence 2.

7. For convenience the passages so far have consisted of only one or two paragraphs. You have to check longer passages for sense too. But you also have to check the order of the paragraphs.

Assume that the short report below is a first draft. As you read it for sense, you will note that one whole paragraph is out of order. You can use the shift symbol to transfer it. CIRCLE the misplaced paragraph and DRAW an arrow from it to its proper place.

(1) An anthropologist, Dr. Alan Harwood, has found that many Puerto Ricans in New York classify diseases, medicines, and foods according to a "hot-cold" theory. A "hot" disease is to be treated with "cold" foods and medicines, and vice versa. So, if a doctor prescribes a treatment running counter to this theory, his advice may be ignored.

(2) As an example, newborn babies often develop rashes, which the Puerto Ricans say are hot diseases caused by eating hot foods. Unfortunately, the evaporated milk that doctors recommend for newborns is a hot food. Whole milk is a cool food, but it is also hard for most newborns to digest. Nevertheless, many new mothers change the formula from evaporated milk to whole milk to prevent their babies from getting rashes.

(3) Dr. Hardwood suggests that doctors treating Puerto Ricans should adapt their remedies to the hot-cold system. To neutralize the infant formula, for instance, they can tell the mothers to add harmless barley water, which is a cool substance. To neutralize the hotness of vitamins or other medicines, they can advise their patients to take them with cool fruit juices or herb teas.

(4) During pregnancy many of the women avoid the hot substances such as vitamins and iron supplements to prevent their babies from having rashes and birth marks. Also, many people refuse to take penicillin, which is a hot medicine, when they have a hot disease like diarrhea or a rash.

- - - - - - - - - - - - - - - - - - -

Paragraphs 3 and 4 should be reversed.

8. Occasionally you may find that several sentences are out of order—not just one—in which case you wouldn't want to use the shift symbol to put the sentences in order because it would be too confusing. One solution is to number the sentences.

Let's take an example of a paragraph that you found was rearranged haphazardly. Instead of rewriting the paragraph, just number all the sentences according to a sequence that you think would be the most sensible.

(a) In 1955, in Montgomery, Alabama, Mrs. Rosa Parks boarded the Cleveland Avenue bus after her day's work as a seamstress. (b) Progress in Civil Rights had a very humble beginning. (c) And the rest of the story is really the story of the sixties. (d) But shortly afterward the bus driver told her that she would have to give her seat to a white person, according to the local custom then. (e) She was tired, and the corns on her feet hurt so much that she folded into an empty seat. (f) Mrs. Parks refused to obey and was arrested. (g) Her arrest triggered the Montgomery bus boycott, led by Dr. Martin Luther King, and the Supreme Court ruling that bus segregation in Montgomery was illegal.

- - - - - - - - - - - - - - - - - - -

Suggestions

2	(a)	7	(c)	3	(e)	6	(g)
1	(b)	4	(d)	5	(f)		

A REPETITIOUS SENTENCE

9. Something else to look for as you read for sense is a sentence that is merely repetitious. Because you use different words, you may repeat an idea without realizing it.

The passage below illustrates. READ it and see if you can figure out which sentence was unnecessary.

---

(1) The Korean language has no articles (a word like a, an, or the). (2) As a result, Koreans learning to speak English have an especially difficult time learning when to use the and when to leave it out. (3) Their own language doesn't have this concept. (4) Many of them take the easy way out and simply omit the article. (5) This is one solution; however, it is a solution that can make even complex speech patterns sound immature.

Did you see that sentence 3 was just another way of saying what sentence 1 said? It added nothing except some interference with the sense of the paragraph.

We can also use the delete symbol to take out an unnecessary sentence. Draw a delete line through sentence 3 above.

- - - - - - - - - - - - - - - - - -

(3) ~~Their own language doesn't have this concept.~~

10. You wouldn't intentionally bore your reader by telling him the same thing twice. But you might do it unintentionally—and even fool yourself—because you've changed some of the words.

READ the passage below, assuming that one sentence merely repeats an idea that was said earlier. USE a delete line to cross it out.

(1) One surprising aftershock of an earthquake is its psychological effect on children. (2) The change is sudden and complete in one day. (3) Children who were happy and secure right before an earthquake become insecure right after it. (4) Unexpectedly, they get a psychological reaction from the earthquake. (5) Psychologists feel that somehow the children's shaky emotions are related to a fear of being separated from their parents.

- - - - - - - - - - - - - - - - - -

...insecure right after it. (4) ~~Unexpectedly, they get a psychological reaction from the earthquake.~~ (5) Psychologists feel ....

COPYEDITING PARAGRAPHS

11. This passage includes some paragraphing errors. Make the changes that will improve it:

(a) First, separate different thoughts into different paragraphs.

(b) Next, transfer any misplaced sentences to their proper places.

(c) Last, cross out any sentences that are repetitious.

(1) Truman Capote, well-known author of Breakfast at Tiffany's and In Cold Blood, has some unusual writing habits. (2) He claims that he is a "completely horizontal author." (3) In fact, he says that he can't think unless he is lying down, either in bed or on a couch. (4) He must also have his cigarettes and coffee as he writes, so that he can puff and sip. (5) But as the day progresses, he too progresses—to mint tea, to sherry, and on to martinis. (6) He must be lying down, however. (7) As you would expect, Mr. Capote doesn't use a typewriter for his early drafts. (8) Then he completely revises his first draft—again in longhand. (9) He writes his first draft in longhand and in pencil.

- -

Suggestions

(a) ¶(7).
(b) Sentence 9 belongs right before sentence 8.
(c) Delete sentence 6.

You might want to leave in a sentence like sentence 6, just for a humorous effect. But this would depend on what you want to achieve, as we'll discuss in later chapters.

Now go on to the review of Chapter 1.

REVIEW

1. The passage below has not been paragraphed. Put a paragraphing symbol beside each sentence that you think should begin a new paragraph.

(1) Once just a loud noise that thrilled the young, rock music has become respectable. (2) It has a history, a culture, and even an encyclopedia. (3) And, besides, it has some academic recognition. (4) The New School for Social Research now has a course called "Atomic Youth and the Rock Mushroom." (5) "What is rock saying? (6) How did it take root? (7) Where is it going?" (8) These are the question that the course description asks. (9) It attempts to discover answers to these questions by informal methods. (10) These methods include invitations to makers of the rock culture to come in and "rap" with the students. (11) Among the guests are disk jockeys, record company executives, promoters, and performers. (12) The instructor is Michael

Luckman, a self-styled radical. (13) Luckman regards rock music as "the music of liberation." (14) And he believes that by ignoring rock music older people fail to get the message of the lyrics, which "express better than any other medium what young people are thinking."

2. One of the sentences in this paragraph is probably out of place. Use the shift symbol to indicate where it would fit in better.

(1) In a strange way the New School was responsible for importing Beatlemania to New York in the sixties. (2) Sid Bernstein, the promoter who did it, was taking a class there that required the reading of British newspapers. (3) Bernstein paid the Beatles $6,500 for two shows in Carnegie Hall back in 1964. (4) And in 1965 he paid them $180,000 for one concert in Shea Stadium. (5) He read of the Beatles and the phenomenal happening in Liverpool long before the trade magazines here picked up the story.

3. Two sentences in this paragraph say just about the same things. Decide which of them you think is the better sentence and delete the other.

(1) Sid Bernstein worries about the attitudes of young rock stars who cancel a show because it's "too far away." (2) He believes that these kids don't know the value of money. (3) Some of these stars are making $15,000 a night. (4) They don't appreciate how much money that is. (5) But before they made it big, they were happy to do four shows a night, 45 minutes each. (6) And they never finished in 44 minutes for fear that someone might throw something. (7) In fact they continued for 48 minutes, just to be sure.

Suggested Answers

1. You might have started a new paragraph with sentence 4 or 5, and another new paragraph with sentence 12. Another possibility is to start one new paragraph with sentence 8 and another new paragraph with sentence 12.

2. Sentence 5 is probably out of order and would fit in better between sentences 2 and 3.

3. Either sentence 2 or 4 probably should be deleted. Sentence 4 seems to express the idea more precisely.

If your answers were similar, put checks (√) in the REVIEW column of the Self-Evaluation Record for Chapter 1 (page 9) and go on to Chapter 2. Otherwise, study the frames covering material in the questions you didn't check.

CHAPTER TWO

Matching the Sentence to the Idea

Once you're sure that all the paragraphs make sense, you've done the hard part of the writing job. Then you're ready to put the magic into the words.

We say that all writing is partly an art and partly a craft. The original idea and the right approach are the art. So far, nobody who has the art has figured out how to teach it to anyone else. But writing clear and interesting sentences is a craft that can be taught. The rest of this book is devoted to it.

Look at the first example. Do you see any difference in meaning between samples (1) and (2)?

(1) Conservationists got a judicial ban in Morris County. Nine towns can no longer use Jersey City's water supply. It was already overtaxed. Many conservationists have tried to halt pollution in this way. New Jersey conservationists have scored the first success.

(2) New Jersey conservationists were first to score against pollution by getting a judicial ban that prevented nine towns in Morris County from using Jersey City's already overtaxed water supply.

These samples present the same information. Sample 1, however, has five sentences, all short and following the same rhythm (or pattern), as if the five ideas they express were equally important. Sample 2, on the other hand, has only one sentence, which shows that there is only one main idea here: that New Jersey was first to score against pollution. The less important ideas clustering around the main one are in other forms, indicating that they are merely supportive.

As you saw in Chapter 1, most paragraphs have more than one important idea. Maybe they have four or five. Later, in Chapter 3, we'll consider some ways to express the relationship between them. But here we're going to look at only single main ideas. In particular, you should learn

(a) how to express a main idea,
(b) some ways to add supporting ideas and details to a main idea to make it more meaningful,
(c) how to combine two or three short sentences with only one main idea so that the reader can tell what is most important.

To find out how you can make best use of this chapter, turn to the preview of Chapter 2.

PREVIEW

1. Underline the subject once and the verb twice in the supporting clause only.

(a) Although the men liked her, she wouldn't date them.

(b) When I heard the rain, I closed the windows.

(c) There would still be hostility even if we ended the war.

2. Any of the words listed below can be inserted in the following sentence. Match each word with the description of its function.

Children like to work ________ they think that it's play.

________ (a) if
________ (b) while
________ (c) since
________ (d) so that
________ (e) although

(i) Makes the supporting clause a condition for the main idea of the sentence.
(ii) Makes the supporting clause give a reason for the main idea.
(iii) Shows that the main event occurs despite the supporting clause.
(iv) Makes the supporting clause suggest when the main event occurred.
(v) Makes the supporting clause give the purpose for the main idea.

3. Punctuate these sentences:

(a) After trying on every dress in the store she finally bought one that was too big.

(b) Students today as everybody knows are very different from students ten or even five years ago.

(c) When I read the commencement address in the newspaper I was surprised to find it so sympathetic to the conservative point of view.
(d) The Democratic Party which convened in Chicago in 1968 put on a lively show that year.

4. Rewrite this foolish sentence to make it sensible:

As a liberal, many of his arguments sound racist to me.

5. Rewrite these three sentences as one sentence, with only one main idea:

Hard-cover books are expensive nowadays. Many people buy paperback novels. Paperback novels are within reach of their pocketbooks.

Suggested Answers

1. (a) Although the men liked her, she wouldn't date them.
   (b) When I heard the rain, I closed the windows.
   (c) There would still be hostility even if we ended the war.

2. i (a) ii (c) iii (e)
   iv (b) v (d)

3. (a) After trying on every dress in the store, she finally bought one that was too big.
   (b) Students today, as everybody knows, are very different from students ten or even five years ago.
   (c) When I read the commencement address in the newspaper, I was surprised to find it so sympathetic to the conservative point of view.
   (d) The Democratic Party, which convened in Chicago in 1968, put on a lively show that year.

4. As a liberal, I think many of his arguments sound racist ~~to me.~~

5. Since hard-cover books are expensive nowadays, many people buy paperback novels which are within reach of their pocketbooks.

If you got all the answers right in the preview of Chapter 2, you can go quickly through the chapter. Otherwise you should map out a more thorough plan on your Self-Evaluation Record for Chapter 2. In the PREVIEW column put a check (✓) beside any question that you could already handle.

SELF-EVALUATION RECORD FOR CHAPTER 2

	PREVIEW	FRAMES	REVIEW
Questions 1 and 2		1 through 8	
Questions 3		9 through 12 17 through 22	
Question 4		13 through 16	
Question 5		23 through 26	

This record shows what frames you should concentrate on. Now on to frame 1.

MAIN CLAUSES AND SUPPORTING CLAUSES

1. As young children, we first think, then speak, and later write in simple sentences. But, when we're grown, we speak in more complex sentence patterns to fit our more complex thoughts and feelings. So that we can consider how to put these ideas together in our writing, we first need to take them apart.

The two big divisions of a sentence are the main clause and the supporting clause. (Maybe you call a main clause a "simple sentence" or an "independent clause" and a supporting clause a "dependent clause.") Actually, the two clauses are alike, except that a main clause can be a sentence by itself and a supporting clause cannot. So you would probably use a main clause to express what you feel is a main idea and a supporting clause for what you feel is supportive—something that isn't important enough to be a sentence by itself.

To illustrate, look over these clauses. Together they make a sentence. But one clause could also be a sentence by itself, with a period after it, because it's a main clause carrying a main idea. Which do you think it is?

(a) While Abe Fortas was a Supreme Court justice
(b) He wrote a brilliant explanation of the right to dissent

You were right if you said "sample (b)." Sample (a) is just a supporting clause. As a test, you can read the two samples aloud. At the end of sample (a) your voice trails off, as if you were expecting something else; but at the end of sample (b) your voice drops, as if you had come to some sort of natural ending.

Did you notice that without the word while sample (a) would be a main clause too? And note that we could easily turn sample (b) into a supporting clause just by adding a special starting word, as here:

(c) Because he wrote a brilliant explanation of the right to dissent

Try the voice test on these two ideas. (The period was purposely left out.) WRITE "M" beside the clause you think expresses a main idea:

________ (a) When Martin Luther King chose to break the rules of dissent
________ (b) He always accepted the consequences with grace

- - - - - - - - - - - - - - - - - -

M (b)

MAIN CLAUSES

2. When you combine two ideas, the idea that you think is most important should be expressed as the main clause.

As a writer, you set the stage for what you want to say, just as a director of a play sets the stage for his drama. You also work with the same raw materials. In a drama

(a) there is some primary action;
(b) some actor controls it;
(c) everyone else is part of the supporting cast, and every other thing is part of the supporting props or background.

Similarly in writing, every main clause has some primary action and an actor to handle it. A verb expresses the action. The person or thing controlling this verb, or performing this action, is called the subject, and it may be either a noun or its pronoun. All the other words are a part of the supporting background.

First, let's consider the basic parts of a main clause. These are labeled in samples (a) and (b) as "S" for "subject" and "V" for "verb."

(a) The voting age was changed to eighteen.
S V

(b) Logic guides the thoughts of a reasonable man.
S V

Notice that all the unlabeled words in each sample are a part of the supporting background for the subject (noun or pronoun) and the verb.

See if you can IDENTIFY the subject and the verb in each main clause. DRAW one line beneath the subject, two lines beneath the verb.

(1) Long hair is putting many barbers out of business.

(2) He smokes "pot" regularly.

(3) The best teachers are not always the most popular ones.

(4) Ecology has recently become a key political issue.

(5) Young people often feel bitter about their elders.

- - - - - - - - - - - - - - - - - -

(1) hair is putting

(2) He smokes

(3) teachers are

(4) Ecology has become

(5) people feel

3. Suppose we could put all English sentences into a computer to find out which kind is most common. We would probably discover it is a main clause by itself, arranged with the subject first, the verb next, and the result of all the action last; for example,

(a) John James wrote his autobiography.

We call the word autobiography the object because it receives the action.

But sample (a) gives us only the basics—who did what. We could develop it, however, and make it more meaningful. One of the many ways to do this is to add single descriptive words, as in sample (b).

(b) John James painstakingly wrote his excellent autobiography.

As you may remember from English classes, painstakingly is an adverb describing the action and excellent is an adjective describing the book. Notice how much more information these two words have given us: Now we know that the book has quality and that John James wrote with extreme care.

Your decision about whether to use these descriptive adjectives and adverbs rests on whether you think they would give the reader more information than you could pack into the subject and the verb. If you do decide you need them, you then have to decide which words would be best. (You don't want to make the mistake of describing something mediocre as fabulous or fantastic.) There are some good reference books to help you find the exact meaning you want. One is Webster's Dictionary of Synonyms. Another is Roget's Thesaurus of the English Language.

Let's see what you can do with sample (a). ADD an adjective or an adverb that will give the clause a different meaning from the one sample (b) gave us:

John James wrote his autobiography.

- - - - - - - - - - - - - - - - - - - -

Suggestions

John James wrote his autobiography. *flippantly* ___________

John James wrote his *flippant* autobiography. ___________

4. Here is another way to develop a basic main clause. If we decide that the reader must know where or when the action took place, we can easily add this information. To continue with the preceding example,

(a) In 1966 John James wrote his excellent autobiography from his death bed in a federal jail.

Notice how the plot has thickened! The three short, underlined units are called prepositional phrases because they start with words called prepositions. Some other common prepositions are by, to, of, for, with, close to, and during. (As you'll see later, prepositional phrases can be used for other kinds of descriptions too.)

In sample (a) notice that the when phrase is at the beginning and the two where phrases are at the end. Are you wondering why? These phrases were placed where the writer felt they fitted in smoothly. There aren't any fixed rules about this. In general, you should put phrases where they will achieve the meaning you want and where they don't sound awkward to you.

But watch out for this sort of shift in meaning:

(b) In the spring a young man's fancy turns to thoughts of love.
(c) A young man's fancy turns to thoughts of love in the spring.

Did you see the difference? Sample (a) explains what happens to a young man in the spring: He thinks about love. Sample (b) explains what always happens to a young man: He thinks about a seasonal kind of love. In other words, in sample (b) the phrase of love runs into the phrase in the spring and the meaning changes.

LOOK AT these sentences:

(a) The police in Boston are known as "Our Finest."
(b) The police are known as "Our Finest" in Boston.
(c) In Boston the police are known as "Our Finest."

Two of those sentences have essentially the same meaning. But one is slightly different. Which is it? ________

- - - - - - - - - - - - - - - - - - -

In sentences (a) and (c) the meaning is that the Boston police are known as "Our Finest." In sentence (b), however, the meaning is that Bostonians call police everywhere "Our Finest."

5. A short prepositional phrase describing where or when the action occurred is usually essential information. To show its importance, you write it without any separating punctuation, as here:

(a) We planted corn in the spring.
(b) In the spring we planted corn.

If you say either of these sentences aloud, you show that the phrase is important by not dropping your voice until you get to the period.

WRITE a main clause about each item of information below. Also add the specified phrase (or phrases) and any descriptive word that you feel is necessary. You can follow this example:

Subject, game; verb, drew; object, crowds; phrase, where.

The Championship Game drew huge crowds to the stadium.

(1) Subject, New Yorkers; verb, abandon; object, city; phrase, when.

(2) Subject, practice; verb, was established; phrase, when.

(3) Subject, they; verb, were married; phrases, where and when.

(4) Subject, suburbanites; verb, work; phrase, where.

(5) Subject, children; verb, learn; phrase, where.

Suggestions

(1) In the summer exhausted New Yorkers abandon their overheated city.

(2) This law practice was established in 1932.

(3) They were married in June in Central Park.

(4) Suburbanites often work in large cities.

(5) Children learn best in a pleasant environment.

SUPPORTING CLAUSES

6. Still another way to develop a main clause is to add a supporting clause that expresses a supporting idea.

As you know, a supporting clause cannot be a sentence by itself. Otherwise, though, it is just like a main clause. This means it always has a subject and a verb, and often it has an object. We can also add any necessa adjective, adverb, or prepositional phrase to it.

In samples (a) and (b) the subject and the verb were underlined.

(a) Although many girls wear hot pants these days

(b) When the Black Panthers were freed

See if you can identify the subjects and verbs of the following clauses. UNDERLINE the subject once and the verb twice.

(1) If men could have babies

(2) Although the new flowers are lovely

(3) Because he has written an excellent article

(4) Even if marijuana were legal here

(5) Since our boys haven't won a football game yet this year

(6) When I saw the swaying chandelier

(7) After we had won the award two years in a row

- - - - - - - - - - - - - - - - - -

(1) men could have

(2) flowers are

(3) he has written

(4) marijuana were

(5) boys haven't won

(6) I saw

(7) we had won

7. When you write a supporting clause to supplement a main one, you should choose the first word of the supporting clause carefully to see that it carries the exact shade of meaning you want. Notice how each different starter changes the meaning of the sentence here:

(a) Prices rose as soon as war had begun.
(b) Prices rose after war had begun.
(c) Prices rose even though war had begun.
(d) Prices rose because war had begun.

We'll review just the most common starting words for supporting clauses that can come anywhere in the sentence—beginning, middle, or end.

As an example, suppose you want to give a reason for the main idea. You can then start the supporting clause with either since or because. But if you want to suggest that the main idea occurred in spite of something else, you can start with even though or although. Samples (e) and (f) illustrate:

(e) Many students live here because it is so close to campus.
(f) The Mets won a championship one year even though they were in the cellar the year before.

The word while is sometimes used instead of because or although. This can be confusing, however, because while more often has another meaning that suggests a time relationship. You should reserve while for this meaning. Some other words you can use appropriately to indicate a time relationship are after, when, as, before, and as soon as.

Samples (g) and (h) illustrate two more situations. If you want to supply a condition for the main idea, you can start the supporting clause with if, provided that, or provided; and, to suggest a purpose for the main clause idea, you can start with so that.

(g) You must work hard if you expect to win.
(h) He worked hard so that he could save money for college.

Later in the chapter you'll learn other starting words for supporting clauses that can come anywhere in the sentence except at the beginning.

8. This table summarizes common starters for supporting clauses.

ON THIS CONDITION	AT THIS TIME	FOR THIS REASON	FOR THIS PURPOSE	IN SPITE OF THIS
If	While	Since	So that	Even though
Provided that	As	Because		Although
Provided	Before			Even if
When	When			
Once	Until			
	Once			
	As soon as			
	Since			

CHOOSE a starter for each supporting clause that will fulfill the meaning specified in the direction. (Of course, consult the table above whenever you need to.)

(1) The novel The Godfather is especially appealing __________ it is so immoral. (The supporting clause gives a reason for the main idea.)

(2) Many people cannot do The New York Times crossword puzzle __________ they are good in English. (The main event occurs despite the supporting clause.)

(3) Men have difficulty getting jobs __________ they have prison records. (The supporting clause is a condition for the main idea.)

(4) Most people thought a four-minute mile was impossible __________ Roger Bannister proved them wrong. (The supporting clause suggests a time when the main event happened.)

(5) Racing fans rooted for Canonero II to win the Belmont ________ the horse had already won the Kentucky Derby and the Preakness. (The supporting clause suggests a time when the main event occurred.)

- - - - - - - - - - - - - - - - - -

Suggestions

(1) because (2) even though (3) if (4) before (5) after

9. When you do have some choice about where to put the supporting clause, maybe you're wondering if there are any rules about where it will fit best.

Again the answer is "No" and you're the judge. There are a few guidelines you may follow, however.

(a) Usually a supporting clause in the middle of a main clause is an interruption; and, like any interruption, it can destroy the flow of thought. You should therefore reserve this middle position for the supporting clause that you really want to call to your reader's attention.
(b) The next-most-prominent place for the supporting clause is at the beginning.
(c) Last, the least conspicuous place for the supporting clause is at the end.

You should also keep in mind that sometimes the overriding consideration about where to put the supporting clause depends on how the sentence will fit with the other sentences of the paragraph.

Look at these sentences:

(a) War broke out when Cliff was only seven.
(b) When Cliff was only seven, war broke out.

Which sentence arrangement would you choose if you wanted to stress Cliff's age? ________

Which sentence arrangement would you choose if you wanted to stress world affairs? ________

- - - - - - - - - - - - - - - - - -

(b) (a)

A SUPPORTING CLAUSE THAT FOLLOWS A MAIN CLAUSE

10. Suppose you want to buttress a main idea with a minor one—that is, you want to mention the main idea first. You can follow a main clause with a supporting clause, and nine times out of ten you won't need any punctuation between them. Here's an example:

(a) The players needed a kind word after they returned to the bench.

There is a simple test to help you tell. Read the sentence with and without the main clause. If you feel that the main clause alone is meaningful, and the supporting clause is merely extra information, put a comma after the main clause. But, if you feel that the supporting clause makes the main clause more specific, you shouldn't use any punctuation. Then the reader will know it's important, too, and he won't drop his voice until he gets to the end of the sentence.

TRY COPYEDITING these sentences. Insert a comma after the main clause if you think it's just extra information. Of course, keep in mind that we often find it hard to judge what is essential in sentences someone else has written.

(1) We will have a chance only if everybody helps.
(2) The dean didn't leave his office although he had threatened to.
(3) He asked for references before she left.
(4) He slipped while he was shoveling snow.
(5) We stayed home last summer since we didn't have enough money for a vacation.

Suggestions

(1) CORRECT
(2) CORRECT or office, although
(3) CORRECT
(4) CORRECT
(5) CORRECT or summer, since

A SUPPORTING CLAUSE THAT INTRODUCES A MAIN CLAUSE

11. Now let's consider the situation in which you want to emphasize a supporting idea, so you write a supporting clause to introduce a main one.

As samples (a) and (b) show, a comma always follows an introductory supporting clause. To prove to yourself that it's necessary, read each sentence aloud twice: once with a pause; next, without one.

(a) After they returned to the bench, the players needed a kind word.
(b) Although the players needed a kind word, the coach didn't have a single one for them.

Hopefully, you noticed that both times the comma helped to clarify the sentence because it told you when to drop your voice. Otherwise you might have continued awhile before realizing you were reading nonsense.

When we speak, everyone understands us because we can separate two ideas that might be confused by dropping our voices appropriately at the end of the first idea. We can also use a suggestive eye movement or hand gesture. But we don't have these natural aids when we write, and we must rely on punctuation marks instead.

COPYEDIT each sentence by putting the comma where it belongs.

(1) After I see a good soap opera I'm ready for real life.
(2) Although I took Latin for four years I can't remember a word of it.
(3) Before I came to college I despised mathematics.
(4) Although many college students are politically active most are not militant.
(5) When you write you should look for a quiet working place.

\- - - - - - - - - - - - - - - - - - -

(1) opera,^ I'm (2) years,^ I (3) college,^ I (4) active,^ most
(5) write,^ you

A LONG PHRASE THAT INTRODUCES A MAIN CLAUSE

12. Occasionally you may want to vary an introductory supporting clause by using a shortcut. One shortcut is to delete the subject and turn the verb into its -ing form. Sample (a) illustrates the resulting long phrase:

(a) After ~~he thought~~ thinking about it all night, Tom decided to return to school.

Notice that the original sentence and the copyedited version have the same meaning. Notice, too, that a comma belongs after both introductions.

You can also turn a supporting clause into a long prepositional phrase by beginning with a preposition and using an <u>-ing</u> form of the verb. Look at these examples:

(b) ~~When I told~~ In telling him about the accident, I omitted the ugly details.

(c) ~~Because I studied~~ By studying all night, I became too tired to take the exam.

Notice that a comma follows the long prepositional phrase too.

COPYEDIT each sentence by using a shortcut for the supporting clause. Be careful to punctuate appropriately.

(1) After she served dinner the maid left for the day.

(2) When you make your bed you should fold hospital corners.

(3) When you apply for school you should always have a second choice.

(4) If she weighs herself every day she is able to stick to her diet.

(5) After he made all the arrangements Dad left the camp.

\- - - - - - - - - - - - - - - - - - -

Suggestions

(1) After ~~she served~~ serving dinner the maid left for the day.

(2) ~~When you make~~ In making your bed you should fold hospital corners.

(3) When ~~you~~ applying for school you should always have a second choice.

(4) ~~If she~~ By weigh~~s~~ing herself every day she is able to stick to her diet.

(5) After ~~he made~~ making all the arrangements Dad left the camp.

13. With the shortcut version of a supporting clause, you should be on the lookout for a common pitfall. Remember that the shortcut phrase no longer has a subject, but it needs one. What it does is to take the easy way out and attach itself to the first good noun in the main clause. Naturally, the reader expects this noun to be the subject of the phrase. But if the writer has changed gears, the results can be ridiculous. Look at this one:

While reading the morning newspaper, the dog got loose.

So the dog is reading the morning newspaper. This has to be a neat trick!

READ these sentences and pick out those with phrases that attach themselves to ridiculous subjects. CHECK each one.

_______ (1) By dieting strenuously, the pounds melted away.
_______ (2) In walking along the beach, the hot sun scorched our bodies.
_______ (3) After slamming the door, she stormed off.
_______ (4) When walking the dog late at night, the streets are usually deserted.
_______ (5) After listening to his story, I was almost ready to believe him.

- - - - - - - - - - - - - - - - -

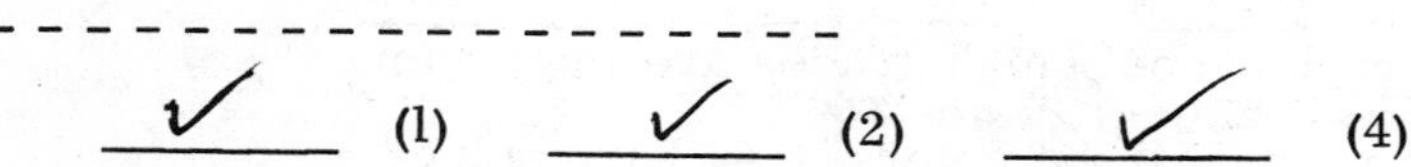
___✓___ (1) ___✓___ (2) ___✓___ (4)

14. Of course, if you're always careful about writing phrases, you won't let them attach themselves to the wrong subjects. Otherwise there is no easy way to recognize the problem, if you have it, except to be on the lookout for foolish attachments as you copyedit.

However, you will become more sensitive to such faulty alliances if you correct a few. There are three ways to get a proper subject for a phrase that has somehow attached itself to the wrong one:

(a) Turn the phrase into a supporting clause with a suitable subject.
(b) Rearrange the sentence so that the phrase is at the end.
(c) Find a suitable subject and insert it in the main clause.

Samples (b), (c), and (d) are possible cures for sample (a)—in which a bank balance borrows money, but not needlessly.

(a) After <u>borrowing</u> some money, my <u>bank balance</u> looked good.
(b) After I had borrowed some money, my bank balance looked good.
(c) My bank balance looked good after I had borrowed some money.
(d) After borrowing some money, I liked the look of my bank balance.

Note in sample (c) that a simple rearrangement wasn't enough to fix up the sentence. Sample (d) also needed more than a new subject.

Each sentence here has a phrase that has attached itself to the wrong subject. COPYEDIT by using one of the three cures:

(1) While making the wish, the candles flickered.

(2) For getting through school, high grades are important.

(3) In decorating a room, all the colors must harmonize.

- - - - - - - - - - - - - - - - - - -

Suggestions

(1) ~~While making the wish~~, the candles flickered [as he made the wish].

(2) For getting through school, high grades are important. [you must be sure that]

(3) In decorating a room, all the colors ~~must~~ harmonize.

15. Before we go on, see if you can recognize a phrase that has attached itself to the wrong subject. COPYEDIT to correct it:

(1) After hearing the bell ring, the class was dismissed.

(2) After listening to his lecture, I knew that he was a bore.

(3) Although worrying all night, the exam was easy.

(4) While eating dinner, the news broadcast was on.

(5) After indicting six of the Harrisburg Thirteen, they waited to come to trial.

- - - - - - - - - - - - - - - - - - -

Suggestions

(1) After hearing the bell ring, the class was dismissed [Miss Dunn]

(2) CORRECT

(3) Although [I had] ~~worrying~~ [worried about it] all night, the exam was easy.

(4) While [he ate] ~~eating~~ dinner the news broadcast was on.

(5) After ~~indicting~~ six of the Harrisburg Thirteen [were indicted], they waited to come to trial.

A PHRASE THAT INTRODUCES THE MAIN CLAUSE

16. While we're talking about phrases that can form foolish alliances, here's another kind of introductory phrase that can do this too: one that describes the subject of the main clause. Sample (a) illustrates the way it should be, and sample (b) illustrates the pitfall.

(a) As the daughter of a millionaire, she suffered from much insincere romantic attention.
(b) As the daughter of a millionaire, the boys feigned great romantic interest in her.

The underlined phrase in sample (b) should describe the girl, as it does in sample (a). Instead it describes boys!

Here are two other ways to fix sample (b).

(c) Because she was the daughter of a millionaire, the boys feigned great romantic interest in her.
(d) The boys feigned great romantic interest in her because she was the daughter of a millionaire.

Notice that the cure in these cases was to turn the phrase back into a clause.

Note too that in sample (a) the phrase is followed by a comma, just like any introductory clause or phrase except one containing essential information.

COPYEDIT any of these phrases that have formed foolish alliances:

(1) As hospital workers, the hospital expects us to follow hospital rules.

(2) By himself, we trained him to fetch the newspaper.

(3) As the son of a mathematician, we expected him to be good in math.

- - - - - - - - - - - - - - - - - -

Suggestions

(1) As hospital workers, ~~the hospital expects us~~ *we are expected* to follow hospital rules.

(2) By himself, we trained him to fetch the newspaper.

(3) ~~As~~ *because he is* the son of a mathematician, we expected him to be good in math.

A SUPPORTING CLAUSE OR LONG PHRASE THAT INTERRUPTS A MAIN CLAUSE

17. Now let's see how to make a big splash by adding a supporting clause or long phrase in the middle of the main clause. Do you need commas around the interrupting clause or phrase?

If it begins with one of the common starters, it probably interrupts the flow of the sentence and should be set apart from the main clause by commas, as here:

(a) That house, as I told you earlier, is too big for us.
(b) My friend, after asking for a raise, was fired instead.

You can read these sentences aloud to prove that commas are needed. And, when you reach them, your voice drops— fortunately. Otherwise, samples (a) and (b) would be gibberish.

Nine times out of ten the commas are necessary around this kind of interrupting supporting clause. But watch out for an exception like this:

(c) Tom's grades, since you asked, were good.
(d) Tom's grades since you asked were good.

What a difference a comma makes! With the commas [sample (c)] the interruption is a kind of side remark, suggesting a reason for the main statement. Without the commas [sample (d)] this sentence means that Tom's grades became good <u>after</u> you inquired about them. Whether or not you would use commas here would depend on the meaning you wanted to express.

COPYEDIT these sentences by punctuating the interrupters:

(1) The cottage I decided is too expensive for us to rent.
(2) Jobs as you know are becoming hard to get down here.
(3) The dean although he threatened to resign didn't leave his office.

---

(1) cottage, I decided, is
(2) Jobs, as you know, are
(3) dean, although he threatened to resign, didn't

A SPECIAL SUPPORTING CLAUSE THAT DESCRIBES A PERSON OR THING IN THE MAIN CLAUSE

18. There is a special kind of supporting clause that you can use to describe a word in the main clause. Consequently, it either interrupts the main clause or follows it. Primarily what's different about it is that the starting word can also be its subject. Let's look at some examples.

Suppose you want to describe a person. You should start the description with who, if who is going to be its subject; if not, you should start with whom.

(a) Wayne Morse, who ran successfully as both a Democrat and a Republican, was a senator from Oregon.
(b) Wayne Morse, whom we admired, was a senator from Oregon.

[You might note that a description starting with who can also stand by itself as a question followed by a question mark. If you like, you can test this out on sample (a).]

Commas go around the descriptions in samples (a) and (b) to show that they were just extra pieces of information. But, when descriptions are essential and commas aren't needed, you can also start with that. As an example, try the following:

(c) The chairman is the man that (whom) we met last night.
(d) The chairman is the man that (who) met us at the door.

Again in sample (d) notice that the who clause could also be a question.

Now suppose you want to describe a "thing" in the main clause. If the description needs commas because it's just extra information, you must start it off with which. Without commas you can start with that.

(e) The book that you just bought is Mary McCarthy's latest novel.
(f) Headaches, which may be a side effect, are annoying.

Two other starting words are useful: where, for a description of a place; why, for a description of a reason. Another one is what.

The descriptive clause in sample (f) can be a sentence by itself. WRITE it that way here:

Which may be a side effect?

19. These points can be summarized easily, as follows:

If the description is extra information (with commas) and describes a		If the description is essential information (without commas) and describes a	
PERSON	THING	PERSON	THING
start with who as the subject; whom otherwise.	start with which.	start with who or that as the subject; whom or that otherwise.	start with that.

PRACTICE on these sentences. PUT in commas if you think they're needed. (Remember that it's often hard to tell what is necessary information and what isn't in sentences someone else has written, but do the best you can.) Also INSERT an appropriate starter. Of course, refer to the table above as you need it.

(1) The clothes ________ she buys are too expensive for me.

(2) The reason ________ Abe Fortas resigned from the Supreme Court is obvious.

(3) The French ________ are known for their cuisine always serve wine with dinner.

(4) The woman ________ is sitting in the chair is my teacher.

(5) Yesterday he gave the opening speech ________ was a great success.

(6) Mr. Jones ________ all the students seemed to admire was dismissed without reason.

- - - - - - - - - - - - - - - - - - - -

Suggestions

(1) clothes that she buys are (You could delete that here.)

(2) reason that Abe Fortas resigned from the Supreme Court is . . . . (You can use why instead of that here, or you could delete that.)

(3) The French, who are known for their cuisine, always

(4) The woman who is sitting in the chair is . . . . (You can also use that.)

(5) speech, which was a

(6) Jones, whom all the students seemed to admire, was

USING CHART 2

20. That about covers the situations we'll deal with in this chapter. When you write your own ideas, punctuation is easier because then you know for sure what is essential and what isn't.

But you're also going to forget some of the rules—especially those you don't use so often. Take heart: They're all summarized for you in Chart 2 (page 316). And it's never cheating to consult this chart, any more than it's cheating to use the dictionary or any other reference. Here are the entries so far:

SITUATION	IF	THEN	EXAMPLE
1. ANY SUPPORTING CLAUSE OR PHRASE THAT INTRODUCES A MAIN CLAUSE	(a) it is a clause or any phrase except an essential one,	(a) set it off by a comma.	(a) After he warned us, he left. After seeing me, he left. By herself, she's hard to take. In a way, he was right.
	(b) it is a short, essential phrase,	(b) don't set it off by a comma.	(b) In the fall the leaves turn.

SITUATION	IF	THEN	EXAMPLE
2. ANY SUPPORTING CLAUSE OR PHRASE THAT INTERRUPTS OR FOLLOWS A MAIN CLAUSE	(a) it interrupts the sentence flow or it's not essential,	(a) set it off by comma(s).	(a) The law, as I found out, isn't clear on it. The law isn't clear on it, as I found out.
	(b) it follows the main clause and is probably essential,	(b) don't set it off by a comma.	(b) I cried when I saw him. We drove to the airport.
3. A SPECIAL SUPPORTING CLAUSE THAT DESCRIBES A PERSON OR THING IN THE MAIN CLAUSE	(a) it is extra information,	(a) set it off by comma(s); for a person use <u>who</u> (as subject) or <u>whom</u>; for a thing use <u>which</u>.	(a) Mr. Smith, who is only fifty, retired. Mr. Smith, whom we just met, retire[d]. My check, which was late, finally came.
	(b) it is essential information.	(b) don't set it off by comma(s); use <u>that</u> (or nothing) for everything; for a person use <u>who</u> (as subject) or <u>whom</u>.	(b) He is the boy who (<u>that</u>) we met. He is the boy whom (<u>that</u>) we met. This is the book that we read.

Let's make sure you can interpret this chart correctly. Find the rule in column "IF" that applies to each example, and WRITE the identifying number and letter in the blank.

__________ (1) This is the house that I like better.
__________ (2) They went to the beach.

- - - - - - - - - - - - - - - - - - -

3b (1) 2b (2)

21. Now refer to your own copy of Chart 2 and use the first three entries to help you COPYEDIT these sentences:

(1) When the smoke cleared I could see the heavy damage.
(2) The Darrens as I have said before have lots of money.
(3) I haven't seen him since he moved.
(4) In the last year the neighborhood has improved.
(5) The apartment that we can afford is not nearly so nice.
(6) Baseball which is my favorite sport is easier to follow.
(7) You need to qualify before you can enter the Indianapolis 500.
(8) After many years of scratching for a living he finally made it big.
(9) The woman whom we just passed was my fourth-grade teacher.
(10) Mary McCarthy also wrote <u>The Group</u> which was a bestseller and a movie.

- - - - - - - - - - - - - - - - - -

(1) cleared,I (1a)
(2) Darrens,as I have said before,have (2a)
(3) CORRECT (2b)
(4) CORRECT (1b)
(5) CORRECT (3b)
(6) Baseball,which is my favorite sport,is (3a)
(7) CORRECT (2b)
(8) living,he (1a)
(9) CORRECT (3b)
(10) Group,which (3a)

As you may have guessed, the reference beside each answer is to the entry in Chart 2 that explains it. If you missed any of them, you should review the rules in the chart.

22. The rules in Chart 2 also apply to longer sentences with more than one supportive phrase or clause; for example, consider the following:

(a) After expressing his opinion, he stalked out of the room, although he had promised to stay longer.

The first comma follows the introductory phrase; the second one precedes some information that the writer tells us is merely nice to know and not essential.

TRY to punctuate these sentences yourself. Use Chart 2, of course.

(1) Although the *Saturday Evening Post* failed twice it recently came out as a quarterly that is probably intended for the noncollege market.
(2) When children learn a new language they usually speak with a more accurate accent than adults because they have less knowledge that would compete.
(3) Although few people realize this the United States went into Vietnam when John Kennedy was president.
(4) Baseball which for most people is a spectator sport probably has more fans in the United States than basketball which is another spectator sport.
(5) I would say that John Barth who wrote *The Sotweed Factor* is the best American writer although I haven't seen anything he has written for a long time.

- - - - - - - - - - - - - - - - - - -

Suggestions

(1) twice ^, it (1a)
(2) language ^, they (1a)
(3) this ^, the (1a)
(4) Baseball ^, which (3a) sport ^, probably (3a), basketball ^, which (3a)
(5) Barth ^, who (3a) Factor ^, is (3a) writer ^, although (2a)

COMBINING IDEAS

23. Much earlier (on page 21) you saw a passage in which five sentences all of one pattern were turned into one great sentence. Those original sentences weren't wrong: They presented correct information, and they presented it correctly. What was wrong was that they suggested five main ideas when in fact there was only one.

You don't have to use complicated forms to show what is more important and what is less so. All you need is good, simple prose in an appropriate form, the kind our best writers use.

Compare samples (a) and (b). As you can see, sample (a) has one main idea—that the state of Delaware has adopted a new conservation measure. Even though the other two ideas merely support this main idea, they are written as main clauses too. Clearly, they don't match the ideas they express. Sample (b) shows one way to handle the situation:

(a) Delaware has adopted a new conservation measure. It bars heavy industry from its coasts. This preserves the coastlines of Delaware Bay and the Atlantic Ocean for tourism and recreation.

(b) Delaware has adopted a new conservation measure that will preserve its coastlines for tourism and recreation by barring heavy industry from the coast.

Sample (b) is better, but not the only alternative. Using the tools you learned in this chapter, EXPRESS the information in sample (a) as one sentence:

- - - - - - - - - - - - - - - - - -

Suggestions

Delaware has adopted a new conservation measure that will bar heavy industry from the coast to preserve it for tourism and recreation.

24. Again, using good prose and the forms you learned here, WRITE each set of three short sentences as one sentence with one main idea. Remember, decide which is the main idea and express it as a main clause. Then write supportive forms like phrases and supporting clauses to express the supportive ideas.

(1) The students support radical ideas. They talk with other radical students. They don't support militant tactics.

(2) The book is usually more enjoyable than the movie. The movie may be more spectacular. The book can have better characterization.

- - - - - - - - - - - - - - - - -

Suggestions

(1) Although the students share radical ideas with other radical students, they don't support militant tactics.
(2) Although the movie may be more spectacular, the book is usually more enjoyable because it can have better characterization.

25. Try these. Using what you've learned so far, WRITE each set of short sentences as one sentence with one main idea.

(1) The Central Park Zoo is interesting. It even has a children's zoo. It is operated by the New York Department of Parks.

(2) Edgar Allan Poe lived in a cottage from 1846 to 1849. It is called the Poe Cottage. He wrote many of his poems there.

- - - - - - - - - - - - - - - - -

Suggestions

(1) The New York Department of Parks operates the interesting Central Park Zoo, which even has a children's zoo.
(2) From 1846 to 1849 Edgar Allan Poe lived in Poe Cottage, where he wrote many of his poems.

26. Once more, try to improve each set of sentences here by EXPRESSING the ideas as one sentence, with one main idea.

(1) Many women prefer to marry and raise families. They don't want to work. But they believe in equal employment opportunities for women.

(2) A proofreader is not expected to be creative. He is not responsible for originating ideas. He is responsible for correct form.

- - - - - - - - - - - - - - - - -

Suggestions

(1) Even though many women prefer to marry and raise families instead of working, they believe in equal employment opportunities for women.

(2) Since a proofreader is responsible only for correct form, he isn't expected to have creative ideas.

Now turn to the review of Chapter 2. You may use Chart 2, of course, to help you answer the questions.

REVIEW

1. Underline the subject once and the verb twice in the supporting clause:

   (a) Dr. William McGill, who is the new president of Columbia University, is a psychologist.
   (b) The belief that people are all good or all bad is naive.
   (c) Integration in many Southern schools has progressed well, although it was slow to start.

2. Any of the words listed below (on the left) can be inserted into the following sentences. Match each word with the description of its function:

   He will buy any record ______________ it is successful.

________	(a) provided	(i)	Shows that the main action happens in spite of the supporting clause.
________	(b) after	(ii)	Makes the supporting clause give a reason for the main idea.
________	(c) because	(iii)	Makes the supporting clause give a condition for the main idea.
________	(d) so that	(iv)	Makes the supporting clause suggest when the main event occurred.
________	(e) although	(v)	Makes the supporting clause give a purpose for the main idea.

3. Punctuate these sentences:

   (a) These children as you can easily see are playing happily.
   (b) Because city living is getting so difficult many people are moving to the suburbs.
   (c) Pollution which is threatening our environment is now a popular political issue.
   (d) If you want to leave the city you must have something to leave for.

4. Copyedit this ridiculous sentence to make it sensible:

After trying to see me all day, I finally talked to him on the telephone.

5. Rewrite these three sentences as one sentence, with only one main idea:

The Greenwich Village artists hold a sidewalk art show. They even hold it in the rain. They exhibit their wares to prospective buyers.

Suggested Answers

1. (a) Dr. William McGill, who is the new president of Columbia University, is a psychologist.

(b) The belief that people are all good or all bad is naive.

(c) Integration in many Southern Schools has progressed well, although it was slow to start.

2. iii (a) provided ii (c) because i (e) although
iv (b) after v (d) so that

3. (a) These children, as you can easily see, are playing happily.
(b) Because city living is getting so difficult, many people are moving to the suburbs.
(c) Pollution, which is threatening our environment, is now a popular political issue.
(d) If you want to leave the city, you must have something to leave for.

4. After ~~trying~~ he tried to see me all day, I finally talked to him on the telephone.

5. Even if it rains the Greenwich Village artists hold a sidewalk art show where they exhibit their wares to prospective buyers.

If you got all the answers right or you know how to correct your errors, put checks (✓) in the REVIEW column of the Self-Evaluation Record for Chapter 2 (page 24) and continue to Chapter 3.

(a) If you missed parts of questions 1 and 2, review frames 1 through 8 first.
(b) If you missed parts of question 3, review frames 9 through 12 and frames 17 through 22.
(c) If you didn't copyedit question 4 satisfactorily, review frames 13 through 16.
(d) If you couldn't do question 5, review frames 23 through 26.

You may also want to make your copy of Chart 2 (page 316) a more personal reference by putting a check beside any entry in the SITUATION column that you either had some trouble with or that you think you might forget later. Then you won't have to search through entries you already know before you can find the forgettable things.

CHAPTER THREE

Linking Main Ideas

Chapter 2 covered some basic techniques. You learned how to write a main idea as a main clause and also how to add a few essentials to make it into a more meaningful sentence. Then you learned how to combine major and minor ideas.

Now we're going to consider how to tie main ideas so they sound as if they belong together. There are many ways to do this. The sample copyedited paragraph illustrates some:

(1) In 1861 Mayor Fernando Wood wanted New York City to secede from New York State. (2) Abraham Lincoln had just become president. (3) Mayor Wood figured that the United States was doomed anyway. (4) The second reason was more important. (5) He was displeased with state legislators who exercised tight control over New York City.

As you can see, it took only minimal changes to bind these separate-sounding main ideas into an interesting, unified story:

(a) The phrase in the first place links us to sentence 1 and tells us we're going to get the first explanation.
(b) Next, the semicolon (;) and the word and link sentence 3 to the same explanation.
(c) The pronoun he is just a substitute for Mayor Wood back in sentence 1.
(d) The word however prepares us to expect some kind of change in sentence 4.
(e) The colon (:) is a dramatic link between sentences 4 and 5. By itself sentence 4 doesn't say much, but with the colon we anticipate something important
(f) Finally, the repetition of Mayor Wood is a dramatic way to remind us who is the chief character of the whole paragraph.

Chapter 3 explains the basic tools you will need in order to make similar transformations in your own writing.

You will learn how to

(a) link two consecutive clauses in various ways to point out their relationship;

(b) link the sentences in a paragraph to achieve a unified effect;

(c) rewrite a set of short, similar sentences and turn them into a unified paragraph in which the main ideas are expressed as main clauses and supporting ideas are expressed in various other ways.

As you did in the first two chapters, you can use the preview of Chapter 3 to help you find out how the chapter can best fulfill your needs. Do the preview now, and then complete the Self-Evaluation Record which follows.

PREVIEW

1. Any of the words listed below (on the left) can be inserted in the following sentence. Match each word with the description of its function:

He wanted to be more experimental this year; ________ he wanted to take extra courses.

________ (a) however,	(i) It indicates that the second statement will give additional information.
________ (b) nevertheless	(ii) It indicates that the second statement is the result of the first.
________ (c) furthermore,	(iii) It shows that despite the first statement the second statement is true.
________ (d) therefore,	(iv) It indicates that the second statement will be in contrast with the first.

2. Punctuate these sentences:

(a) He was the school's star athlete he broke track records and he won several basketball trophies.
(b) After seeing his name on the program I asked him to get me some tickets however he refused.
(c) Since they don't swim well they don't often go to the beach they play golf instead.
(d) I have heard that swimming which is my favorite sport is good exercise but I haven't been swimming once this year.
(e) I registered for school but all the classes I wanted were already filled.

3. You can assume that the following passage has been punctuated correctly. However, it doesn't read like a unit. Unify the passage by combining short sentences and inserting any words or expressions that you think will link one sentence to another.

(1) The cheapest way to extract coal is by strip mining. (2) It is desolating thousands of acres of beautiful mountain country. (3) There is little hope that the damage will ever be repaired. (4) The Department of Interior reports that only 58,000 of the 1.8 million stripped acres have been restored. (5) It may be outlawed. (6) Many conservationists recommend it. (7) The only alternative is deep mining. (8) It is three times more expensive. (9) It is much more dangerous. (10) More than 80,000 miners have died in deep mine accidents since 1910. (11) Safety precautions might make it more acceptable. (12) Safety precautions would make it even more expensive.

Suggested Answers

1. iv (a) iii (b) i (c) ii (d)

2. (a) He was the school's star athlete: He broke track records, and he won several basketball trophies.

(b) After seeing his name on the program, I asked him to get me some tickets; however, he refused.

(c) Since they don't swim well they don't often go to the beach they play golf instead.

(d) I have heard that swimming which is my favorite sport is good exercise but I haven't been swimming once this year.

(e) I registered for school but all the classes I wanted were already filled.

3. (1) The cheapest way to extract coal is by strip mining.

(2) It is desolating thousands of acres of beautiful mountain country.

(3) There is little hope that the damage will ever be repaired.

(4) The Department of Interior reports that only 58,000 of the 1.8 million stripped acres have been restored.

(5) It may be outlawed.

(6) Many conservationists recommend it.

(7) The only alternative is deep mining.

(8) It is three times more expensive.

(9) It is much more dangerous.

(10) More than 80,000 miners have died in deep mine accidents since 1910.

(11) Safety precautions might make it more acceptable.

(12) Safety precautions would make it even more expensive.

Of course, there are many other ways to revise this paragraph

If you got the questions right or your revisions compared well with the suggestions, you can read through Chapter 3 very quickly. In the PREVIEW column of the Self-Evaluation Record for Chapter 3, put a check beside a question that you answered to your satisfaction. Remember, a blank will indicate where you need to concentrate your efforts.

SELF-EVALUATION RECORD FOR CHAPTER 3

	PREVIEW	FRAMES	REVIEW
Questions 1 and 2		1 through 10	
Question 3		11 through 25	

TWO MAIN CLAUSES JOINED: WITHOUT A LINKING ADVERB

1. As you know, all the main ideas in the same paragraph must be related somehow even if they are in separate sentences. There are many ways to show these relationships. But before we consider how to unify a whole paragraph, let's consider how to link two sentences that follow one another.

One common device is to put them together in one sentence, with a semicolon replacing the period. Notice that the words in these two samples are exactly the same:

(a) Tricia Nixon was the eighth presidential daughter to marry in the White House. She was the first to marry outdoors.

(b) Tricia Nixon was the eighth presidential daughter to marry in the White House; she was the first to marry outdoors.

In sample (a) the main clauses are separate, like Tricia Nixon and Edward Cox; in sample (b) they're married, like Mr. and Mrs. Edward Cox.

If you were to read these samples aloud, you would pause longer after the period than you would after the semicolon. But, as is so often the case, there aren't any rules about which is better, period or semicolon. This would depend on the emphasis you want.

Find the two main ideas in each of these examples. Then SEPARATE them by a semicolon as a clue that they are closely related and can be in one sentence.

(1) A woman in Australia made history by giving birth to nine babies seven of them were born alive.

(2) James Michener said that the language of girl students at Kent angered the Guard the soldiers had never heard anything like it.

(3) The raccoon is one of the earth's most lovable creatures favorite children's stories give him almost human qualities.
(4) The American and British system of justice assumes that the accused is innocent the European system assumes that he's guilty.
(5) Believers in scientology say that man is good he must free himself from negative memories of the past, however.

- - - - - - - - - - - - - - - - - - -

(1) babies; seven (2) Guard; the (3) creatures; favorite
(4) innocent; the (5) good; he

TWO MAIN CLAUSES JOINED: WITH A LINKING ADVERB

2. Another way to link two consecutive main ideas is to begin the second one with a linking word like and, but, or however that explains how the second idea will be related to the first. Then you can either put the two ideas together in one sentence or keep them separate.

You may have learned somewhere that you must never begin a new sentence with a word like and or but. Nonsense—do it anyway! Sometimes we don't know where a rule came from, yet we continue to follow it slavishl

Maybe you're wondering when to join the main ideas in a single sentence and when to keep them separate if you also use a linking word between them. Again, this depends on the effect you want to achieve. Compare these samples. Which do you think is a more forceful way to prepare the reader for a contrast?

(a) I wanted to get a job this summer to help pay my tuition at school next year. However, summer jobs are almost impossible to find.
(b) I wanted to get a job this summer to help pay my tuition at school next year; however, summer jobs are almost impossible to find.

Most people would say "sample (a)." In reading the two samples aloud, you would probably put extra stress on the word however in sample (a).

A linking word is a particularly effective sentence starter because it tells the reader what to expect. However, like any other attention-getter, it loses its effect if it is overused.

What is another appropriate word you might use instead of however in samples (a) and (b)? ______________

- - - - - - - - - - - - - - - - - - -

Suggestions

But or perhaps Yet

3. There are many different linking words—or linking adverbs, as they are often called. The right one to use depends mostly on the relationship the two clauses have to each other. Let's consider some.

Suppose you want to tell the reader that despite what you said earlier the next idea you will present is still true. Then you would start this next idea with yet or nevertheless, as here:

(a) He failed algebra last year. Nevertheless, he graduated in the top 20 percent of his class.
(b) He failed algebra last year. Yet he graduated in the top 20 percent of his class.

Notice that yet doesn't require a comma, but that nevertheless does. There is a handy rule to help you remember when to use the comma: If the linking adverb is four letters or longer, put a comma after it; a comma isn't necessary otherwise.

To continue with the linking adverbs, suppose you want to warn the reader that the next statement is a result of what you said before. Samples (c) and (d) are two ways to show this:

(c) He had saved his money during his working years. Therefore, he was able to retire comfortably.
(d) He had saved his money during his working years. Consequently, he was able to retire comfortably.

Two more possibilities are so and thus. If you want to signal the reader to expect additional facts, you can use either and or furthermore. (Occasionally you might use moreover, although this word is too stiff and formal for most statements.)

Which of these linking adverbs would not be followed by a comma: and, furthermore, besides, or moreover? ________________

- - - - - - - - - - - - - - - - - -

and (It is not a four-letter word.)

4. Now SELECT an appropriate linking adverb for each example. WRITE it on the blank and USE the appropriate punctuation with it.

(1) He has worked hard all his life. __________ he doesn't work hard any longer.
(2) At the last minute he decided he really should take English 101. __________ he was too late to register.
(3) Registration had closed in all the English classes. __________ he was able to persuade Mr. Edmonds to admit one more student.
(4) He has some minor physical handicaps. __________ he is excused from regular gymnasium classes.
(5) I voted for Harold Jenkins. __________ I wasn't happy to see him win.
(6) He works hard in school and on the job. __________ he doesn't have much time to socialize.
(7) New Jersey was one of the thirteen original colonies. __________ it was one of the first states to ratify the Constitution.
(8) Some people thought that the Kent State shootings were justified. __________ at least one of the students who were killed was merely on his way to class.
(9) Rightists and leftists were outraged by the conviction of Lieutenant Calley. __________ their reasons for the outrage were totally different.
(10) Spring semester is exactly as long as the fall semester. __________ it always seems a lot longer.

- - - - - - - - - - - - - - - - - - - -

Suggestions

(1) But or However^ (2) But or However^ (3) Yet or Nevertheless^ or But or However^ (4) Consequently^ Therefore^ or Thus^ (5) Yet or Nevertheless^ or But or However^ (6) So or Consequently^ Therefore^ or Thus^ (7) Consequently^ Therefore^ Thus^ And or Furthermore^ (8) However^ or But (9) However^ or But (10) But or However^ or Yet or Nevertheless^

5. As you saw in the last frame, you usually have a range of linking adverbs to choose from. How do you decide which one is best? Once more, it is writer's choice. Most of the time you should probably be informal and use the simpler linking adverbs like <u>and</u> and <u>but</u>. You can then save the longer, more formal linking adverbs, like <u>however</u> and <u>consequently</u>, for emphasis or variety.

Remember that you can also put two main clauses together in one sentence even when they are already linked by a linking adverb. The right punctuation to join them, in fact, depends on the linking adverb you've selected. Fortunately, the rule of the four-letter words holds here too:

(a) If you use a linking adverb of four letters or more, put a semicolon after the first clause and a comma after the linking adverb.
(b) If you use a shorter linking adverb, put a comma after the first clause and nothing after the linking adverb.

Compare these samples:

(a) He waited a long time; however, nobody came.
(b) He waited a long time, but nobody came.

You can test the rule by reading the samples aloud. You would pause longer before the semicolon in sample (a) than before the comma in sample (b).

COPYEDIT these sentences. (Don't forget the comma after some of the linking adverbs.)

(1) His grades were high but his morale was low.
(2) You need to write a first draft however anyone can do that.
(3) He gave blood last week therefore he couldn't do it again today.
(4) He gave blood three weeks ago and he should wait a week before giving it again.
(5) He wears expensive clothes but they never fit right.

- - - - - - - - - - - - - - - - - -

(1) high, but his (2) draft; however, anyone (3) week; therefore, he (4) ago, and he (5) clothes, but they

6. To summarize, we use a four-letter linking adverb and a semicolon to join two clauses when we need some variety in our sentences or when we want to be particularly emphatic. Most of the time, though, we use a shorter linking adverb and a comma.

COPYEDIT the sentences on the next page. But watch out! Some may already be correct, just as this one is:

The group bought fifty acres and started a commune.

Notice that a comma isn't necessary after acres because we're joining two verbs (bought and started) and not two clauses. Here, the one group did two things.

(1) Some students believe in a lottery for the draft but others don't.
(2) He expressed many reasons however he never mentioned the real one.
(3) He bought a house and moved to the country.
(4) He bought some land and he expects to build a house on it.
(5) He didn't get any volunteers nevertheless he was satisfied.
(6) This was a terrible storm and five-hundred people are now homeless.
(7) He asked for a new watch and a new band to go with it.
(8) In summer we ski too however we have to go to South America to do it.
(9) He remembered my birthday but he didn't buy me a gift.
(10) Every sentence must have a subject and a complete verb.

- -

(1) draft, but others (2) reasons ; however , he (3) CORRECT
(4) land , and he (5) volunteers ; nevertheless , he (6) storm , and five
(7) CORRECT (8) too ; however , we (9) birthday , but he (10) CORRECT

7. Suppose you're joining two main clauses, and at least one of them already has a comma to set off a phrase or other supporting form. Unless you use a semicolon to join the two main clauses, the reader won't be able to tell which are the main ideas.

Look at this example:

When the rain stopped, the flooding stopped too; and we went about our daily business shortly after.

As you can see, the semicolon was used to join the main clauses even though we would ordinarily use a comma before the linking adverb and.

LOOK FOR the major ideas in each sentence, and join them with a semicolon.

(1) After waiting a long time, he finally left but nobody came.
(2) The Barrens, who have lots of money, send their children to the public schools and they are proud to do so.
(3) After many years of trying to like my brother-in-law, I gave up trying and we have been getting along better ever since.
(4) Although the cottage is simple, it is adequate however, it is too far away.
(5) If you work hard at something, you aren't bound to succeed yet you know that you at least tried.

- -

(1) left ; but (2) schools ; and (3) trying, and
(4) adequate ; however, (5) succeed ; yet

TWO MAIN CLAUSES JOINED: WITH A COLON

8. Look at sample (a) below, which is punctuated according to one suggestion we've just discussed. Then look at sample (b). This treatment of the same sentence attracts much more attention:

(a) Our reference book, A Manual of Style, is complete; it helps the writer as well as the editor.
(b) Our reference book, A Manual of Style, is complete: It helps the writer as well as the editor.

If you read sample (b) aloud, you stop abruptly when you reach the colon. The colon is a more dramatic way to show the break between the first statement and its explanation. And the capital letter starting the explanation dramatizes the situation even further.

You can also use the colon between a main clause and its explanation even if the explanation is not a main clause, as in sample (c):

(c) The student thought the teacher was only one thing: an idiot.

But this time the first word after the colon isn't capitalized because what follows the colon is not a main clause.

As is usually the case with dramatic things, however, you should use the colon sparingly. Otherwise it would soon lose all of its drama.

COPYEDIT these sentences to achieve a dramatic effect. (Don't forget to capitalize the first word of the explanation if it's also a main clause.)

(1) The notes are personal they are from my husband during the time he was courting me.
(2) I have had only one goal all my life to be a doctor.
(3) Golf is my favorite pastime it's my way to relax.
(4) The Frick Museum in New York is a fine small museum it has major paintings by such artists as Vermeer and Goya, as well as outstanding collections.
(5) The demonstrations were for Angela Davis the demonstrators felt that she was imprisoned unfairly.

- - - - - - - - - - - - - - - - - -

(1) personal: they
(2) life: to
(3) pastime: it's
(4) museum: it
(5) Davis: the

USING CHART 2

9. Again, don't worry about remembering all the rules. The two entries here, reprinted from Chart 2, summarize everything we've covered in this chapter so far (except for 4b, which is explained in frame 12). LOOK them over first:

SITUATION	IF	THEN	EXAMPLE
4. ADVERB	(a) it links two main clauses,	(a) put a comma after it only if it has four or more letters. (Don't put a comma after <u>and</u>, <u>so</u>, <u>but</u>, <u>or</u>, <u>nor</u>, <u>yet</u>.)	(a) I like English, but I like math more. I like English; however, I like math more.
	(b) it is not a linking adverb,	(b) set it off by comma(s) only if the reader should pause to emphasize it.	(b) Sometimes I like to watch TV. Sometimes, I like to watch TV.
5. TWO MAIN CLAUSES JOINED	(a) no linking adverb is used to indicate a close relationship,	(a) put a semicolon between the two main clauses.	(a) I worked late many nights; I hated it.
	(b) a short linking adverb (<u>and</u>, <u>but</u>, <u>yet</u>) is used to be informal,	(b) put a comma between the two main clauses.	(b) He wore a coat, but he was cold.
	(c) a four-letter linking adverb (or longer) is used for variety or for emphasis,	(c) put a semicolon between the two main clauses .	(c) He wore a coat; however, he was cold.

SITUATION	IF	THEN	EXAMPLE
5. TWO MAIN CLAUSES JOINED (Continued)	(d) at least one main clause has a phrase or supporting clause set off by commas,	(d) put a semicolon between the two main clauses no matter what the linking adverb is.	(d) Even though he wore a coat, he was cold; but he stayed on the post.
	(e) the second clause is an explanation of the first, for a dramatic effect,	(e) put a colon after the first clause and capitalize the first word of the second. (If the explanation is not a clause, don't capitalize the first word.)	(e) He won three letters: He is a talented athlete. (He won two letters: in track and in fencing.)

See how well you can interpret these entries. On the blank WRITE the identifying letter for entry 5 that applies. Then COPYEDIT the sentences according to the rules in entries 4 and 5.

_____ (1) I have forgiven him however he has not forgiven me.

_____ (2) Although I see him often, he has not forgiven me but I forgave him years ago.

_____ (3) We married in the Depression we divorced then too.

_____ (4) I flunked English last year but I'll never do that again.

_____ (5) He bought three books all three are novels.

- - - - - - - - - - - - - - - - -

c (1) him; however, he

d (2) me; but I

a (3) Depression; we

b (4) year, but I'll

a or e (5) books: All

books; all

RUN-ON SENTENCES

10. You may have heard an English teacher talk about a <u>run-on</u> sentence. This is merely a string of main and supporting ideas put together in one sentence without any attempt to separate them so the reader will know what they are. If you follow all the suggestions in this book, you won't write run-on sentences yourself. However, just for practice in using Chart 2, try your hand at copyediting the run-on sentences below.

The best way to proceed through each tangle is to LOOK FOR THE MAIN IDEAS FIRST. The rest is easy. You can follow this example:

While gardening yesterday, we noticed a huge snake; but it wasn't poisonous.

(1) When I read that book I thought it was exceptional but now I think I was wrong.

(2) After a year in this town I was ready to leave but I stayed because of the great people I met here.

(3) Although he said at first he would testify he refused when he was asked however he gave in eventually.

(4) He was as I pointed out fifth in his graduating class but he couldn't get into Harvard.

(5) Because they participated in peace marches they were considered radicals however they were actually conservative on other issues.

- - - - - - - - - - - - - - - - - -

(1) When I read that book, (1a) I thought it was exceptional; (5d) (4a) but now I think I was wrong.

(2) After a year in this town, (1a) I was ready to leave; (5d) (4a) but I stayed because of the great people I met here.

(3) Although he said at first he would testify, (1a) he refused when he was asked; (5d) however, (4a) he gave in eventually.

(4) He was, (2a) as I pointed out, (2a) fifth in his graduating class; (5d) (4a) but he couldn't get into Harvard.

(5) Because they participated in peace marches, (1a) they were considered radicals; (5d) however, (4a) they were actually conservative on other issues.

USING YOUR JUDGMENT

11. You must have heard the comment "The operation was a success, but the patient died."

Quite possibly you could follow all the suggestions you learned so far, yet your writing would somehow miss the target. In a sense, it might be too perfect, like the girl who is so well groomed that she looks unnatural. The urge to mess her hair is irresistible. The perfect sentence may need some well-planned messing too.

As an example, do you recognize Julius Caesar's account of his conquest of Gaul?

(a) I came, I saw, I conquered.

Sample (a) doesn't strictly obey the punctuation rules you have learned. But, aside from punctuation, do you suppose you could improve on this sentence by using a phrase or a supporting clause? Look at these:

(b) After I came and saw, I conquered.
(c) Having come and seen, I conquered.

Obviously, Caesar knew best, and never mind the rules. And obviously, too, you need to exercise a lot of judgment when you write.

The rules and various suggestions are intended only to help you. They do this by providing a kind of skeleton that you can use as a base to structure your own thoughts. In general, you should follow the rules and suggestions because they make the writing easier and usually better. But you shouldn't let a rule prevent you from trying something that you think will be more effective. In short, break a rule if you have a special reason for doing so.

In the next pages we're going to consider ways to link the sentences of the paragraph to make a unit. If some of the linking devices seem to be contradictory, keep in mind that you must exercise judgment in applying them too—that one device may work beautifully in one situation, but not in the other.

TO INTRODUCE A SET OF UNLINKED SENTENCES: LINK WITH TRANSITIONS

12. One very helpful way to link sentences of the paragraph is to use some standard phrases and adverbs that are called *transitions* because they act as a bridge between two ideas. Here are a few examples; maybe you can think of others:

TO INTRODUCE AN ILLUSTRATION	TO ADD ANOTHER ASPECT OF THE SAME IDEA	TO POINT OUT A CONTRAST OR QUALIFICATION	TO INDICATE A CONCLUSION OR RESULT	TO INDICATE A TIME
For example,	Besides,	Otherwise,	In conclusion,	At the same time,
For instance,	Again,	In contrast,	To sum up,	Nowadays,
To illustrate,	Next,	On the other hand,	In other words,	Up to now,
As an illustration,	In the second place,	Instead,	As a result,	So far,
	Similarly,	Meanwhile,	Accordingly,	From then on,
	In addition,	Still,	In short,	Until then,
	Finally,	Despite this,	Obviously,	Today,
	Also,	Just the same,	Clearly,	
	First,	But	Thus,	
	And	However,	Consequently,	
	Furthermore,	Yet	Therefore,	
	Moreover,	Nevertheless,	So	

Notice that the linking adverbs were included because they are transitions too. Other transitions that don't seem to fit any of these categories are *in a way*, *in a sense*, *as you know*, *as you see*, *in the first place*, *in fact*, and *of course*. (These can be varied to fit the sentence.)

Most of the time you would put the transition at the beginning of the sentence because it attracts more attention there. And, since it isn't essential, you should set it off by a comma unless for some reason you *don't* want the reader to pause. (On the other hand, you might want to put a comma after a short linking adverb if you *do* want the reader to pause.) To illustrate, consider the following:

(a) Usually, we stay home on holidays.
(b) Usually we stay home on holidays.
(c) So everyone had a good time.
(d) So, everyone had a good time.

All four sentences are punctuated to show where the emphasis should be. You might want to read these sentences aloud according to the directions given by the comma or the lack of one.

You can also put a transition in the middle of the sentence. In that case you often have a choice about whether to set it off by commas, depending on the emphasis you want. Occasionally the commas would change the meaning. As an example, how would you punctuate the transition in this sentence?

She of course demanded alimony.

- - - - - - - - - - - - - - - - - - -

It is writer's choice here. With the commas around of course the sentence suggests that "she" is that special type of woman who would demand alimony. Without the commas it suggests that alimony is the customary demand.

13. Transitions can certainly be lifesavers to your paragraphs! On the other hand, as you'll see later, you should use them cautiously. They should provide easy transition from idea to idea, but not clutter up your passages. The best rule is to use all techniques in moderation.

Look at this paragraph with the underlined transitions sprinkled in. READ it aloud twice, once with and once without the transitions.

A day-care center used to be a place where parents could park their kids for a few hours. However, a new kind of center has sprung up that is more than custodial. Nowadays, the day-care center usually has organized programs to encourage the children's development. In a sense, by shifting some of the responsibility for child rearing to the community, it is helping the parents as well as the children.

Didn't you think the transitions here were helpful?

See if you can GIVE a reasonable substitute transition for those in the paragraph:

(1) However ____________________
(2) Nowadays ____________________
(3) In a sense ____________________

- - - - - - - - - - - - - - - - - - -

Suggestions

(1) But
(2) These days
(3) In a way

14. Read over this paragraph. As an exercise to see what effect transitions alone can have, use them exclusively to improve it. Of course, you may consult the table in frame 12.

(1) The sound of the trumpet varies with the length of the tube. (2) Trumpets made before 1500 were straight and as much as eight feet long. (3) Until about 1813 most of them were like today's bugle, which is capable of only a limited number of tones. (4) Modern players, like Miles Davis and Cootie Williams, use valved trumpets. (5) They can produce all the tones of the chromatic scale.

\- - - - - - - - - - - - - - - - - - -

Suggestions

(1) The sound of the trumpet varies with the length of the tube. (2) Trumpets made before 1500 were straight and as much as eight feet long. (3) *From then* until about 1813, most of them were like today's bugle, which is capable of only a limited number of tones. (4) *However,* modern players, like Miles Davis and Cootie Williams, use valved trumpets. (5) *With them* they can produce all the tones of the chromatic scale.

(Notice that the transition from sentence 2 to sentence 3 helps to clarify the meaning. However, the transition from sentence 3 to sentence 4 makes the sentence smoother. The transition from sentence 4 to sentence 5 again helps to clarify the meaning.)

A SET OF UNLINKED SENTENCES: LINK WITH PRONOUN REPLACEMENTS

15. We can spoil the sound of a passage just by repeating one noun unnecessarily. The cure is to substitute a pronoun for this noun *if*—and this is a big if—the reader knows for sure which noun is being replaced and what it means.

Read this passage and note all the repetitions of an expression with the word *millionaires*:

According to the Treasury Department, 1203 American *millionaires* didn't file an income tax return in 1969. Of the 1203 million American *millionaires*, 56 *millionaires* didn't pay any taxes because these *millionaires* were able to take advantage of one or more of eight different loopholes in the tax laws.

Now read the same passage, but with some pronoun replacements, and note how much better it sounds:

According to the Treasury Department, 1203 American *millionaires* didn't file an income tax return in 1969. Of these, ~~the 1203 million American millionaires,~~ 56 *millionaires* didn't pay any taxes because they ~~these millionaires~~ were able to take advantage of one or more of eight different loopholes in the tax laws.

As you can see, two repetitions of the expression with the word *millionaires* were replaced at great profit to the readability. You might also delete the word *millionaires* in the second sentence, after *56*.

16. Remember, you can replace a noun that is repeated too often, *provided* the reader would know for sure exactly what noun is being replaced.

COPYEDIT these paragraphs by replacing nouns with pronouns whenever you can:

(1) A woman made the first telephone bet for the nation's first legalized off-track gambling system. Using a code name, the woman bet ten dollars on Title Song to show. When Title Song actually won the race, the woman made a profit of four dollars.

(2) Robert E. Peary, who discovered the North Pole, began exploring in 1886 on Greenland, when Peary was thirty years old. With Peary's

headquarters at McCormick Bay, Peary explored Greenland's coast from 1891 to 1892. The first time he tried for the North Pole, in 1893, he wasn't successful. However, Peary made a successful dash for the North Pole on March 1, 1909. Peary reached the North Pole on April 6, 1909, when Peary was fifty-four years old.

\- - - - - - - - - - - - - - - - - - - -

Suggestions

(1) A woman made the first telephone bet for the nation's first legalized off-track gambling system. Using a code name, the woman bet ten dollars on Title Song to show. When Title Song actually won the race, the woman made a profit of four dollars. (In the last sentence you might have said, "When he actually won the race, the woman made a profit of four dollars.")

(2) Robert E. Peary, who discovered the North Pole, began exploring in 1886 on Greenland, when Peary was thirty years old. With Peary's headquarters at McCormick Bay, Peary explored Greenland's coast from 1891 to 1892. The first time Peary tried for the North Pole, in 1893, he wasn't successful. However, Peary made a successful dash for the North Pole on March 1, 1909. Peary reached the North Pole on April 6, 1909, when Peary was fifty-four years old.

A SET OF UNLINKED SENTENCES: REPETITIONS FOR EMPHASIS

17. Underlying all the techniques for linking sentences is the premise that we're going to make the passage more interesting as well as more unified. Maybe you're thinking that some topics are naturally dull, like mathematics—maybe even English.

But few topics are either naturally exciting or naturally dull. Most topics become exciting when the writer presents them in an interesting way. An uninteresting presentation can make the same topics dull. Even sex can be made to sound dreary. And the paragraph below illustrates how a usually unattractive topic - - garbage - - can be interesting.

Sometimes by purposely repeating a word from a previous sentence the writer tells the reader that he is continuing the same train of thought. UNDERLINE the word, or words, that are repeated here for emphasis and interest.

Garbage threatens to bury us. Garbage is responsible for filling in acres of our natural wetlands. Garbage is polluting our harbors and waterways. And garbage is stripping our land of natural resources and leaving unsanitary landfills and litter in their places.

\- - - - - - - - - - - - - - - - - - -

Garbage in each sentence

A SET OF UNLINKED SENTENCES: VARIETY OF SENTENCE PATTERNS AND LENGTHS

18. In addition to all the devices you've learned so far to make sentences sound as if they belong together, we have one more. This is to vary the patterns and lengths of the sentences, unless you want them to sound alike for a special effect. This technique wasn't specifically mentioned earlier because variety often occurs naturally as a by-product of other techniques.

Still, it is another approach to help you construct a paragraph—another way of looking at things.

In the original version of the paragraph below, the sentences form a monotonous pattern because each one begins with a phrase. Although you could improve the paragraph in other ways too, the technique of varied sentence patterns and lengths was applied exclusively in the copyediting here. Mostly, a phrase was shifted or left out and short sentences were combined. READ this paragraph with and without the copyediting to see how much better the copyedited version sounds:

In World War II flak was the British term for "antiaircraft fire." And the In German ~~flak was the~~ abbreviation for "antiaircraft cannon." In World War I combat fliers had used this word as part of their private language. And in In slang, also flack means "press agent," ~~In slang~~ flak is just "hot air."

(1) Briefly explain how the first two sentences were improved:

____

(2) Explain how the third sentence was improved:

____

(3) Explain how the last two sentences were improved.

____

- - - - - - - - - - - - - - - - - - - -

(1) The first two sentences were combined.
(2) The starting phrase was shifted to avoid the in beginning phrase.
(3) The last two sentences were combined.

19. In the following paragraph the sentences form a monotonous pattern so that we don't get the feeling of a complete unit. Briefly describe that pattern in your own words. Then see what you can do to relieve the tedium by using different sentence patterns and different sentence lengths.

If city pedestrians carry special alarm buttons, they can probably reduce the crime rate in the street considerably. If they squeeze these buttons, a sound goes off. If this sound is pitched high enough, only dogs can hear it. If patroling dogs are specially trained to respond, they can run to attack whoever moves first—hopefully, the attacker.

- - - - - - - - - - -

- - - - - - - - - - - - - - - - - - - -

All the sentences start with a supporting if clause.

Suggestions

~~If~~ city pedestrians carry special alarm buttons, ~~they~~ can probably reduce the crime rate in the street considerably. If they squeeze these buttons, a sound goes off. ~~If this sound is~~ pitched high ~~enough,~~ only dogs can hear it. If patroling dogs are specially trained to respond, they can run to attack whoever moves first—hopefully, the attacker.

20. COPYEDIT this paragraph to make it "sound" better. You may use every device you've learned so far: add transitions; substitute pronouns for nouns that are repeated unnecessarily; and repeat nouns for emphasis. You may also shift sentence parts if you think they would sound better elsewhere.

The child-labor problem is apparently growing. Most violations are in agriculture, on farms employing migrant labor. In both light and heavy industry, investigators have turned up a surprising number of violations. In Detroit investigators found a motel owner who illegally employed seventy-two minors, or about half of his work force. In New York City investigators found an employer who hired eight minors to clean large chemical barrels containing pesticides and formaldehyde. The employer did not give them any protective clothing.

\- - - - - - - - - - - - - - - - - -

Suggestions

Even today, the child-labor problem is apparently growing. Most violations are in agriculture, on farms employing migrant labor. However, in both light and heavy industry investigators have turned up a surprising number of violations. For example, in Detroit they found a motel owner who illegally employed seventy-two minors, or about half of his work force. In New York City they found an employer who hired eight minors to clean large chemical barrels containing pesticides and formaldehyde. But he did not give the eight minors any protective clothing.

(There are, of course, many possible revisions. For example, you might also have joined the last sentence to the preceding one. Or you might have shifted the phrases in Detroit and in New York City to follow owner and employer.)

USING CHART 2

21. For your convenience, all the techniques you practiced for linking sentences are summarized as entry 6 in Chart 2. Look this entry over:

SITUATION		EXAMPLE
6. A SET OF UNLINKED SENTENCES	(a) Sentences may be linked by linking adverbs and other transitions. (b) A pronoun is substituted for a noun if the reference is clear. (c) A word or phrase is repeated purposely for emphasis. (d) The patterns and lengths of the sentences are varied.	After a lifetime of exposure to many pesticides, human beings may have accumulated enough to suffer genetic effects. ~~After the deposit of~~ As an example, so much mercury has been deposited in ~~human beings,~~ our waterways that swordfish have unsafe concentrations. ~~Among~~ other ~~excessive~~ unsafe ~~deposits~~ concentrations in foods ~~have been~~ are the result the additions of artificial preservatives and flavors.

LOOK AT the example and answer these questions about it.

(1) Was any word or word group repeated for emphasis? ________
If so, what? ________________

(2) Was any transition used? ________
If so, what? ________________

(3) Was any pronoun substituted for a noun? ________
If so, what? ________________

- - - - - - - - - - - - - - - - - -

(1) Yes; unsafe concentrations
(2) Yes; As an example,
(3) Yes; our (for human beings')

LINKING MAIN IDEAS

22. COPYEDIT this passage to improve it. USE any device you've learned, any reference chart, and any reference book. (As background, you should know that Charles Rangel is a black congressman from New York.)

According to Charles Rangel, President Nixon's plan for a volunteer army was a device to get young whites off his back. According to him, the army would make America's militarism more palatable to middle-aged whites. As an inducement to join, former President Nixon offered a $3000 bonus for combat duty. By this offer, President Nixon had recommended a mercenary army.

According to Representative Rangel, white boys of the middle class wouldn't join. According to him too, the army would consist mostly of blacks and Spanish-Americans, with a handful of poor whites. Representative Rangel wondered about the President's shortsightedness. The soldiers would realize that the soldiers would be doing the white civilians' killing. Representative Rangel says that the Russian Revolution began when an oppressed army and navy revolted.

- - - - - - - - - - - - - - - - - - -

Suggestions

According to Charles Rangel, President Nixon's plan for a volunteer army was a device to get young whites off his back. ~~According to him, the army would~~ make America's militarism more palatable to middle-aged whites. As an inducement to join, former President ~~Nixon~~ offered a $3000 bonus for combat duty. ~~By this offer, President Nixon~~ had recommended a mercenary army.

~~According to~~ Representative Rangel, white boys in the middle class wouldn't join. ~~According to him too,~~ the army would consist mostly of blacks and Spanish-Americans, with a handful of poor whites. Representative Rangel wondered about the President's shortsightedness. The soldiers would realize that the soldiers would be doing the white civilians' killing. Representative Rangel says that the Russian Revolution began when an oppressed army and navy revolted.

23. In Chapter 2 you took two or three short sentences, all alike, and made them into one big sentence. First, you decided what you wanted to emphasize, and you wrote this idea as a main clause. Then you added the supporting ideas in various suitable forms.

You're ready to develop this skill now that you know how to treat several ideas and how to link them together into one unified passage.

Look at this set of short sentences. Notice that originally all thirteen sentences looked alike, as if they were all equally important. But they were combined in the copyedited version to show that there are really many fewer than thirteen main ideas—only five, in fact.

(1) Scott Nearing taught economics at the University of Pennsylvania for ten years. (2) He had a public fight against child labor. (3) He was dismissed from his teaching post. (4) He got a job at the University of Toledo. (5) He was a pacifist in World War I. (6) He was fired from his job. (7) He was thrown out of the Communist Party (8) His views were too individualistic. (9) By 1932 he was in the midst of a Depression. (10) He was unable to teach or get his writings published. (11) He married and took to the hills. (12) He has lived the simple, rural life since then. (13) Many young people today would like to emulate it.

Describe the main ideas briefly in your own words.

(1) ____

(2) ____

(3) ____

(4) ____

(5) ____

Suggestions

(1) Nearing was dismissed from his job at the University of Pennsylvania.
(2) He was dismissed from his job at the University of Toledo.
(3) He was dismissed from the Communist Party.
(4) He got married and took to the hills.
(5) He has lived the simple, rural life ever since.

24. Now let's see how you do with this set of sentences. Remember, decide which are the main ideas and make them the main clauses. Then add supporting ideas expressed in the various forms you learned. To tie everything together, use any of the techniques covered in this chapter.

(1) The college magazines seem to be short of funds. (2) The college magazines seem to be short of humor too. (3) The Princeton Tiger was once an awesome beast. (4) It was founded in 1882. (5) It boasted humor from Booth Tarkington and F. Scott Fitzgerald. (6) Now it must beg for humorous contributions. (7) There is a simple theory. (8) People are more involved in social issues. (9) This makes them more sensitive. (10) Humor must be aimed only at college deans. (11) Who cares if you make fun of college deans? (12) Any issue of the magazine could be the last.

- - - - - - - - - - - - - - - - - - - -

Suggestions

(1) The college magazines seem to be short of funds. (2) The college magazines seem to be short of humor too. (3) The Princeton Tiger was once an awesome beast. (4) It was founded in 1882. (5) It boasted humor from Booth Tarkington and F. Scott Fitzgerald. (6) Now it must beg for humorous contributions. (7) There is a simple theory. (8) People are more involved in social issues. (9) This makes them more sensitive. (10) Humor must be aimed only at college deans.

(11) Who cares if you make fun of college deans?

(12) Any issue of the magazine could be the last.

25. Try this set. As background, "Jim Crow" refers to segregation practices against black people since the Civil War.

(1) Whites and blacks in the South are caught up in living non-Jim Crow. (2) They are caught up in varying degrees. (3) One thing can be said for segregation. (4) Everyone knew how to act then. (5) Walls are now partially broken down. (6) People are less sure about how to act. (7) Th situation has created its own anxieties and frustrations. (8) It has its humorous moments. (9) A black woman went to the placement office at the University of North Carolina. (10) Her photographs were larger than the space provided on the application. (11) The blonde applicant next to her sensed the problem. (12) Her suggestion was to cover up a part of the application. (13) This part said "U.S. citizenship? Yes... No...." (14) The blond said there couldn't be any doubt of the black woman's U.S. citizenship. (15) The black woman would have been angry in the old days. (16) She laughed now and accepted the suggestion. (17) People are playing by their own rules.

- - - - - - - - - - - - - - - - - - - -

Suggestions

(1) Whites and blacks in the South are caught up in living non-Jim Crow. (2) They are caught up in varying degrees. (3) One thing can be said for segregation. (4) Everyone knew how to act then. (5) Walls are now partially broken down. (6) People are less sure about how to act.

(7) The situation has created its own anxieties and frustrations. (8) It has its humorous moments. (9) A black woman went to the placement office at the University of North Carolina. (10) Her photographs were large

than the space provided on the application. (11) The blonde applicant next to her sensed the problem. (12) Her suggestion was to cover up a part of the application. (13) This part said "U.S. citizenship? Yes... No...." (14) The blonde said there couldn't be any doubt of the black woman's U.S. citizenship. (15) The black woman would have been angry in the old days. (16) She laughed now and accepted the suggestion. (17) People are playing by their own rules.

Now do the review of Chapter 3.

REVIEW

1. Any of these words listed below (on the left) can be inserted in the following sentence. Match each word with the description of its function.

   Daniel Ellsberg knew beforehand that he would be prosecuted for disclosing the Pentagon secrets; ______________ he intended to take full responsibility without implicating his friends.

________	(a) consequently,	(i)	It indicates that the second statement will be in contrast with the first.
________	(b) furthermore	(ii)	It indicates that despite the first statement the second statement is true.
________	(c) however,	(iii)	It indicates that the second statement will give additional information.
________	(d) nevertheless,	(iv)	It indicates that the second statement is the result of the first.

2. Punctuate these sentences:

   (a) I usually vote with the Democrats but this year I voted for a Republican.
   (b) English which is a required course here is usually easy for me but this year I didn't get a good grade.

(c) When the votes were counted we were surprised to learn that he won we even considered asking for a recount.
(d) He wrote two books by the time he was thirty a biography and a novel.
(e) He was too young for the draft however he wasn't too young to work.

3. You can assume that the following passage has been punctuated correctly. However, it isn't a smooth, easy-to-follow unit. Unify the passage by combining short sentences and inserting words or expressions that will link one sentence to another.

(1) Right now we rely heavily on petroleum as a source of energy. (2) Petroleum presents some difficulties for the future. (3) Petroleum costs are rising. (4) The cause is the search for new petroleum supplies. (5) The search for oil extends to the poles. (6) The search extends out on the continental shelf. (7) The price of fuel oil in Boston has doubled in a year. (8) Oil will run out in a century or so. (9) Oil may need to be rationed before that. (10) Oil would be used for transportation and the manufacture of plastics. (11) It would not be used to produce electricity or to heat homes. (12) Another problem is a growing dependence on foreign sources for it. (13) By 1985 the American demand will reach 28 million barrels a day. (14) Only 11 million barrels are expected to be produced domestically. (15) More than 30 percent of it already comes from abroad. (16) It comes mostly from the Caribbean. (17) Many foreign governments have a major voice in the price and flow of American fuel.

Suggested Answers

1. iv, (a) iii, (b) i (c) ii (d).

2. (a) I usually vote with the Democrats, but this year I voted for a Republican.

(b) English which is a required course here is usually easy for me but this year I didn't get a good grade.
(c) When the votes were counted we were surprised to learn that he won we even considered asking for a recount.
(d) He wrote two books by the time he was thirty a biography and a novel.
(e) He was too young for the draft however he wasn't too young to work.

3. (1) Right now we rely heavily on petroleum as a source of energy. (2) Petroleum presents some difficulties for the future. (3) Petroleum costs are rising. (4) The cause is the search for new petroleum supplies. (5) The search for oil extends to the poles. (6) The search extends out on the continental shelf. (7) The price of fuel oil in Boston has doubled in a year. (8) Oil will run out in a century or so. (9) Oil may need to be rationed before that. (10) Oil would be used for transportation and the manufacture of plastics. (11) It would not be used to produce electricity or to heat homes. (12) Another problem is a growing dependence on foreign sources for it. (13) By 1985 the American demand will reach 28 million barrels a day. (14) Only 11 million barrels are expected to be produced domestically. (15) More than 30 percent of it already comes from abroad. (16) It comes mostly from the Caribbean. (17) Many foreign governments have a major voice in the price and flow of American fuel.

(As usual, many other revisions are possible.)

If you answered the questions correctly, and your revision of the passage in question 3 compared well with the suggested sample, check these questions in the REVIEW column of the Self-Evaluation Record for

Chapter 3 (page 57), and go on to Chapter 4. If not, mark your own copy of Chart 2 (pages 317–318), so you will know which entries to concentrate on. Check entries 4 and 5 if you missed parts of questions 1 and 2; check entry 6 if you feel you could use more practice on unifying paragraphs by linking the sentences.

CHAPTER FOUR

Improving Emphasis

A sculptor chisels a rough piece of stone until he gets some general shape of what he eventually wants to produce. Slowly he refines his work until, at last, he has fashioned a beautifully formed statue. This is much like what you're doing in this book. You have already learned how to organize paragraphs and link sentences. Now you're going to learn ways to refine your basic ideas to make them sharper.

As an example, STUDY this copyedited passage:

Nader's

(1) ~~The~~ Raiders, ~~of Nader, who are~~ the champions of consumers, have made some alarming discoveries. (2) The Raiders claim that industries

--especially the big ones--

are exploiting us. (3) ~~This is especially true of the big ones.~~ (4) (Apparently, they have always exploited us.) (5) Nader has had a big effect wherever he has probed. (6) First comes Nader; next, ~~comes~~ reform.

Now look at the original and compare it with the copyedited version.

(1) The Raiders of Nader, who are the champions of consumers, have made some alarming discoveries. (2) The Raiders claim that industries are exploiting us. (3) This is especially true of the big ones. (4) Apparently, they have always exploited us. (5) Nader has had a big effect wherever he has probed. (6) First comes Nader; next comes reform.

As you see, only very small changes sharpened the original passage.

(a) Nader's in sentence 1 simplifies Raiders of Nader, which was awkward.
(b) The words who are can be deleted in this same sentence without any loss in meaning.
(c) Dashes emphasize sentence 3 and simplify it so much that we can put it into sentence 2 next to industries.
(d) Parentheses around sentence 4 show that it is just a side remark.
(e) Finally, in sentence 5 a comma marks the place where the word comes used to be, The word comes can be dropped because the reader will know it belongs there.

As a summary, in this chapter you're going to learn

(a) some ways to emphasize or de-emphasize details, and
(b) some ways to simplify phrases and clauses.

As always, you can use the preview of Chapter 4 to help you plan how to use the chapter to give you maximum benefits. First, do the preview, and then fill out the Self-Evaluation Record for Chapter 4.

PREVIEW

1. Punctuate the following sentences:

   (a) Roy Wilkins a black civil rights leader writes a newspaper column.
   (b) John Howard Griffin wrote the book Black Like Me.
   (c) Franklin D. Roosevelt the only man to be elected president four times is remembered for his "fireside chats."
   (d) The expression "Do as I say, not as I do" is my favorite.
   (e) Lillian Hellman wrote her autobiography The Unfinished Woman.

2. Here you're going to insert the (a) description (a love story) into the first three sentences, after the word play. Next, you're going to insert the (b) description (do you remember) into the last two sentences after the word house. Punctuate each insertion according to the emphasis suggested.

   (a) Description: a love story
      (i) The second play was better than the first. (Treat the description in the usual way.)
      (ii) The second play was better than the first. (Emphasize the description.)
      (iii) The second play was better than the first. (De-emphasize the description.)
   (b) Description: do you remember
      (iv) When I saw the house I knew I had to have it. (Emphasize the description.)
      (v) When I saw the house I knew I had to have it. (De-emphasize the description.)

3. Reduce each of these sentences as much as you can, and punctuate it correctly.

   (a) Tom was born in Durham in the state of North Carolina on January 3 in the year 1927.

   (b) I believe in the rights of women.

   (c) I want to borrow the book belonging to Chris.

   (d) This cup is made of china that cup is made of earthenware.

   (e) The dog lost the bone it had.

Suggested Answers

1. (a) Roy Wilkins, a black civil rights leader, writes

   (b) CORRECT

   (c) Roosevelt, the only man to be elected president four times, is

   (d) CORRECT

   (e) wrote her autobiography, The Unfinished Woman.

2. (a-i) The second play, a love story, was better than the first.

   (a-ii) The second play—a love story—was better than the first.

   (a-iii) The second play (a love story) was better than the first.

   (b-i) When I saw the house—do you remember?—I knew I had to have it.

   (b-ii) When I saw the house (do you remember?) I knew I had to have it.

3. (a) Tom was born in Durham, ~~in the state of~~ North Carolina, on January 3, 1927.

   (b) I believe in ~~the~~ women's rights ~~of women~~.

   (c) I want to borrow ~~the~~ Chris's book ~~belonging to Chris~~.

   (d) This cup is made of china; that cup, ~~is made~~ of earthenware.

   (e) The dog lost ~~the~~ its bone. ~~it had.~~

If you answered all the questions satisfactorily, you need only a light skim through this chapter. Otherwise put a check in the PREVIEW column of the Self-Evaluation Record for Chapter 4 beside any question that you can handle well enough. As usual, the blanks will then show those frames that you should study more thoroughly.

SELF-EVALUATION RECORD FOR CHAPTER 4

	PREVIEW	FRAMES	REVIEW
Question 1		1 through 4	
Question 2		5 through 10	
Question 3		11 through 19	

DESCRIPTIONS

1. In earlier chapters you learned how to add many different kinds of basic details to a main idea. And you used many different forms, such as adjectives and adverbs, phrases explaining where or when the action happened, and clauses describing someone or something in the main clause. All of these details were descriptions.

Now we're going to consider some other special kinds of descriptions One is just a shortcut for a descriptive clause. As an example, compare samples (a) and (b):

(a) Eldridge Cleaver belonged to the Black Panthers, which is a militant faction.

(b) Eldridge Cleaver belonged to the Black Panthers, a militant faction.

Did you notice that sample (b) meant exactly what sample (a) meant even though the words which is were dropped?

(c) The girl who is standing in the corner used to be the class president.

(d) The girl standing in the corner used to be the class president.

Here, samples (c) and (d) have exactly the same meaning too, even though the words who is were dropped in sample (d).

Shortcut descriptions can be very effective, as you'll see. LOOK AT these examples. UNDERLINE the words that can be dropped with no loss of meaning whatever.

(1) The movie, which is based on The Godfather, cannot mention the Mafia.

(2) The Newark that is in Ohio is far different from the Newark in New Jersey.

- - - - - - - - - - - - - - - - - - -

(1) which is (2) Newark that is

(You'll see later that other words can be deleted too.)

A SPECIAL DESCRIPTION: NOT A SENTENCE

2. Here are two examples of special descriptions that are just short-cuts of descriptive clauses. Can you tell whether the description has the main emphasis in samples (a) and (b)?

(a) The burning of Atlanta is one scene we associate with the movie Gone With the Wind.

(b) Mr. Gulch, the principal of Technical High School, is the first speaker.

Out of context, in sample (a) we really can't tell; the main emphasis may be on this specific movie or on the movie as opposed to the book. But in sample (b) the emphasis is surely on Mr. Gulch, and the words principal of Technical High School describe him.

We might also write sample (b) this way:

(c) Mr. Gulch, or the principal of Technical High School, is the first speaker.

The emphasis is still on Mr. Gulch. But now the word or is the tip-off that the description will be coming next.

Still another way to rewrite sample (b) is as here:

(d) The principal of Technical High School, Mr. Gulch, was the principal speaker.

Now which words have the main emphasis?

____

- - - - - - - - - - - - - - - - - -

The principal of Technical High School

3. Suppose a friend says she has something vital to tell you. You're all primed to listen, but she begins this way:

"Last week, or was it the week before? I can't remember exactly. No, it must have been last week because that was when...."

Are you still listening? No. When you write, it is even more important to include only relevant descriptions because you can lose your audience even faster.

Of course, there aren't any rules about the kinds of things you should describe. As the writer, you have to decide, and your decision depends on the circumstances. Will the description clarify the meaning and make it more interesting? If so, include it. Will the description interfere with the main point? Then don't include it.

There are really only two kinds of relevant descriptions:

(a) A description that is essential.
(b) A description that is helpful and nice to know.

When you decide to use a description, you also have to signal your reader to let him know how important it is. If you want to tell him that a description is essential because it narrows the meaning and makes it more specific, then you wouldn't set it off by punctuation. But if you want to tell him that it's nice to know but not absolutely essential, you would set it off.

LOOK AT these sentences:

(a) I prefer the proverb "Haste makes waste."
(b) A mystery, or a detective story, is fun to read.
(c) Mr. Clark, the dean, used to be a good athlete.

Which sentence has an essential description? ________________

- - - - - - - - - - - - - - - - - -

(a)

4. If a description needs to be set off, most of the time we would use commas. The rule is simple.

(a) The description is set off by commas if it is merely extra information.
(b) It is not set off by commas if it narrows the meaning of the entire sentence and makes it more specific.

To test out the rule in a sentence, you can read that sentence twice: once with the description and once without it.

Now COPYEDIT these sentences:

(1) Mr. James the foreman voted to strike.
(2) He is remembered for the statement "I do not choose to run."
(3) The policeman an argumentative fellow was too busy talking to see the accident.
(4) The winner of the scholarship was Tom Freed the winner of the award for high achievement in mathematics.
(5) Ibsen's play Hedda Gabler was recently produced on Broadway.
(6) He subscribes to the statement "Clothes make the man."
(7) The expression "colossus on the Hudson" describes Columbia University.
(8) Margaret Mead a well-known American anthropologist has written a book about the generation gap.
(9) Ti-Grace Atkinson a supporter of women's lib spoke at Catholic University.
(10) Many people feel that drug laws should distinguish between the soft drug marijuana and the hard drug heroin.

- - - - - - - - - - - - - - - - - -

(1) Mr. James^,the foreman^,voted
(2) CORRECT
(3) policeman^,an argumentative fellow^,was
(4) Freed^,the winner of the award
(5) CORRECT
(6) CORRECT
(7) CORRECT
(8) Mead^,a well-known American anthropologist^,has
(9) Atkinson^,a supporter of women's lib^,spoke
(10) CORRECT

5. But a comma is not the only way to set off a helpful but not absolutely essential description. We can also use dashes or parentheses.

COMPARE the following:

(a) Mr. Johnson, the new bank teller, comes from Indiana.
(b) Mr. Johnson (the new bank teller) comes from Indiana.
(c) Mr. Johnson—the new bank teller—comes from Indiana.

The commas look familiar, don't they? The parentheses seem to tuck the description away—to de-emphasize it—as if it weren't really very important. The dashes are attention-getters. Like all attention-getters, though, they can stop getting attention if they're used unnecessarily.

All three punctuation marks can be used interchangeably. The most appropriate one on any given occasion depends on the kind of effect you want to achieve.

Judging from the punctuation mark that sets off each description here, label the effect the writer probably wanted to give. WRITE "U" if it's the usual type of description; WRITE "E" if it's emphasized; and WRITE "D" if it's de-emphasized.

_____ (1) The children disliked the dogs, a pair of French poodles.
_____ (2) You have to wear tennis shoes (sneakers) on a clay court.
_____ (3) His wife—a real beauty—is two years older than he.
_____ (4) The second story (a mystery) was better than the first.
_____ (5) His hobby, wood carving, takes most of his time.

- - - - - - - - - - - - - - - - - - - -

U (1) D (2) E (3) D (4) U (5)

6. Now PUNCTUATE the description in each sentence according to the given direction:

De-emphasize
_____________ (1) Senator Robert Kennedy the junior senator from New York was assassinated in June 1968.

Emphasize
_____________ (2) Willis Reed our star player was injured last week.

De-emphasize
_____________ (3) The book a textbook was on his desk.

Usual
_____________ (4) The leader of the opposition Senator Fulbright delivered that speech.

Usual ________________ (5) Her boyfriend a medical student has a high draft number.

De-emphasize ________________ (6) Betty Friedan a leader of women's lib probably started the movement off by writing a book.

Emphasize ________________ (7) Today, the Senate will vote on the new bill a pressing issue.

Emphasize ________________ (8) The speakers two politicians don't get along well.

Usual ________________ (9) The private school here a progressive place had to close.

Usual ________________ (10) The book a fictionalized account of World War II could be a bestseller.

- -

(1) Kennedy (the junior senator from New York) was
(2) Reed--our star player--was
(3) book (a textbook) was
(4) opposition, Senator Fulbright, delivered
(5) boyfriend, a medical student, has
(6) Friedan (a leader of women's lib) probably
(7) bill--a pressing issue.
(8) speakers--two politicians--don't
(9) here, a progressive place, had
(10) book, a fictionalized account of World War II, could

A SPECIAL DESCRIPTION: A SENTENCE

7. All along we've said that main ideas are expressed as main clauses and supporting ideas are expressed in other forms. However, we can also use a main clause for a special description that isn't a part of the main train of thought, provided we set it off in some special way.

We can't use commas because the result would be too confusing. But dashes or parentheses are fine, depending on whether we want to emphasize or de-emphasize. COMPARE these examples:

(a) The boy is very tall, he is at least 6 feet 10, but he weighs only 160 pounds.

(b) The boy is very tall—he is at least 6 feet 10—but he weighs only 160 pounds.

(c) The boy is very tall (he is at least 6 feet 10), but he weighs only 160 pounds.

The commas just don't work. In sample (b) the dashes emphasize the description. But note that they cancel all other punctuation—even the comma that ordinarily joins two clauses. In sample (c) the comma is still there, but notice that it follows the closing parenthesis.

Notice, too, in both samples (b) and (c) that the description does not begin with a capital letter or end with a period, even though it is a sentence. The only exception is a description that is a question or an exclamation. In such cases the "?" or the "!" is retained, as here:

(d) Some musicians—remember Woodstock!—never seem to tire.

(e) Some schools (can it be true?) have a rule against long hair.

(Whether it is a description or not, an exclamation is reserved for the most attention-getting situations, of course.)

For some practice in using parentheses to de-emphasize a description and dashes to emphasize one, each example here is repeated twice. COPYEDIT by emphasizing the (a) example and de-emphasizing the (b):

(a) He told me his story it was in strict confidence but I had heard it before.

(b) He told me his story it was in strict confidence but I had heard it before.

(c) He comes from a distinguished family his mother was the daughter of a senator and he is very proud.

(d) He comes from a distinguished family his mother was the daughter of a senator and he is very proud.

- - - - - - - - - - - - - - - - - -

(a) story—it was in strict confidence—but

(b) story (it was in strict confidence), but

(c) family—his mother was the daughter of a senator—and

(d) family (his mother was the daughter of a senator), and

Notice the comma after the closing parenthesis in (b) and (d). This comma links the two main clauses.

8. Recall that a description enclosed in parentheses and buried in another sentence does not begin with a capital letter or end with a period.

(a) He is the highest-paid player on the team. (His salary is $150,000 a year.)

This is a good treatment because the description doesn't interrupt the main thought. Notice that it begins with a capital letter and ends with a period, as a sentence should.

Recall that a description enclosed in parentheses and buried in another sentence does not begin with a capital letter and it does not end with a period.

(b) He is the highest-paid player on the team (his salary is $150,000 a year).

Let's assume that the following descriptions are a part of some long report. Judging from the form of each, decide whether the writer has set it off by itself. If so, put a CHECK MARK beside it.

________ (1) (He works in Greensville.)
________ (2) (he works in Greensville)
________ (3) (He hasn't organized his work well.)
________ (4) (He goes to Indiana University.)
________ (5) (we deserve a better deal)

- - - - - - - - - - - - - - - - - - -

(1) ✓ (3) ✓ (4) ✓

USING CHART 2

9. As you've seen, you can handle most special descriptions however you like. But once you choose a particular form, you should apply it according to the rules. As usual, these rules are very easy to forget. Chart 2 will be particularly helpful though. STUDY the two entries:

SITUATION	IF	THEN	EXAMPLE
7. A SPECIAL DESCRIPTION: NOT A SENTENCE	(a) it narrows the meaning and makes it more specific,	(a) don't set it off.	(a) The book Rebecca was also a movie.
	(b) it is the usual nice-to-know, extra information,	(b) set it off by commas.	(b) His first book, a novel, was a success.
	(c) it is extra information that should be emphasized,	(c) set it off by dashes, which cancel all punctuation except ? or !.	(c) His first book—a novel—was a success. This was his first book—a novel—and it was a great success.
	(d) it is extra information that should be de-emphasized,	(d) set if off by parentheses. No punctuation goes before the opening parenthesis. No punctuation goes before the closing parenthesis except ? or !.	(d) His first book (a novel!) was a success. This was his first book (a novel), and it was a great success.
8. A SPECIAL DESCRIPTION: A SENTENCE	(a) it is set off by itself,	(a) enclose it in parentheses. (It begins with a capital and ends with a period.)	(a) The photo was great. (It was of his father.)
	(b) it is within another sentence and it needs to be emphasized,	(b) same as 7c.	(b) He is tall—is he over 6 feet?—and he's fat.

SITUATION	IF	THEN	EXAMPLE
8. A SPECIAL DESCRIPTION: A SENTENCE (continued)	(c) it is within another sentence, and it needs to be de-emphasized.	(c) same as 7d.	(c) He is tall (he's over 6 feet), and he's fat.

To make sure you can interpret this chart, WRITE the number and letter in the IF column that applies to each example here.

_______ (1) As soon as he was alone (it was hours later), he fell asleep.
_______ (2) He notified the two students, the fullback and the quarter-back, that he wouldn't attend the rally.

- - - - - - - - - - - - - - - - - - -

(1) 8c (2) 7b

10. Take out Chart 2 and use it to COPYEDIT the following sentences. In some examples you have a choice of punctuation mark. Whatever mark you select, be sure you follow the rules.

(1) He asked advice from his brother a third-year law student.

(2) It was colored brightly I'd say it was between yellow and red and it looked well made too.

(3) The newspapers we have four of them are all bad.

(4) The public school here P.S. 75 is considered very good.

(5) They go to a good school Ohio State University.

(6) This is Mr. James the music teacher.

(7) His grades are good they are almost too good and I know he'll graduate.

(8) The movie it was <u>Divorce Italian Style</u> was on television last night.

(9) New York the best city in the world is my home town.

(10) The student studying over there is a star football player.

- - - - - - - - - - - - - - - - - - -

Suggestions

(1) brother a third-year law student. OR brother a third-year law student. OR brother a third-year law student.

(2) brightly I'd say it was between yellow and red and OR brightly I'd say it was between yellow and red and

(3) newspapers we have four of them are OR newspapers we have four of them are

(4) here P.S. 75 is OR here P.S. 75 is OR here P.S. 75 is

(5) school Ohio State University OR school Ohio State University Or school Ohio State University

(6) James the music teacher OR James the music teacher OR James the music teacher

(7) good they are almost too good and OR good they are almost too good and

(8) movie it was Divorce Italian Style was OR movie it was Divorce Italian Style was

(9) York the best city in the world is OR York the best city in the world is OR York the best city in the world is

(10) CORRECT

A SPECIAL DESCRIPTION: EXPRESSES OWNERSHIP

11. Another kind of special description expresses ownership. (You probably use it already.) Look at these examples:

(a) The rights of man
(b) The rights that man owns
(c) The rights that man possesses
(d) The rights belonging to man

We can also use a shortcut that will replace any of the longer forms, as here:

(e) Man's rights

Notice that the apostrophe replaces the words or letters that were left out. You can use all these forms interchangeably. However, the form in sample (e) is usually more informal than the others.

The rule is simple. To show ownership

(a) Add an apostrophe plus s to any singular noun owner, even if it already ends in s.
(b) Add an apostrophe alone to a plural noun owner ending in s.
(c) Add an apostrophe plus s to a plural noun that does not end in s.
(d) Use a special word without an apostrophe for a pronoun owner.

Now compare these descriptions of ownership.

NOUN OWNERS	PRONOUN OWNERS
Bess's house	Her house
Teacher's pet	His pet
Cat's paw	Its paw
Players' roles	Their roles
Women's rights	Their rights

Note particularly the description with the "it" owner—the its. Many people confuse this form with "it's," which is actually a shortcut—a contraction—for "it is." Remember, the apostrophe is used in descriptions of ownership only when nouns are the owners.

PUT A CHECK MARK beside any of these words that you think are a part of an ownership description:

_______ (1) who's
_______ (2) its
_______ (3) whose
_______ (4) our
_______ (5) it's

- - - - - - - - - - - - - - - - - -

✓ (2) ✓ (3) ✓ (4)

12. Remember the rule: When the owner is a noun, you can shorten a description of ownership by adding an apostrophe plus s to a single noun (or to a plural noun that does not end in s) and just the apostrophe to a plural noun ending in s. When the owner is a pronoun, however, you have to use a special word without an apostrophe.

See if you can APPLY this rule and CHANGE each long expression to the appropriate shorter form. First make a noun the owner and then the pronoun. Follow this example:

EXAMPLE: the car belonging to Charles.

Charles's car

his car

(1) The ear of the pig ________ ________

(2) The book that Mr. Sams owns ________ ________

(3) The ears of the pigs ________ ________

(4) The book belonging to the school ________ ________

(5) The dresses of the girls ________ ________

(6) The eyes of the girl ________ ________

- - - - - - - - - - - - - - - - - - - -

(1) The pig's ear
Its ear

(2) Mr. Sams's book
His book

(3) The pigs' ears
Their ears

(4) The school's book
Its book

(5) The girls' dresses
Their dresses

(6) The girl's eyes
Her eyes

A SPECIAL DESCRIPTION: OBVIOUS WORDS ARE LEFT OUT

13. Some special descriptions are so clear that we can leave the obvious parts out. This kind of simplification accounts for the comma between city and state and between day and year.

Look at this sample:

(a) We honeymooned in Charleston in South Carolina.

As you can see, the phrase in South Carolina is essential because it defines the Charleston we mean. We might have honeymooned in another Charleston in another state—West Virginia, for instance. This, of course, is why a comma doesn't follow Charleston in sample (a).

But we would rarely write this long form. We would write the shortcut in sample (b) instead.

(b) We honeymooned in Charleston, South Carolina.

In sample (b) the obvious in was dropped, and the comma was left in its place. And this is where our rule about separating city from state came from.

Now look at this sample:

(c) The United States achieved its independence July 4 in 1776.

Again, a comma doesn't follow 4 because the year is essential. Independence wasn't achieved on just any July 4. However, more often, we're likely to write this:

(d) The United States achieved its independence July 4, 1776.

Here, too, the obvious in was dropped and a comma was left in its place. And this is where our rule about separating day from year came from. (There is a second reason for the comma between the 4 and 1776, however: to separate two sets of numbers that could otherwise become confused.)

COPYEDIT these sentences by dropping the obvious words.

(1) He lives in Kansas City in the state of Missouri.
(2) He was born on January 26 in the year of 1926.

- - - - - - - - - - - - - - - - -

(1) He lives in Kansas City, ~~in the state of~~ Missouri.
(2) He was born on January 26, ~~in the year of~~ 1926.

14. Obvious words can be left out in other situations too, with a comma again acting as a marker to show where the words used to be.

Look at sample (a). Can you tell what words the comma represents?

(a) He read three books last week; this week, only one.

Right you are if you thought the comma stands for the words he read, as in sample (b):

(b) He read three books last week; this week he read only one.

Remember, the comma can replace only those words that the reader already knows. Otherwise he wouldn't be able to make sense of the sentence. Often, these words have just been said in the same kind of situation. As you see in samples (a) and (b), the replaced words he read were already used in a similar way (in the first part of the sentence).

SEE if you can tell what word, or words, the comma in each sentence represents. WRITE the word, or words, on the blank:

______________ (1) His grade was 86 in math; in English, 92.

______________ (2) The price of coffee is 98¢ a pound; the price of milk, 30¢ a quart.

______________ (3) In France the national drink is wine; in Germany, beer.

______________ (4) They prefer the sea; we, the mountains.

______________ (5) The table was unfinished; the dresser, in mint condition.

- - - - - - - - - - - - - - - - - - -

(1) his grade was
(2) is
(3) the national drink is
(4) prefer
(5) was

15. This time, read over the sentence to see if you can leave out any words. If so, delete them and mark their place by a comma. Remember, you can't take out any words unless the reader can understand the sentence without them.

FOLLOW this example:

The boys' dormitory is old; the girls', ~~dormitory is~~ brand new.

(1) Girls are considered neat; boys are considered messy.
(2) The rent in August was $350; the rent in September was $250.
(3) Our vacation this year was two weeks; last year it was ten days.
(4) He drives a Ford; she drives a Volkswagen.
(5) She works downtown; he works in the local bookstore.

- - - - - - - - - - - - - - - - - - -

(1) Girls are considered neat; boys ~~are considered~~ messy.

(2) The rent in August was $350; ~~the rent~~ in September ~~was~~ $250.

(3) Our vacation this year was two weeks; last year ~~it was~~ ten days.

(4) He drives a Ford; she ~~drives~~ a Volkswagen.

(5) She works downtown; he ~~works~~ in the local bookstore.

16. The entries in Chart 2 for the last two special descriptions are as follows:

SITUATION	IF	THEN	EXAMPLE
9. A SPECIAL DESCRIPTION: EXPRESSES OWNERSHIP	(a) a noun is the owner,	(a) add 's to all singular nouns, even one that ends in s. Add ' alone to all plural nouns ending in s. Add 's to plural nouns not ending in s.	(a) Mary's bell Tess's bell The girls' bell The children's bell
	(b) a pronoun is the owner,	(b) use the special form without an apostrophe: my, our, your, his, her, their, its, or whose.	(b) This is its home now.
10. A SPECIAL DESCRIPTION: OBVIOUS WORDS ARE LEFT OUT	(a) a word or words are obvious between city and state or between day and year,	(a) drop the obvious word or words, and insert a comma instead.	(a) I was born in Newark ~~in the state of~~ Ohio, on June 8 ~~in~~ 1932.

SITUATION	IF	THEN	EXAMPLE
10. A SPECIAL DESCRIPTION: OBVIOUS WORDS LEFT OUT (Continued)	(b) other words are obvious or are repeated from a similar situation.	(b) same as 10a.	(b) This bowl is ~~made of~~ pewter; that bowl,~~is made of~~ silver.

Just to make sure you're interpreting the chart correctly, WRITE IN the identifying number and letter that each example represents:

_______ (1) The dog lost its collar.
_______ (2) Last week he earned $80; this week, $60.
_______ (3) This is George's date.
_______ (4) He is from Miami, Ohio.

- - - - - - - - - - - - - - - - - -

9b (1) 10b (2) 9a (3) 10a (4)

USING CHART 2

17. Now look at Chart 2 and use it to help you COPYEDIT this passage. Assume that all the punctuation is right except in situations pertaining to entries 7 through 10.

Do you know the difference between a proofreader and a copyeditor? A proofreader even a good one hasn't much chance to be creative: He must just be sure that the printed version matches the authors final copy exactly. A copyeditor can be creative by suggesting changes creative changes. In fact, changing is the copyeditors whole job or responsibility. He corrects punctuation the author generally appreciates this and style too. The author and copyeditor work together they should, anyway to produce a better product. And proofreader and copyeditor work together too: The copyeditor is responsible for style; the proofreader is responsible for form.

- - - - - - - - - - - - - - - - - -

Suggestions

Do you know the difference between a proofreader and a copyeditor?

A proofreader even a good one hasn't much chance to be creative: He must just be sure that the printed version matches the authors final copy exactly. A copyeditor can be creative by suggesting changes creative changes. In fact, changing is the copyeditors whole job or responsibility. He corrects punctuation the author generally appreciates this and style too. The author and copyeditor work together they should, anyway to produce a better product. And proofreader and copyeditor work together too: The copyeditor is responsible for style; the proofreader is respon- sible for form.

(Of course, you could have used alternative forms for examples of entries 7 and 8.)

COPYEDITING DESCRIPTIONS

18. Now see if you can apply what you've learned in this chapter. Note that the sample fails to differentiate between the main issue and descriptions:

(1) Many people argue that bussing children to school is not a permanent solution to segregation. (2) The solutions of Southerners was often bussing. (3) They bussed white children to white schools. (4) The real solution is completely open housing. (5) This would mix the children first at home. (6) This is the important place to mix them.

At first you might imagine that some of the sentences don't actually belong in this passage. At second look you see that they do. The solution is to decide which are the main thoughts and which ideas are really descriptions, and to use the techniques you learned to present these descriptions simply and effectively.

COPYEDIT this passage according to the following suggestions. (This, of course, is only one of the many ways to revise the paragraph.)

(1) In sentence 2 you can use a shortcut form for the phrase <u>solutions of Southerners</u>.

(2) Sentence 2 is a side remark; and so is sentence 3, which is a description of sentence 2. Mark these sentences appropriately.

(3) Sentence 4 is a main thought. So is sentence 5. However, sentence 6 is a description of sentence 5. Indicate this.

- - - - - - - - - - - - - - - - - - -

Suggestions

(2), (3) (The ~~solutions of~~ Southerners' solution was often bussing -- ~~They~~ bussing white children to white schools.)

(4)-(6) The real solution is completely open housing. This would mix the children first at home, ~~This is~~ the important place to mix them.

19. TRY this one yourself. See how much you can improve it just by handling descriptions appropriately.

Briggs and five other gorillas had just moved into new cages. These are experimentally designed to test the adaptability of the apes to an artificial environment. Briggs is an orangutan from Borneo. Briggs was having trouble deciding whether he liked the new quarters he had. These new quarters were indoor cages with a simulated treetop. There were plenty of vines for him and the others to swing on, and the cage was big enough. It was 20 x 20 feet. But Briggs was curious. He was destructively curious. He tried to rip the artificial vines and break the artificial branches. At the end of the first day they had lasted him out. They won the first round at least!

- - - - - - - - - - - - - - - - - - -

Suggestions

Briggs (an orangutan from Borneo) and five other gorillas had just moved into new cages, ~~These are~~ experimentally designed to test the apes' adaptability ~~of the apes~~ to an artificial environment. ~~Briggs is an orangutan from Borneo~~ Briggs was having trouble deciding whether he liked ~~the~~ his new quarters ~~he had~~ ~~These new quarters were~~ indoor cages with a simulated treetop. There were plenty of vines for him and the others to swing on, and the cage was big enough ~~It was~~ 20 x 20 feet. But Briggs was curious ~~He was~~ destructively curious. He tried to rip the artificial vines and break the artificial branches. At the end of the first day they had lasted him out They won the first round at least!

After you have compared your passage with the copyedited sample, do the review of Chapter 4.

REVIEW

1. Punctuate the following sentences:

    (a) Many women support Betty Friedan one of the first women in "the movement."
    (b) Professor Ashley Montagu a well-known anthropologist was an early champion of the ladies.
    (c) Graduates of Columbia College reminisce over the song "Roar, Lion, Roar."
    (d) General Douglas MacArthur was remembered for the promise "I shall return!"
    (e) Dick Cavett the host of a popular television talk show has also been a television writer and actor.

2. Insert the (a) description in the first three sentences (after <u>book</u>) and the (b) description in the last two sentences (before <u>and</u>). Punctuate each one according to the emphasis suggested.

    (a) Description: a novel

        (i) He wrote his first book soon after he graduated from college.

        (Treat the description in the usual way.)

(ii) He wrote his first book soon after he graduated from college.

(Emphasize the description.)

(iii) He wrote his first book soon after he graduated from college.

(De-emphasize the description.)

(b) Description: it was dramatic.

(iv) In World War II General Douglas MacArthur made headlines with a promise to return and in the Korean War Harry Truman made headlines with a promise to return MacArthur.

(Emphasize the description.)

(v) In World War II General Douglas MacArthur made headlines with a promise to return and in the Korean War Harry Truman made headlines with a promise to return MacArthur.

(De-emphasize the description.)

3. Reduce each of these sentences as much as you can, and punctuate them correctly:

(a) I visited the city of Concord in the state of Massachusetts on July 4 in the year 1950.

(b) Last month he earned $300 this month he earned only $200.

(c) This is the television set belonging to the class.

(d) The school colors of the University of Tennessee are orange and white the school colors of the University of South Carolina are garnet and black.

(e) The children lost the shoes that belonged to them.

Suggested Answers

1. (a) Friedan, one of the first women in "the movement."
   (b) Montagu, a well-known anthropologist, was
   (c) CORRECT
   (d) CORRECT
   (e) Cavett, the host of a popular television talk show, has

2. (a-i) He wrote his first book, a novel, soon after he graduated from college.
   (a-ii) He wrote his first book---a novel---soon after he graduated from college.
   (a-iii) He wrote his first book (a novel) soon after he graduated from college.
   (b-iv) In World War II General Douglas MacArthur made headlines with a promise to return--it was dramatic!--and in the Korean War Harry Truman made headlines with a promise to return MacArthur.
   (b-v) In World War II General Douglas MacArthur made headlines with a promise to return (it was dramatic!), and in the Korean War Harry Truman made headlines with a promise to return MacArthur.

3. (a) I visited ~~the city of~~ Concord, ~~in the state of~~ Massachusetts, on July 4, ~~in the year~~ 1950.
   (b) Last month he earned $300; this month, ~~he earned~~ only $200.
   (c) This is the class's television set ~~belonging to the class~~.
   (d) The University of Tennessee's school colors ~~of the~~ are orange and white; ~~the school colors of~~ the University of South Carolina's ~~are~~ garnet and black.
   (e) The children lost ~~the~~ their shoes ~~that belonged to them~~.

If you answered the questions correctly, put checks beside the questions in the REVIEW column of the Self-Evaluation Record for Chapter 4 (page 88), and go on to Chapter 5. In marking your own copy of Chart 2 (pages 319-321), put checks beside entries 7 and 8 if you missed any parts of questions 1 and 2; put a check beside entry 9 or 10, whichever is appropriate, if you missed parts of question 3.

CHAPTER FIVE

Simplifying Descriptions

In order to write good prose, you know you must reserve the main clauses for the main ideas. But, once you do that, you have many alternate ways of handling the important details—and particularly if these details are descriptions, as you saw in Chapter 4.

Besides those techniques you have already learned, however, another valuable tool is to cluster a few key words describing someone or something important in the sentence. This kind of construction can frequently replace a long descriptive phrase—even a descriptive clause—and become a giant pep pill for your prose. At the least, it will be more concise.

COMPARE these, for example:

(a) We often hear of liberals who have high principles.
But she is a conservative who has high principles.

(b) We often hear of high-principled liberals.
But she is a high-principled conservative.

Out of context we can't say for sure that sample (b) is much better than sample (a). But we can say for sure that it's a shorter, more direct way to say exactly what sample (a) says. And writing that's direct and concise is usually an improvement because it has a better chance of making its points.

In this chapter you'll learn how to reduce some phrases and clauses to two-word descriptions and also how to punctuate them to get your meaning across.

But first turn to the preview of Chapter 5 to find out what you already know about special descriptions like these.

PREVIEW

1. Punctuate the description in each of the following sentences:

   (a) It was a cold chilling day in November.
   (b) Those are three smart boys.
   (c) That is a high tension wire.

(d) He bought three ill fitting suits.
(e) He bought a white orlon sweater.
(f) He stepped on a sharp carpet tack.
(g) I read a four or five page article in that magazine.
(h) You need a three inch margin.
(i) She heard a high piercing scream.
(j) They are two perfectly matched players.

2. Reduce each sentence by using a two-word description instead of a longer descriptive phrase or clause:

(a) Some Americans believe that only citizens who are politically active elect our politicians.

(b) By using techniques in which he applied a lot of pressure to the customers, Mr. Jones became a salesman who sold a lot of insurance.

Suggested Answers

1. (a) a cold, chilling day
(b) CORRECT
(c) a high-tension wire
(d) bought three ill-fitting suits
(e) CORRECT
(f) CORRECT
(g) a four-or five-page article
(h) a three-inch margin
(i) a high, piercing scream
(j) CORRECT

2.

(a) Some Americans believe that only politically active citizens ~~who are politically active~~ elect our politicians.

(b) By using high-pressure techniques, ~~in which he applied a lot of pressure to the customers,~~ Mr. Jones became a high-selling salesman ~~who sold a lot a lot of insurance.~~

Did you get everything right? If so, you can skim over the chapter. Otherwise, mark the Self-Evaluation Record for Chapter 5 to indicate frames you need to concentrate on.

SELF-EVALUATION RECORD FOR CHAPTER 5

	PREVIEW	FRAMES	REVIEW
Question 1		1 through 9	
Question 2		10 through 14	

A TWO-WORD DESCRIPTION

1. You can really streamline your writing by condensing descriptive phrases and clauses into two-word descriptions. But you need to punctuate them so that everyone will interpret them exactly as you intend.

As an example, in Newsweek magazine a two-word description had two possible interpretations because the print was so blurred that you couldn't tell whether the blurred print concealed a hyphen or a comma. Samples (a) and (b) illustrate the two possibilities:

(a) a still, deadly weapon
(b) a still-deadly weapon

Sample (a) means a quiet and deadly weapon—a grenade? But sample (b) means a weapon that remains deadly. Out of context you would never know which meaning the writer had intended.

Look at these examples. Notice how the hyphen joins the underlined words so that they act as if they were actually one word; without the hyphen each word has a separate meaning.

WITHOUT A HYPHEN	WITH A HYPHEN
(c) A major league owner (It means "an important owner in the league.")	(d) A major-league owner (It means "an owner of a team in the major leagues."

No skating sign	No-skating sign
(It means "there was no sign about the skating.")	(It means "a sign that said there was no skating.")

Once you become sensitive to possible misinterpretations of two-word descriptions, you're likely to hear and read some humorous things. As an example, in a recent television discussion about black people in sports, sports announcer Howard Cosell reminded us that we still haven't had a "black head coach." Try reading that one with a hyphen joining black and head!

SEE if you can INTERPRET the two-word descriptions below. WRITE what you think each one means.

(1) A small change purse ______________________________

(2) A small-change purse ______________________________

- - - - - - - - - - - - - - - - - - -

Suggestions

(1) A change purse that is small.

(2) A purse for small change.

2. Now let's consider how to punctuate a two-word description so that it will say exactly what you mean and the reader won't have to figure everything out for himself.

Only two of the possible relationships between the three words require punctuation to make them clear:

(a) The two descriptive words act together to describe the noun.

He is a tough-looking boy.

(b) The two descriptive words act separately to describe the same characteristic of the noun.

He is a tall, strong boy.

In (a) notice that the hyphen joining the two descriptive words shows that they act as if they were actually one word: The boy isn't tough or looking—but tough-looking. In (b) the two descriptive words describe the same characteristic—the boy's physique. This means we could join them by and, just as we can join any other units that are alike. We insert a comma to show where the and can go. Only in this relationship can the two descriptive words be reversed.

Two other relationships are possible. The two descriptive words can act separately to describe two different characteristics of the noun, as here:

(c) He saw three smart boys.

No punctuation is necessary in (c); the three describes the number of boys, and smart describes their ability. Nor is any punctuation necessary when the last two words act as a unit, as here:

(d) He is an awkward old man.

Some languages have only one word for old man. Note that in these last two relationships the two descriptive words cannot be reversed.

Describe in your own words the relationship between these two-word descriptions, judging from the punctuation:

(1) An angry young man ______________________________

(2) An angry, young man ______________________________

\- - - - - - - - - - - - - - - - - -

Suggestions

(1) The last two words act as a unit.

(2) The first two words act separately to describe the same characteristic of the noun. Since you could insert and between the two words, you need the comma. (Note that here the two words could be reverse

3. Let's summarize. In order to punctuate a two-word description, you need to test the relationships between the words:

(a) Do the first two words act together to describe the noun as if they were actually one word? If so, join them by a hyphen. (They cannot be reversed or joined by and.)

(b) Do the first two words act separately to describe the same characteristic of the noun? If so, set them off by a comma. (They can be joined by and, and they can be reversed.)

The other two relationships don't require punctuation: The first two words act separately to describe two different characteristics of the third word, or the last two words act as a unit. In these relationships the first two words cannot be reversed.

However, you don't need to test these relationships if one descriptive word is an -ly adverb, as here:

(a) He is a politically active student.
(b) This is a racially mixed community.

Notice that both descriptions are clear without any punctuation between the descriptive words. Notice too that these words cannot be reversed.

See if you can follow these guidelines to PUNCTUATE the following two-word descriptions:

(1) He ran an incredibly naive campaign.
(2) He bought a grotesque brick house.
(3) This is a slow laborious process.
(4) He lives in a "one horse" town.
(5) He took three demanding courses last semester.
(6) This is a recently published book.
(7) Donations are a tax exempt expense.
(8) They want a one family house in the suburbs.
(9) He took an advanced math course.
(10) She is a new inexperienced teacher.

- - - - - - - - - - - - - - - - - -

(1) CORRECT
(2) CORRECT
(3) a slow, laborious process
(4) a "one-horse" town
(5) CORRECT
(6) CORRECT
(7) a tax-exempt expense.
(8) a one-family house
(9) CORRECT (You might have put a hyphen between advanced and math on the assumption that these words acted as a unit.)
(10) a new, inexperienced teacher.

4. Try PUNCTUATING the following two-word descriptions:

(1) He bought two old cars so that he could repair them.
(2) They are bright capable boys.
(3) He is an ill mannered child.
(4) It is a highly developed process.
(5) You should use a water soluble paint.
(6) He is in a high income bracket.
(7) We took a long refreshing swim.
(8) Those are well matched teams.
(9) What you need is a strong energetic man.
(10) She wore a new red sweater.
(11) He wrote a one act play.
(12) I like clay tennis courts.
(13) Mays had a near perfect day at the plate.
(14) He is a nearly perfect player.
(15) I enjoy good rock music.

- - - - - - - - - - - - - - - - - - -

(1) CORRECT
(2) are bright, capable boys.
(3) an ill-mannered child.
(4) CORRECT
(5) a water-soluble paint.
(6) a high-income bracket.
(7) CORRECT or a long, refreshing swim.
(8) are well-matched teams.
(9) a strong, energetic man.
(10) CORRECT
(11) a one-act play.
(12) CORRECT
(13) a near-perfect day
(14) CORRECT
(15) CORRECT

JOINING TWO-WORD DESCRIPTIONS

5. Here is a special case that is handy to know about. Suppose you were writing about inflation, and you wanted to say that it affected lower-income people and middle-income people most, as in sample (a):

(a) Inflation hurts lower-income people and middle-income people most.

You can shorten this sentence and get to the point more quickly if you drop the obvious words, as in sample (b):

(b) Inflation hurts lower- and middle-income people most.

Note that we must keep the hyphen to show that lower still belongs with the words income and people.

Here is the rule covering this special situation: To join two similar two-word descriptions, we can reduce the first one to the beginning word—plus a hyphen if the hyphen is needed.

APPLY the rule to these examples: Don't forget the hyphen in the short form if it was necessary in the long form.

(1) The dress has a two inch hem or a three inch hem.
(2) That applies to both tight fitting clothes and loose fitting clothes.
(3) Most teachers expect four page reports or five page reports.
(4) I need two white mice or three white mice for this experiment.

- - - - - - - - - - - - - - - - - -

(1) The dress has a two inch hem or a three inch hem.
(2) That applies to both tight fitting clothes and loose-fitting clothes.
(3) Most teachers expect four page reports or five-page reports.
(4) I need two white mice or three white mice for this experiment.

A THREE-WORD DESCRIPTION

6. Two more variations will crop up from time to time. One is a three-word description, with three descriptive words instead of the usual two. However, the same relationships hold between the descriptive words.

(a) She has her old pencil-slim figure.
(b) She wore a new elegant, graceful dress.
(c) I have three white cardigan sweaters.

Once we decide that a hyphen is needed in (a) between pencil and slim, we can consider the two-word description composed of old, pencil-slim, and figure. No further punctuation is then needed between the two descriptive units because they separately describe different characteristics of figure.

In (b) the words elegant and graceful are set off by a comma because they describe the same characteristic of dress. However, no further punctuation is needed between the descriptive unit elegant, graceful and that of new because these describe different characteristics.

In (c) the three descriptive words describe three different characteristics of sweaters.

The second variation of the two-word description occurs when the descriptive words follow the noun. Although we still have a two-word description, punctuation isn't necessary because the description is already clear.

(d) Her new figure is pencil slim.

Try to PUNCTUATE these variations:

(1) They live in a large old fashioned house.
(2) These two teams are well matched.
(3) We have two old stone houses for sale.
(4) He wore sorry looking blue jeans.
(5) I spotted the two happy smiling children.

- - - - - - - - - - - - - - - - - - -

(1) They live in a large old-fashioned house (OR large, old-fashioned).
(2) CORRECT
(3) CORRECT
(4) He wore sorry-looking blue jeans.
(5) I spotted the two happy, smiling children.

USING CHART 2

7. All the details for handling two-word descriptions are summarized here as they appear in Chart 2:

SITUATION	IF	THEN	EXAMPLE
11. A TWO-WORD DESCRIPTION	(a) a descriptive word is an -ly adverb,	(a) no punctuation is necessary.	(a) He is a politically active student.
	(b) two descriptive words or units separately describe different	(b) same as 11(a).	(b) He has two new pens. He has two red wool sweaters.

SITUATION	IF	THEN	EXAMPLE
11. A TWO-WORD DESCRIPTION (Continued)	characteristics of the noun (you can't reverse them),		
	(c) a descriptive word or unit describes another descriptive word plus a noun acting as a unit (you can't reverse the descriptive words),	(c) same as 11(a).	(c) They bought a new beach house. They bought a new frame beach house.
	(d) two descriptive words or units act together to describe the noun as if they were really one word,	(d) join the descriptive words by a hyphen. (With two descriptions alike except for the beginning word, shorten the first to the beginning word plus hyphen.)	(d) He makes short-range plans. He makes many short-range plans. (English is either a two- or three-credit course.)
	(e) two descriptive words or units separately describe the noun, but both describe the same characteristic (you can insert and between them and you can reverse them),	(e) put a comma between them to mark where the and was dropped.	(e) It was a dull, dreary day. We spent three dull, dreary days there.

COPYEDIT each example by inserting appropriate punctuation if it is needed. Also WRITE the identifying letter of the entry matching it.

______ (1) He has a high pitched voice.
______ (2) He is a highly respected teacher.
______ (3) He wrote three satisfactory papers.
______ (4) He is a deep brooding fellow.
______ (5) He wore dirty blue jeans.

- - - - - - - - - - - - - - - - - -

d (1) a high-pitched voice
a (2) CORRECT
b (3) CORRECT
e (4) a deep, brooding fellow
c (5) CORRECT

A TWO-WORD DESCRIPTION

8. Using Chart 2, COPYEDIT these examples:

(1) He ordered two boiled eggs.
(2) They have front or top loading machines.
(3) He bought two used bird cages.
(4) He asked a double barreled question.
(5) This is a well lit room.
(6) He borrowed a worn soiled tie.
(7) Math is a five credit course.
(8) He graded twenty term papers.
(9) He read a three or four page article.
(10) She is cold icy woman.
(11) This is the old apple tree.
(12) She was a strikingly beautiful girl.
(13) Napoleon was a short stocky man.
(14) He bought a new blue shirt.
(15) They need able bodied men.

- - - - - - - - - - - - - - - -

(1) CORRECT (11b)
(2) have front-or top-loading machines. (11d)
(3) CORRECT (11c)
(4) a double-barreled question. (11d)
(5) a well-lit room. (11d)
(6) a worn, soiled tie. (11e)

(7) a five-credit course. (11d)
(8) CORRECT (11b)
(9) a three-or four-page article. (11d)
(10) a cold, icy woman. (11a)
(11) CORRECT (11c)
(12) CORRECT (11a)
(13) a short, stocky man. (11a)
(14) CORRECT (11b)
(15) need able-bodied men. (11d)

9. You can assume that the punctuation in the following passage is correct except for missing hyphens or commas between descriptive words. First, UNDERLINE each two-word description, and then COPYEDIT by inserting any appropriate punctuation.

(a) In 1920 only about 20 percent of all qualified young people went to high school. (b) This extra advanced schooling was a privilege that they didn't pay for. (c) Nowadays, almost 50 percent of our high school graduates go to college. (d) Yet we make them pay for something that is no longer reserved for the few privileged people.

(e) Henry Steele Commager, the noted historian, gives two principal arguments supporting tuition free education. (f) One is that a liberal or democratic type government cannot work without well educated men and women. (g) Next, his equally convincing argument is that as our fast growing society becomes more complex, more expertise is required to run it. (h) Those who train themselves for highly technical jobs are necessary public servants learning the skills that the society must have in order to survive.

(i) Every Western country except the United States provides a free university education. (j) Poorer countries give grants to deserving university students on the hard headed principle that highly educated men and women serve their country just as soldiers do. (k) Besides, they pay back later what they take now in high income taxes and in high property taxes too.

- - - - - - - - - - - - - - - - - -

(a) all qualified young people

(b) extra, advanced schooling

(c) high-school graduates

(d) few privileged people

(e) two principal arguments tuition-free education

(f) liberal-or democratic-type government well-educated men

(g) equally convincing argument fast-growing society

(h) highly technical jobs necessary public servants

(i) Every Western country free university education

(j) deserving university students hard-headed principle highly educated men

(k) high income taxes high property taxes

Note: Situation (a) could also have a comma after qualified, depending on the writer's intention. Situation (c) is very common without the hyphen—probably because everyone understands what it means here.

10. Now let's see if you can turn some unnecessarily long clauses and phrases into neat two-word descriptions.

Compare these, for example. Sample (b) has a lot more punch, don't you think?

(a) Mohammed Ali is a fighter who is a smooth talker.
(b) Mohammed Ali is a smooth-talking fighter.

Or look at these:

(c) Businessmen prefer words like utilize and finalize that sound impressive rather than words that sound plainer like use and finish.
(d) Businessmen prefer impressive-sounding words like utilize and and finalize rather than the plainer-sounding use and finish.

Notice that in each example we have reduced a supporting clause to a two-word description. TRY one yourself:

Students who were naïve about politics revolutionized the 1968 presidential campaigns.

- - - - - - - - - - - - - - - - - - -

Suggestion

Politically naïve

Students ~~who were naïve about politics~~ revolutionized the 1968 presidential campaigns.

11. Out of context you can't tell whether a two-word description is better than a supporting clause saying the same things. However, it often sounds smoother, and it is always more direct.

Now TRY these:

(1) The boys who are built powerfully won't necessarily be the athletes who will break records.

(2) The low value of the dollar is a complaint these days that is persistent and nagging.

(3) The watch has been specially treated with a substance that resists rust.

(4) He wrote a report that is seven or eight pages.

- - - - - - - - - - - - - - - - - -

Suggestions

powerfully built ... record-breaking

(1) The boys ~~who are built powerfully~~ won't necessarily be the athletes ~~who will break records~~.

persistent, nagging

(2) The low value of the dollar is a complaint these days ~~that is persistent and nagging~~.

rust-resistant

(3) The watch has been specially treated with a substance ~~that resists rust~~.

seven-or eight-page

(4) He wrote a report ~~that is seven or eight pages~~.

12. Often, we can reduce sentences cluttered with long phrases and other unnecessary words to a simpler form by substituting a with phrase, plus a two-word description, for something more unwieldly.

(a) By having the government subsidize housing, we may be able to solve the acute shortage.

(b) With government-subsidized housing, we may be able to solve the acute shortage.

Other phrases that are good substitutes for long phrases may start with because of, instead of, by, or after.

Sometimes we can be more inventive, as here:

(c) The World Almanac is a reference book that is sold more frequently than any other reference book in the world.

(d) The World Almanac is the world's largest-selling reference book.

Note how we shortened the expression in the world by an expression of ownership. We also used knowledge about book-selling here: A "book sold more frequently than any other" must be the largest-selling book.

There are no rules you can follow so you'll be creative. But when you have a long phrase or clause, and you see you have had to repeat words, look for a way to reduce the sentence with a two-word description. (You may want to consult your Thesaurus too.)

TRY REDUCING this sentence:

By getting a job that pays better, he will be able to afford a car.

- - - - - - - - - - - - - - - - - - - -

Suggestion

With a better-paying

~~By getting~~ a job ~~that pays better~~, he will be able to afford a car.

13. Try REDUCING these sentences to a simpler form with a two-word description:

(1) With an order that was for a thousand dollars, Mr. Jenkins won the prize.

(2) By keeping to foods that don't cost much, we were able to scrape by on a salary that was small and insufficient.

(3) Philip Roth is one writer of novels who has sold more books than most writers of novels in this country.

(4) By making a decision quickly and wisely, he was able to have a happy life in his home.

- - - - - - - - - - - - - - - - - -

Suggestions

(1) With ~~an order that was for a~~ *his* thousand*-*dollar~~s~~ *order*, Mr. Jenkins won the prize.

(2) By keeping to *low-cost* foods ~~that don't cost much,~~ we were able to scrape by on a ~~salary that was~~ small~~ and~~*,* insufficient *salary*.

(3) Philip Roth is one ~~writer~~ of *this country's best-selling* ~~novels who has sold more books than most writers of novels in this country~~ *novelists*.

(4) *Because of a quick, wise* ~~By making a~~ decision ~~quickly and wisely,~~ he was able to have a happy *home* life ~~in his home~~.

14. You may also be able to simplify sentences by using two-word descriptions and other devices you learned in earlier chapters.

As an example, compare these:

(a) The sea islands of Georgia are beautiful. They have filmy Spanish moss that drips from the trees. The trees are huge. They are called "live oaks."

(b) The sea islands of Georgia are beautiful, with filmy Spanish moss dripping from the huge "live oaks."

Here we could reduce four sentences to one because we could use two-word descriptions. Note that we don't put a comma between huge and live in huge "live oaks" because live and oaks are a unit—the name of a species of oaks; the word live here does not mean living.

USE two-word descriptions and other devices to reduce these four sentences to one sentence with exactly the same meaning.

Housing shortages in large cities are acute.

This is true for renters who have low incomes.

It is also true for renters who have middle incomes.

The reason is that building costs are high.

- -

Suggestions

Housing shortages in large cities are acute.

low- and middle-income

~~This is true~~ for renters ~~who have low incomes~~.

~~It is also true for renters who have middle incomes~~.

Because of high

~~The reason is that~~ building costs ~~are high~~.

Now turn to the review of Chapter 5.

REVIEW

1. Punctuate the description in each of the following sentences:

    (a) I saw three white men dash down the road.
    (b) He bought a black wool sweater.
    (c) He bought a two door car.
    (d) I heard a loud grating noise.
    (e) It was a delightfully cool day.
    (f) He is the new vice president.
    (g) She has a sweet looking sister.
    (h) He is a clever eager student.
    (i) We sell either pint or quart size Mason jars.
    (j) Each person was served one cold rubbery chicken,

2. Reduce each sentence by using a two-word description instead of a longer descriptive phrase or clause:

(a) He can read a novel that is a thousand pages in an evening.

(b) The employees who work hard will eventually get the jobs with the highest pay in the company.

Suggested Answers

1. (a) CORRECT
   (b) CORRECT
   (c) a two-door car
   (d) a loud, grating noise
   (e) CORRECT
   (f) CORRECT
   (g) a sweet-looking sister
   (h) a clever, eager student
   (i) either pint- or quart-size Mason jars.
   (j) CORRECT, OR one cold, rubbery chicken

2. (a) He can read a thousand-page novel ~~that is a thousand pages~~ in an evening.
   (b) The hard-working employees ~~who work hard~~ will eventually get the company's highest-paying jobs. ~~with the highest pay in the company.~~

If you had everything right, you can put a check beside each question in the REVIEW column of the Self-Evaluation Record for Chapter 5 (page 112) and go on to Chapter 6. If you missed parts of question 1, however, you may want to check those parts of entry 11 in your copy of Chart 2. Check 11(a) if you missed (e) in question 1; check 11(b) if you missed (b) or (j); check 11(c) if you missed (a) or (f); check 11(d) if you missed (c), (g), or (i); and check 11(e) if you missed (d) or (h).

CHAPTER SIX

Making a List and Checking It Twice

Another way to make your writing more effective is to present a set of similar ideas as a list of items under the same heading. This kind of arrangement tells the reader exactly how all the ideas are related.

To illustrate, look at sample (a):

(a) The conviction of Lieutenant Calley raised the question of a national guilt:

(i) All Germans were told to be guilty after World War I.
(ii) All Germans and Japanese were told to be guilty after World War II.
(iii) Now all Americans are told to feel guilty about Vietnam.

And now look at the original:

(b) The conviction of Lieutenant Calley raised the question of a national guilt. All Germans were told to be guilty after World War I. All Germans and Japanese were told to be guilty after World War II. Now all Americans are told to feel guilty about Vietnam.

The difference is dramatic! With just a minimum number of changes, this passage was turned from a set of seemingly unrelated sentences into a clear, effective list of items under a common heading.

You'll learn how to accomplish similar miracles. Chapter 6 is all about lists: when to use them, and how to make them in order to give your reader the most information about the way your ideas are related. A list is a way to link together a number of main ideas, all of equal importance; a list is also a useful way to handle details.

As usual, do the preview of Chapter 6 first to see how you can make best use of the chapter.

PREVIEW

1. Punctuate the following sentences:

   (a) We visited the following places together Montreal Canada Boston Massachusetts and Buffalo New York.

   (b) As a boy scout he earned three merit badges as follows in swimming in hiking and in canoeing.

   (c) He opened three jars one was spoiled one was all right and the third was good.

   (d) His grades were as follows three A's two B's and one C.

2. Copyedit this sentence so that each item on the list is in the same form:

   We heard that the course could hold our interest, was informative, and accurate.

3. Turn this set of facts into a regular, complete list.

   There is a trend toward nuclear power. It is strong. We now have twenty-one commercial nuclear reactors. There are fifty-four under construction. There are orders for forty-two more.

4. Turn this set of facts into an outline list.

   Nuclear power has its drawbacks. First, its technology is more complex than expected. The capital costs of a large nuclear plant have risen sharply, and nuclear reactors produce even more waste than fossil-fuel generators. People also harbor deep-seated fears about anything atomic.

5. Turn this set of facts into an incomplete list:

   Many states already have nuclear plants. Minnesota is one. So is California. So is Massachusetts. Other states have them too.

Suggested Answers

1. (a) We visited the following places together Montreal Canada Boston Massachusetts and Buffalo New York.

   (b) As a boy scout he earned three merit badges as follows in swimming in hiking and in canoeing.

   (c) He opened three jars one was spoiled one was all right and the third was good.

   (d) His grades were as follows three A's two B's and one C.

2. We heard that the course ~~could hold our~~ interest, ~~was~~ informative, and accurate.

3. ~~There is~~ a trend toward nuclear power ~~It~~ is strong We now have twenty-one commercial nuclear reactors ~~There are~~ fifty-four under construction There are orders for forty-two more.

4. Nuclear power has its drawbacks ~~First,~~ its technology is more complex than expected. The capital costs of a large nuclear plant have risen sharply and nuclear reactors produce even more waste than fossil-fuel generators. People ~~also~~ harbor deep-seated fears about anything atomic.

5. Many states already have nuclear plants Minnesota ~~is one. So is~~ California ~~So is~~ Massachusetts. ~~Other states have them too.~~

If you answered all the questions satisfactorily, skim over the chapter lightly. Mark the PREVIEW column of your Self-Evaluation Record for Chapter 6 by putting a check beside each question you answered correctly. As usual, the blanks will show which frames you should study.

SELF-EVALUATION RECORD FOR CHAPTER 6

	PREVIEW	FRAMES	REVIEW
Questions 1 and 2		1 through 10	
Question 3		11 and 12	
Question 4		13 through 16	
Question 5		17 through 19	

AN INTRODUCTION TO ANY COMPLETE LIST

1. Before we consider how to turn a set of different-looking facts into an orderly list, let's examine the forms we have to work with.

Any list—whether it is long, short, or just an incomplete set of items—always has two parts: the general heading, or introduction, and the set of related items. Generally, the introduction comes first, to show the common thread running through the items.

Although there are several ways to introduce a list, samples (a) and (b) illustrate the major ones:

(a) The three major cities on the East Coast are Boston, New York, and Washington.
(b) The East Coast has three major cities: Boston, New York, and Washington.

Notice in sample (a) that the introduction and the set of items together make a complete sentence. But punctuation isn't necessary between them because the introduction leads into the list of items without any break.

This isn't the case in sample (b). Here the introduction is already a complete sentence, even without the set of items. The colon is used as an abrupt signal that the common heading has been stated and a set of examples is coming up next.

The important difference to remember is that the colon is used ONLY after a complete sentence. (And remember that the colon shouldn't be used too often, or it will lose its effectiveness.)

SEE if you can tell which introductions here need a colon. Then INSERT one if it's needed:

(1) He says that he has three choices to keep his present job, to get another job, or to return to school.

(2) His three choices are to keep his present job, to get another job, or to return to school.

(3) Professor Jones has broken all the rules He has been boring; he has been sarcastic; and he has been late to class every day.

- - - - - - - - - - - - - - - - - - -

(1) choices : to

(2) CORRECT

(3) rules : He

2. The right introduction to use may also depend on the items being listed. If the items are not sentences, you may use either kind of introduction: the informal, sample (a) below, or the more formal, sample (b). But, if the items are sentences themselves, you have no choice except to be formal and use a sentence with a colon, sample (c).

COMPARE these:

(a) The best things in life are said to be expensive, immoral, or fattening.

(b) The best things in life can be described this way: expensive, immoral, or fattening.

(c) The best things in life have these three characteristics: They're expensive; they're immoral; or they're fattening.

Note that in sample (c) the items are sentences separated by semicolons and that the first one begins with a capital.

ASSUME that each of these is the first item of a list. Indicate the kind of introduction you would use: WRITE "C" if you must use the colon; WRITE "E" if you could use either the colon or no punctuation at all.

______ (1) The best things in life are free;

______ (2) New Mexico,

______ (3) riding on an airplane,

______ (4) They defeated the Indians;

______ (5) during the summer,

- - - - - - - - - - - - - - - - - - -

C (1) E (2) E (3) C (4) E (5)

3. Another common way to introduce a list is to add on a formal expression like as follows or the following to the usual introduction. Listen to how the tone changes and becomes more formal:

(a) The three major cities on the East Coast are as follows: Boston, New York, and Washington.
(b) The three major cities on the East Coast are the following:
(c) The East Coast has three major cities, as follows:
(d) The East Coast has the following three major cities:

In each case, now, the introduction is a sentence even without the list. So a colon can be inserted after it. Sample (c) is a special situation, however. Since the introduction was already a sentence without the as follows, this added expression is set off by a comma, just like any other piece of added information would be.

Only the introductions to lists are given here. See if you can COPYEDIT them correctly:

(1) He says he has the following three choices
(2) He says he has three choices as follows
(3) He has three choices
(4) His three choices are as follows
(5) His three choices are
(6) His three choices are the following

- - - - - - - - - - - - - - - - - - - -

(1) choices :
(2) choices, as follows:
(3) choices:
(4) follows:
(5) CORRECT
(6) following:

A REGULAR, COMPLETE LIST

4. Now let's look at the second part of a list—the items themselves. And first we'll consider regular, complete lists.

We need to show that these items are related by the common thread we've stated in the introduction. One way to do this is to put them all in the same form. As an example, look at these regular, complete lists:

(a) She likes to shop, to cook, and to eat.
(b) They traveled together: They went to France; they went to England; and, last, they went to Spain.

In sample (a) all the items are verb parts beginning with to—infinitives. In sample (b) they are short sentences. We say the related items in each sample are "parallel," meaning they're all expressed in the same form. (As you know, two parallel streets run in the same direction.)

The second way to show that the items are related is to punctuate them alike. In sample (a) notice that each item is separated from the next one on the list by a comma. The comma indicates when one item has ended and the next one begins. But in sample (b) the items are separated by semicolons, and the first word of the first item is capitalized because they're short sentences.

SEE if you can sort out the items in these examples and INSERT appropriate punctuation:

(1) He chased a mouse around the barn over the fence and into the yard.
(2) He's impressive he's witty he's handsome and he's charming.
(3) She is a great wife a great mother and a great friend.
(4) I enjoy playing eighteen holes of golf swimming a mile to the float and hiking for twenty miles.
(5) She bought a new hat a new coat and a new pair of shoes.

- - - - - - - - - - - - - - - - - -

(1) barn, over the fence, and
(2) impressive: He's witty; he's handsome; and
(3) wife, a great mother, and
(4) golf, swimming a mile to the float, and
(5) hat, a new coat, and

5. Just so you can see what would happen if you accidentally forgot the commas between the items of a regular, complete list, compare samples (a) and (b):

(a) Representatives met to select a committee, to review current projects, and to recommend future projects.
(b) Representatives met to select a committee to review current projects and to recommend future projects.

Sample (a) is just a list of things the representatives set out to do. But without the commas, as in sample (b), this sentence has another meaning: that the representatives met for the purpose of selecting a committee. And this committee, not the representatives, would review current projects and recommend future ones.

Remember, to clarify a regular list you should put a comma after every item except the last. Some experts advise dropping the last comma. But if you keep it, you'll never go wrong; and you'll never need to worry about inviting this sort of misinterpretation:

(c) I invited Mary and Joe, Peg, Nancy and Jim.
(d) I invited Mary and Joe, Peg, Nancy, and Jim.

In sample (a), without the last comma, Nancy and Jim are invited as a couple. In sample (b), with the comma, Nancy and Jim are invited as singles.

6. Let's see what happens when the items are not in the same form. Look at this list, for example:

(a) His lectures are witty, relevant, and he references them well.

Although the reader expects another adjective after relevant, he gets a clause instead. At first he's put off because he doesn't realize that the clause describes the lectures, just as the adjectives do.

The cure for this kind of misleading set of items is to put all the items in the same form, as here:

(b) His lectures are witty, relevant, and well-referenced.

Now each item is an adjective. What would you suggest for this set?

(c) My hobbies are to embroider, to cook, and gardening.

Samples (d), (e), and (f) show the possibilities:

(d) My hobbies are ~~to~~ embroider^ing^, ~~to~~ cook^ing^, and gardening.
(e) My hobbies are to embroider, to cook, and ^to^ garden~~ing~~.
(f) My hobbies are to embroider, ~~to~~ cook, and garden~~ing~~.

In (d) we changed each item to the -ing form. In (e) we changed each form to the infinitive form and we repeated the to each time for emphasis. In (f) we changed each form to the infinitive form too, but we omitted the to before the last two items because it was obvious.

Sample (g) shows an incorrect form with the infinitive, however:

(g) My hobbies are to embroider, to cook, and gardening.

You may either keep the to before all items for emphasis or drop the to before all items except the last. However, you cannot keep it sometimes and drop it sometimes, as in (g).

7. COPYEDIT these lists and put all items into the same form:

(1) My new goals were to stay in school, to graduate, and then I could get a good job.

(2) My favorite subjects in high school were physics, learning to drive a car, and French.

(3) He told us to read the story, then we had to answer some questions about it, and write a book report.

(4) Professor Jones is middle-aged, he's getting bald, and short.

(5) Boy scouts are supposed to swim well, know how to build fires, and to take Morse code.

\- - - - - - - - - - - - - - - - - -

(1) My new goals were to stay in school, to graduate, and then ~~I could~~ to get a good job.

My new goals were to stay in school, ~~to~~ graduate, and then ~~I could~~ get a good job.

(2) My favorite subjects in high school were physics, ~~learning to~~ driver *education*, ~~a car,~~ and French.

(3) He told us to read the story, ~~then we had~~ *then* to answer some questions about it, and *to* write a book report.

He told us to read the story, then ~~we had to~~ answer some questions about it, and write a book report.

(4) Professor Jones is middle-aged, ~~he's getting~~ bald*ing*, and short.

(5) Boys scouts are supposed to swim well, ~~know how~~ to build fires, and to take Morse code.

Boy scouts are supposed to swim well, ~~know how to~~ build fires, and take Morse code.

8. So far, the items in the lists were simple enough so that commas separated them (or semicolons if they were sentences). But now suppose you want to make a list of items that aren't sentences, but that contain commas themselves to make them clear. If you separate such items by commas too, the reader won't be able to tell which are the main items and which are just parts of items. As an example, COMPARE samples (a) and (b). Which do you think is clearer?

(a) Projected convention dates are June 10, 1976, June 8, 1980, and June 9, 1984.
(b) Projected convention dates are June 10, 1976; June 8, 1980; and June 9, 1984.

You probably said sample (b). Since you need commas between the day and the year, commas between the dates too would be confusing. With the semicolons you can show immediately that the dates are the main items.

The rule is to separate items in a list by semicolons if at least one item already has a comma.

APPLY this rule and COPYEDIT these sentences:

(1) I have lived in Joplin Boise and Topeka.
(2) I have lived in Joplin Missouri Boise Idaho and Topeka Kansas.

(3) His grades are English A math B and history C.
(4) In that salad we used Bermuda onions Boston lettuce and raw mushrooms.
(5) Three professors twenty students and nine outsiders heard his lecture.

- - - - - - - - - - - - - - - - - - - -

(1) Joplin, Boise, and
(2) Joplin, Missouri; Boise, Idaho; and Topeka, Kansas.
(3) English, A; math, B; and history, C.
(4) onions, Boston lettuce, and
(5) professors, twenty students, and

9. COPYEDIT these sentences for practice. Remember, look for the main items first; separate them by commas unless at least one item already has a comma. In that case separate the main items by semicolons.

(1) He worked the first three weeks in June the first and second weeks in July and the third and fourth weeks in August.
(2) She recommended bathing the baby first feeding him next and then putting him down for a nap.
(3) He worked the first second and fourth weeks in June the first and third weeks in July and the second and fourth weeks in August.
(4) Some major earthquakes in the United States were in California on April 19 1906 California on March 10 1933 and Alaska on March 27 1964.
(5) The election returns so far are Jackson *15,000 Pollack 25,000 and Bergman 1920. *(Hint: The word with was dropped from each item.)

- - - - - - - - - - - - - - - - - - - -

(1) He worked the first three weeks in June, the first and second weeks in July, and the third and fourth weeks in August.
(2) She recommended bathing the baby first, feeding him next, and then putting him down for a nap.
(3) He worked the first, second, and fourth weeks in June; the first and third weeks in July; and the second and fourth weeks in August.
(4) Some major earthquakes in the United States were in California on April 19, 1906; California on March 10, 1933; and Alaska on March 27, 1964.
(5) The election returns so far are Jackson, 15,000; Pollack, 25,000; and Bergman, 1920.

If you missed sentences 4 and 5 because you forgot the commas within the items, see entry 10, parts a and b, of Chart 2.

10. PUNCTUATE the following lists. Look back at previous frames, if necessary.

(1) Grants were given to the following Professor Martini Department of Physics Professor Schwartz Department of Psychiatry and Professor Benjamin Department of Anthropology.
(2) The grades were good as follows five A's twelve B's ten C's two D's and no F's.
(3) Prices on some items were high coffee $1.15 per pound milk 35¢ a quart and bread 50¢ per loaf.
(4) The following men received grants Professor Martini Professor Martin and Professor Benjamin.
(5) Grants were given to Professor Martini Professor Schwartz and Professor Benjamin.

- - - - - - - - - - - - - - - - - - - -

(1) Grants were given to the following: Professor Martini, Department of Physics; Professor Schwartz, Department of Psychiatry; and Professor Benjamin, Department of Anthropology.
(2) The grades were good, as follows: five A's, twelve B's, ten C's, two D's, and no F's.
(3) Prices on some items were high: coffee, $1.15 per pound; milk, 35¢ a quart; and bread, 50¢ per loaf. [The word <u>was</u> was dropped from each item. See entry 10(b), Chart 2.]
(4) The following men received grants: Professor Martini, Professor Martin, and Professor Benjamin.
(5) Grants were given to Professor Martini, Professor Schwartz, and Professor Benjamin.

11. A regular, complete list is a compact way to show a relationship, and you can make one up whenever you note a common thread through three or four items. Without the colon, the list doesn't attract undue attention, and you can use it as often as you like. You shouldn't overuse the colon, however.

You can also use a regular, complete list to introduce a report that will discuss three or four items in detail. Or you can use a short list for a summary paragraph.

Here is a set of facts presented in a way that doesn't show any relationships. Let's see if we can turn it into a list that would make a satisfactory introduction to a report on programmed instruction:

(a) Programmed instruction is a fairly new form of learning. It has three advantages. The student can pace himself and go as fast as he likes. He can also study by himself. He can check his answers as he goes to make sure he is learning.

To make a list of sample (a), we have to decide what the main train of thought is, what the examples are, and what is just detail. Sample (b) is one possible treatment:

(b) Programmed instruction, a fairly new form of learning, has three advantages: The student can pace himself and go as fast as he likes; he can study by himself; and he can check his answers as he goes to make sure he is learning.

(1) What was the main train of thought? ____________________
(2) What was treated as detail? ____________________________

---

(1) The advantages of programmed instruction.
(2) That programmed instruction is a fairly new form of learning.

12. Now see if you can turn the following information into a list:

Five contributions of $100, 000 or more went to the 1968 presidential campaign of former Senator Eugene J. McCarthy. Senator McCarthy was the unsuccessful antiwar candidate for the Democratic nomination. Stewart Mott gave $210, 000. He is the son of a founder of the General Motors Corporation. Mr. and Mrs. Jack Dreyfus gave at least $100, 000. Ellsworth T. Carrington gave $100, 000. He is a Wall Street account executive. Mr. and Mrs. Martin Peretz gave $100, 000. Alan Miller gave $108, 000. He is a retired industrialist.

Suggestions

Five contributions of $100, 000 or more went to the 1968 presidential campaign of former Senator Eugene J. McCarthy, he ~~Senator McCarthy~~

was the unsuccessful antiwar candidate for the Democratic nomination. Stewart Mott gave $210, 000. He is the son of a founder of the General Motors Corporation. Mr. and Mrs. Jack Dreyfus gave at least $100, 000. Ellsworth T. Carrington gave $100, 000. He is a Wall Street account executive. Mr. and Mrs. Martin Peretz gave $100, 000. Alan Miller gave $108, 000. He is a retired industrialist.

AN OUTLINE LIST

13. For formal reports and term papers, you might want to emphasize the items by listing them in outline form. The introduction is followed by a colon; each item is numbered or lettered; and the first item starts with a capital letter.

Each item should also be in the same form and followed by the same punctuation mark. Either a comma or a semicolon can be used if the items are not sentences, and either a semicolon or a period can be used if the items are single sentences. A period must be used, however, if an item consists of more than one sentence.

LOOK AT this example:

These pets have the following gestation periods (in days) and life spans (in years):

(a) The monkey has a gestation period of 164 days and a life span of 7 years;
(b) the dog has a gestation period of 61 days and a life span of 16 years; and
(c) the cat has a gestation period of 63 days and a life span of 15 years.

Notice that each item was followed by a semicolon (although a period could have been used), and <u>and</u> was added after item (b). When you use a comma or a semicolon in this outline form, you can tie everything together by inserting <u>and</u> after the next-to-last item. (You should use <u>or</u> if you're giving a list of choices, however.)

ASSUME that each example here is an item on a different list in outline form. PUNCTUATE each one appropriately:

(1) People in small towns are trying to raise money for new airports
(2) A proper curriculum
(3) An entertainment committee consisting of three members

- - - - - - - - - - - - - - - - - -

Suggestions

(1) airports; or airports.
(2) curriculum;
(3) members;

14. In an outline list each item is very noticeable. This means that any item that doesn't belong to the list can be especially misleading.

Here is a list that a manager of a large company set up to explain his training program. Do you see anything wrong with it?

(a) Added training is given to employees who

(1) have previous experience;
(2) transfer from another department; or
(3) return from a leave of absence.

Everything appears to be in good order, as far as form and punctuation are concerned. Offhand, you might have said this was a fine list.

When we examine the items more closely, however, we find that the first item is not an example at all—it is really a part of the rule: All these employees have had previous experience.

Sample (b) shows what this list should look like, with item 1 up in the introduction where it belongs:

(b) Added training is given to employees with previous experience who

(1) transfer from another department; or
(2) return from a leave of absence.

Now each part of the list is related to the introduction in the same way.

Whether you use the outline or the regular, complete form, you should be sure you have properly identified the examples and the common heading.

15. The information below is already assembled as a list. This time, SEE if you can PUT this list into an outline form:

The three largest dams in the world are as follows: The Tarbela in Pakistan is largest, with a volume of 186 million cubic yards; Fort Peck in the United States is second, with a volume of 125.6 million cubic yards; and Oahe in the United States is third, with a volume of 92 million cubic yards.

- - - - - - - - - - - - - - - - - - - -

Suggestions

The three largest dams in the world are as follows: The Tarbela in Pakistan is largest, with a volume of 186 million cubic yards; Fort Peck in the United States is second, with a volume of 125.6 million cubic yards; and Oahe in the United States is third, with a volume of 92 million cubic yards.

If you wrote out the list instead of using copyediting symbols, you might have had something like this:

The three largest dams in the world are as follows:

(1) The Tarbela in Pakistan is largest, with a volume of 186 million cubic yards.
(2) Fort Peck in the United States is second, with a volume of 125.6 million cubic yards.
(3) Oahe in the United States is third, with a volume of 92 million cubic yards.

16. Now PUT this set of information into a formal outline list:

New York City once had many daily newspapers. Now it has only three. The New York Times is a morning newspaper. This is probably the most informative newspaper. It has a liberal viewpoint. The Daily News is also a morning newspaper. It has the highest circulation. It has a conservative viewpoint. The New York Post is an afternoon newspaper. It is the youngest newspaper of the three. It has a liberal viewpoint.

- - - - - - - - - - - - - - - - - - - -

Suggestions

Although New York City once had many daily newspapers, now it has only three. The New York Times is a morning newspaper. This is probably the most informative newspaper. It has a liberal viewpoint. The Daily News is also a morning newspaper. It has the highest circulation. It has a conservative viewpoint. The New York Post is an afternoon newspaper. It is the youngest newspaper of the three. It has a liberal viewpoint.

Here is another possibility. This one doesn't stress the liberal-conservative politics, however.

Although New York City once had many daily newspapers, now it has only three. The New York Times is a morning newspaper. This is probably the most informative newspaper. It has a liberal viewpoint. The Daily News is also a morning newspaper. It has the highest circulation. It has a conservative viewpoint. The New York Post is an afternoon newspaper. It is the youngest newspaper of the three. It has a liberal viewpoint.

AN INCOMPLETE LIST

17. A third major kind of list is the incomplete list. You have to use a special form to let the reader know you are giving him examples and not the whole list.

Sample (a) illustrates one of these forms.

(a) Ian's reading list included many books: Zelda, The Godfather, and As I Lay Dying.

This form is just like a regular, complete list except that included is the main verb of the introduction. This tells the reader that the list is incomplete.

Samples (b), (c), and (d) illustrate other ways to write incomplete lists:

(b) Ian read many books last summer, as for example, Zelda, The Godfather, and As I Lay Dying.

(c) Ian read many books last summer, such as Brazil, The Arms of Krupp, and High Priest.

(d) Ian read many books last summer, including The Beatles, Couples, and Ambassador's Journal.

Notice that the introduction to these incomplete lists is always a sentence, but without a colon following it. Instead, a comma is used and a word suggesting "there are others." A comma also follows an expression that has the word example.

Put a check beside each incomplete list. Then COPYEDIT all three lists.

_____ (1) I have taken several courses including English composition math and American history.

_____ (2) I have taken several courses English composition math and American history.

_____ (3) I have taken several courses for example English composition math and American history.

- - - - - - - - - - - - - - - - - -

_____ (1) I have taken several courses, including English composition, math, and American history.

_____ (2) I have taken several courses: English composition, math, and American history.

_____ (3) I have taken several courses, for example, English composition, math, and American history.

18. Read over this information:

(a) The Yankees play the teams in their division most often.
The Orioles are from Baltimore. They are in the division.
The Red Sox are from Boston. They are in the division.
The Indians in Cleveland are in the division too.

It's all there except that the division has three more teams than the ones that are named in (a). But it's not very inspiring. To turn this information into an incomplete list, you have to pick the main thread running through, just as you do when you make a complete list. You can then put details in parentheses, or in phrases that don't need commas. (Commas would be too confusing.)

Sample (b) is a possible treatment:

(b) The Yankees play the teams in their own division most often, including the Orioles (Baltimore), the Red Sox (Boston), and the Indians (Cleveland).

As you can see, sample (b) is not just briefer and peppier: More importan it is not misleading.

WRITE the first item over again, using a different form: ______________

- - - - - - - - - - - - - - - - - - - -

Suggestions

the Orioles (they're from Baltimore),
the Orioles (from Baltimore),
the Orioles from Baltimore,

19. Try to make TWO incomplete lists from this information.

(a) New York City has many advantages. It has great museums. It also has theater. New movies open there. New York City has disadvantages too. It has a high cost of living. It is also dirty. It also has unsatisfactory air most of the time.

Hint: Use a transition between the two lists.

- - - - - - - - - - - - - - - - - - -

Suggestions

New York City has many advantages, including great museums, theater, and new movies. However, it also has disadvantages, such as its high cost of living, its filth, and its frequently unsatisfactory air.

USING CHART 2

20. Unless you write many papers and reports, you can't expect to remember all the ways to present a list. But you don't need to worry about forgetting them either, since they're summarized for you in Chart 2, as here:

SITUATION	IF	THEN	EXAMPLE
12. AN INTRODUCTION TO ANY COMPLETE LIST	(a) it is not a sentence,	(a) don't put any punctuation after it.	(a) His grades were A, B, and D.
	(b) an expression (as follows or the following) is added to make a sentence,	(b) put a colon after it.	(b) His grades were as follows: A, B, and D.
	(c) it was already a sentence without as follows or the following,	(c) put a colon after it and a comma before as follows.	(c) His grades were fair, as follows: B, C, and D. He got the following grades: B, C, and D.
13. A REGULAR, COMPLETE LIST	(a) no item has a comma and none is a sentence,	(a) use any introduction. Put a comma after each item except the last.	(a) He needs a hat, a coat, and shoes.

SITUATION	IF	THEN	EXAMPLE
13. A REGULAR, COMPLETE LIST (Continued)	(b) at least one item has a comma but none is a sentence,	(b) use any introduction. Put a semicolon after each item except the last.	(b) The train stopped at Hartford, Conn.; Springfield, Mass.; and Pittsfield, Mass.
	(c) each item is a sentence,	(c) use introduction of form 12b or 12c. Put a semicolon after each part except the last. Capitalize the first word of the first item.	(c) He claims this: She was bound; she was gagged; and she was robbed.
14. AN OUTLINE LIST	(a) no item is a sentence,	(a) use any introduction. Number or letter each item; capitalize the first word of the first item; and separate items by commas or semicolons. Add <u>and</u> to next-to-last item (or <u>or</u> in a list of choices).	(a) He expects the following grades: (1) An A in French, (2) an F in math, and (3) a C in history.
	(b) each item is a sentence or more than one sentence,	(b) do the same as in (a) but end with semicolons or periods if items are single sentences; end only with periods if items are more than one sentence. (Don't add <u>and</u>/<u>or</u> to next-to-last item if periods are used.)	(b) He told me this: (1) I want to be a senator; or (2) I want to be a governor.
15. AN INCOMPLETE LIST	(a) the introduction is a sentence followed by <u>such as</u> or <u>including</u>,	(a) put a comma (not a colon) before <u>such as</u> or <u>including</u>, but not after.	(a) His grades were excellent, including three A's.

SITUATION	IF	THEN	EXAMPLE
15. AN INCOMPLETE LIST (Continued)	(b) the introduction is a sentence followed by as an example, for example, etc.,	(b) put a comma (not a colon) before and after the expression with example.	(b) His grades were excellent, for example, three A's.
	(c) the main verb in the introduction is the verb include,	(c) handle the same as a regular, complete list.	(c) His grades include the following: 2 A's and 3 B's. His grades include 2 A's and 3 B's.

Now try to interpret the chart entries. IDENTIFY each example by its number and letter in the IF column.

________ (1) The list is long, as follows: bread, cheese, and wine.
________ (2) He ordered soap, water, and dishes.

- - - - - - - - - - - - - - - - - -

12c (1) 12b (2)

COPYEDITING LISTS

21. USING Chart 2, COPYEDIT the lists and their introductions in the following paragraph. Assume that all other punctuation is correct. (The lines have been numbered to help you check your answers afterward.)

(1) According to the 1970 census, 53 percent of all Americans hug
(2) the coasts . These 107 million people are situated approximately
(3) as follows
(4) 1. About four-tenths of the people live around the
(5) Great Lakes
(6) 2. nearly three-tenths live along the Atlantic Seaboard
(7) 3. Two-tenths live along the Pacific
(8) 4. One-tenth lives near the Gulf of Mexico

(9) But the total distance of this coast is approximately 17,300

(10) miles. This total includes the following areas the Atlantic the

(11) Pacific the Gulf of Mexico the Great Lakes and the Arctic Coast

(12) of sparsely populated Northern Alaska.

(13) As it did in the 1960 census, the West had the highest rate of

(14) growth. This region consists of thirteen states such as Hawaii

(15) Alaska Idaho and New Mexico. The top ten states in 1960 were

(16) still the top ten in 1970. Besides the top ten, though, six

(17) states gained more than 100,000 since 1960 as follows Alabama

(18) Arizona Colorado Connecticut Georgia and Hawaii.

- - - - - - - - - - - - - - - - - -

(3) as follows

(5) Great Lakes OR Great Lakes

(6) nearly ... Atlantic Seaboard OR Atlantic Seaboard

(7) the Pacific OR Pacific

(8) of Mexico

(10) following areas the Atlantic

(11) the Pacific the Gulf of Mexico the Great Lakes and

(14) states such as Hawaii

(15) Alaska Idaho and

(17) 1960 as follows Alabama

(18) Arizona Colorado Connecticut Georgia and

When you have checked your answers, turn to the review of Chapter 6.

REVIEW

1. Punctuate these sentences:

   (a) We ordered the supplies as follows milk two quarts bread one loaf and eggs two dozen.

(b) He ordered these supplies eggs milk and bread.
(c) My claims are as follows the land is overpriced you knew it yet you tried to sell it to me.
(d) The Air France plane goes from Paris France to New York New York to London England and to Mexico City Mexico.

2. Put each item in the following list in the same form:

At one time or another Miss Jones was a dancer, an actress, and taught school.

3. Turn this set of facts into a regular, complete list:

President Nixon has committed us to nuclear power. There are two major reasons why it looks like the best answer to our needs. It will be environmentally better than other fuels. It will also be less costly.

4. Turn this set of facts into an outline list. (Hydroelectric means "electric energy derived from the energy of falling water.")

Damming more rivers cannot fill the need for energy. There are two major reasons why this is true. Hydroelectric power accounts for only 4 percent of our present energy production. Most of the suitable dam sites have already been exploited. The Tennessee Valley Authority was originally a water-power project. Now it derives less than 20 percent of its power from hydroelectric facilities.

5. Turn this set of facts into an incomplete list.

The titles of some recent, widely discussed books reflect public concern about nuclear plants. Perils of the Peaceful Atom is one. Another is The Careless Atom. A third is Population Control through Nuclear Pollution. There are others too.

Suggested Answers

1. (a) We ordered the supplies as follows milk two quarts bread one loaf and eggs two dozen.
   (b) He ordered these supplies eggs milk and bread.
   (c) My claims are as follows the land is overpriced you knew it yet you tried to sell it to me.
   (d) The Air France plane goes from Paris France to London, England to New York New York and to Mexico City Mexico.

2. At one time or another Miss Jones was a dancer, an actress, and taught school

3. President Nixon has committed us to nuclear power There are two major reasons why it looks like the best answer to our needs It will be environmentally better than other fuels It will also be less costly.

4. Damming more rivers cannot fill the need for energy There are two major reasons why this is true Hydroelectric power accounts for only 4 percent of our present energy production. Most of the suitable dam sites have already been exploited. The Tennessee Valley Authority was originally a water-power project Now it derives less than 20 percent of its power from hydroelectric facilities.

5. The titles of some recent, widely discussed books reflect public concern about nuclear plants Perils of the Peaceful Atom is one Another is The Careless Atom A third is Population Control through Nuclear Pollution. There are others, too.

If you answered each question satisfactorily, put a check beside the question in the Self-Evaluation Record for Chapter 6 (page 131). If any question gave you trouble, you may want to check the entry on Chart 2: If you missed any part of questions 1, 2, or 3, you should check entry 12 or 13, whichever is appropriate; if you missed question 4, you should check entry 14; and if you missed question 5, you should check entry 15.

CHAPTER SEVEN

Agreeing To Be Consistent

As everyone knows, a singular subject needs a singular verb and a plural subject needs a plural verb. Subject and verb must be consistent; we say they must agree.

For most people, agreement comes as naturally in writing as it does in speech, provided the sentence is simple enough:

(a) The bell is ringing.
(b) The bells are ringing.

But agreement may not be so obvious. As an example, which of these do you think is right, sample (c) or sample (d)?

(c) Two and three is five or two times three is six.
(d) Two and three are five or two times three are six.

You couldn't miss on this one. Both are right, depending on how you interpret the mathematical subjects. If you're thinking of the entire sum or the entire product, sample (a) with its singular verbs is right. (Remember the expression "two is company—three's a crowd.")

But if you're thinking of the individual figures that make up sum and product, then sample (b) with its plural verbs is right. As you can see, only the writer himself knows for sure.

This chapter covers the situations in which you may not be certain about agreement:

(a) Longer sentences with subjects that are hard to identify at first;
(b) pronouns that sound as if they're plural but are actually singular; and
(c) subjects that sound as if they are singular but actually may be representing a collection of things or people.

You will also learn how to improve your sentences by using either pronouns or singular subjects that represent collections.

But, first—turn to the preview of Chapter 7.

PREVIEW

1. In each of these sentences UNDERLINE the right verb or the right possessive pronoun and the right verb:

   (a) One of the people I wanted to impress (wasn't, weren't) even there.
   (b) Everybody here (has, have) (her, their) own chores to do.
   (c) A number of June graduates (has, have) already found jobs.
   (d) The group (has, have) its own worries.
   (e) One of the principal reasons that I was able to do that job (was, were) that I knew how to type.
   (f) The number of lifeguards on duty (was, were) less than adequate.
   (g) The jury (was, were) unanimous in its decision.
   (h) One of the Irish Catholics who (is, are) making news (is, are) Bernadette Devlin.
   (i) The number of black people employed here (is, are) considerable.
   (j) One of the women who (belongs, belong) to the League of Women Voters (has, have) told me about his voting record.
   (k) A number of our students (was, were) active in McCarthy's 1968 campaign.
   (l) No one (has, have) trouble reading (his, their) own handwriting.
   (m) One of the more serious kinds of food poisoning (is, are) called botulism.
   (n) The team (has, have) refused to play its last home game without the star.
   (o) Nobody (helps, help) them with their homework.

2. Try to combine each set of sentences into a single sentence without using the word <u>not:</u>

   (a) All the things in the store must be sold. We must be out by September. We can't have things left.

   (b) The men and women on the committee pick Miss Cupcake of California. They base the decision on her beauty. They also base it on her talent.

Suggested Answers

1.
(a) wasn't, weren't
(b) has, have her, their
(c) has, have
(d) has have
(e) was, were
(f) was, were
(g) was, were
(h) is, are is, are
(i) is, are
(j) belongs, belong has, have
(k) was, were
(l) has, have his, their
(m) is, are
(n) has, have
(o) helps, help

2.
(a) Everything ~~All the things~~ in the store must be sold, because ~~We~~ we must be out by September, and nothing can be ~~We can't have things~~ left.

(b) ~~The men and women on~~ The committee picks Miss Cupcake of California on the basis of ~~They base the decision on~~ her beauty and ~~They also base it on her~~ talent.

If you answered each question in the preview of Chapter 7 satisfactorily, skim over the chapter quickly. Otherwise, mark the Self-Evaluation Record for Chapter 7, and proceed as usual.

SELF-EVALUATION RECORD FOR CHAPTER 7

	PREVIEW	FRAMES	REVIEW
Question 1		1 through 8	
Question 2		9 through 12	

THE WORD ONE IS THE SUBJECT

1. Sometimes distracting phrases can come between the subject and the verb and affect agreement. As an example, would you say offhand that sample (a) is right or sample (b)?

(a) One of the few good restaurants in town are the Flying Saucer.
(b) One of the few good restaurants in town is the Flying Saucer.

You were right if you picked sample (b). Despite the intervening words, the subject is one and not restaurants; and a singular verb is necessary.

Any time you aren't sure about agreement in a sentence like this you can rearrange the sentence, as sample (c) shows.

(c) The Flying Saucer is one of the few good restaurants in town.

Now the agreement is obvious: a singular verb consistent with the singular subject of Flying Saucer.

Some agreement problems arise when you fail to recognize the subject and the verb because you are distracted by the words between them. To give you some practice, UNDERLINE each subject and also the verb agreeing with it:

(1) Two of the new students weren't on the list.
(2) The reason for the riots was probably the high unemployment.
(3) The noise of the streets is exciting.
(4) The fruits of victory are said to be sweet.
(5) The results of the examination are always posted.

- - - - - - - - - - - - - - - - - -

(1) two weren't
(2) reason was
(3) noise is
(4) fruits are
(5) results are

2. Distractions between subject and verb can multiply. For example,

One of the few good restaurants in town that serve at odd hours is the Flying Saucer.

This is a perfectly good sentence, yet it can offer some dandy agreement problems. Despite all the distractions,

(a) The main subject of the sentence is one, so that the verb is must be singular too.
(b) Because the word that in the supporting clause actually represents the plural word restaurants, the verb serve must be plural to agree.

Here, UNDERLINE each subject and verb in a main clause once and each subject and verb in a supporting clause twice:

(1) One of the girls who live there was in an accident yesterday.

(2) One of the men who are on the school board was arrested.

(3) This is one of the restaurants that always get a three-star rating.

(4) One of the books that are on my reading list is Decline and Fall.

(5) One of the girls who wait on tables here is a student at the college.

- - - - - - - - - - - - - - - - - - - -

(1) one who live was

(2) one who are was arrested

(3) this is that get

(4) one that are is

(5) one who wait is

3. This time, see if you can pick the verb or verb part that would be consistent, and UNDERLINE it. Remember, don't be misled by intervening phrases. You can follow this example:

One of the men who (is, are) up for promotion (says, say) that he (doesn't, don't) deserve it.

(1) One of the gadgets that (is, are) on sale (doesn't, don't) really work.
(2) One of the problems that (was, were) hard to understand in class (wasn't, weren't) on the exam.
(3) (Is, Are) she one of the girls who (is, are) trying out to be cheer leaders?
(4) Two of the basketball players on the team (is, are) more than seven feet tall.
(5) One of the best television shows in those days (was, were) "The Show of Shows."

(6) One of the girls who (goes, go) home weekends (was, were) late getting back last Sunday.
(7) The contestants who (wins, win) all the prizes (is, are) the ones who (has, have) the most confidence.
(8) One of the drug stores that (is, are) open all night (is, are) too far away.
(9) The rule that most students (follows, follow) (isn't, aren't) always the best.
(10) One of the drugs that (is, are) known to be harmful (is, are) heroin.

- - - - - - - - - - - - - - - - - -

(1) (is, are) (doesn't, don't)
(2) (was, were) (wasn't, weren't)
(3) (Is, Are) (is, are)
(4) (is, are)
(5) (was, were)
(6) (goes, go) (was, were)
(7) (wins, win) (is, are) (has, have)
(8) (is, are) (is, are)
(9) (follows, follow) (isn't, aren't)
(10) (is, are) (is, are)

A PRONOUN LIKE EVERYONE IS THE SUBJECT

4. A pronoun like anybody or everybody can present a troublesome agreement problem because it sounds as if it refers to a lot of people, when actually it refers to only one.

To illustrate, what would you say is the right verb in this example?

Everybody (knows, know) about the generation gap.

I hope you chose knows. Although everybody sounds like a lot of people, it actually means "every body," which is clearly a singular notion, like "every single man." Everything is another example. It sounds like a lot of things, but it actually means "every single thing"—again a singular notion.

Other examples of pronoun subjects that always need a singular verb are none, each, everyone, anyone, anything, no one, nothing, or nobody.

In each sentence here, UNDERLINE the subject once, and the verb (or part of the verb) that agrees with it twice. Don't be fooled by any intervening plural phrases!

(1) None of the students (was, were) interested in his course.

(2) Each of the cottages (is, are) painted white.

(3) Everyone in the class (has, have) noticed the teacher's deep depression.

(4) Nobody in the group (has, have) explained the rationale.

(5) None of us (was, were) involved in the violent activities.

- - - - - - - - - - - - - - - - - -

(1) None was

(2) Each is

(3) Everyone has

(4) Nobody has

(5) None was

5. Subjects and verbs aren't the only parts of the sentence that have to agree, of course. A pronoun like his or their, and others used to express ownership, must agree with the subject it refers to. These pronouns are also called possessive pronouns.

Which possessive pronoun in this sample would you say agrees, his or their?

Everyone has (his, their) own peculiar story to tell.

You were right if you picked his.

The rule is that if the possessive pronoun refers to a singular subject, it must be singular too; but if it refers to a plural subject, it must be plural.

In each sentence UNDERLINE the subject once; UNDERLINE the agreeing verb (or part of the verb) twice; and UNDERLINE the agreeing possessive pronoun once.

(1) Everybody in the university (has, have) the right to park (his, their) car in the school parking lot.

(2) Each of the patients in this hospital (has, have) (his, their) own telephone.

(3) Everyone on the eleventh floor (is, are) having (his, their) office painted this morning.

(4) Nobody (is, are) willing to speak for (his, their) rights.

(5) One of the boys (is, are) trying to start (his, their) own business.

- - - - - - - - - - - - - - - - - -

1. Everybody (has, have) (his, their)

2. Each (has, have) (his, their)

3. Everybody (is, are) (his, their)

4. Nobody (is, are) (his, their)

5. One (is, are) (his, their)

THE WORD NUMBER IS THE SUBJECT

6. The word number used as a subject always presents an agreement problem. Is it singular? Is it plural? Samples (a) and (b) illustrate.

(a) A number of students are failing.
(b) The number of failing students is surprising.

In sample (a) the expression a number means "several students," and it needs a plural verb. But in sample (b) the expression the number stands for a total unit, and a singular verb agrees with it,

In each sentence DECIDE whether a singular or plural verb is needed. Then UNDERLINE the verb or part of the verb.

(1) A number of fine students (is, are) in his class.
(2) The number of students on scholarships (has, have) increased this year.
(3) The number of policemen who struck (was, were) less than I thought.
(4) A number of interesting exhibits (is, are) in town for Christmas.
(5) Each year the number of friends I have in school (shrinks, shrink).

- - - - - - - - - - - - - - - - - -

(1) (is, are)
(2) (has, have)
(3) (was, were)
(4) (is, are)
(5) (shrinks, shrink)

A COLLECTIVE NOUN IS THE SUBJECT

7. Do you remember the earlier example of the mathematical computation at the beginning of this chapter? See samples (c) and (d), page 154. The writer can interpret it either as a unit or as separate parts acting individually.

An entire class of nouns called collectives has this characteristic too. Sample (a) illustrates:

(a) The class has already elected its new officers.

The class acted as a unit to elect its officers. But this class consists of twenty individuals too, all of whom can act individually, as sample (b) shows.

(b) The class were divided in their opinions.

Only the writer knows for sure.

Some other similar words that can be either singular or plural, depending on how the writer interprets them, are group, crowd, team, jury, committee, family, or army. If a collective noun represents a unit, a singular verb agrees with it and a singular possessive pronoun. But, if a collective represents individual items, a plural verb and a plural possessive pronoun agree.

DECIDE which possessive pronoun refers to the subject and agrees with it, and UNDERLINE it.

(1) The committee on social activities has decided to have (its, their) dance next month.
(2) The family have gone about (its, their) own activities.
(3) The team has (its, their) annual dinner at the college.
(4) The group have (its, their) own interests.
(5) The army of civil rights workers was the symbol of the sixties and had Martin Luther King as (its, their) leader.

- - - - - - - - - - - - - - - - - -

(1) (its, their)
(2) (its, their)
(3) (its, their)
(4) (its, their)
(5) (its, their)

USING CHART 2

8. You might not remember all the rules about agreement, but the most troublesome situations are summarized in Chart 2 and given here:

SITUATION	IF	THEN	EXAMPLE
16. THE WORD ONE IS THE SUBJECT		the verb is singular, despite any intervening words. (The verb in an intervening supporting clause whose subject is who or that must be plural when who or that represents a plural.)	One of the new students who are auditing the course is really a graduate.
17. A PRONOUN LIKE EVERYONE IS THE SUBJECT	anyone, everybody, each, none, anything, no one, everyone, everything, nothing, nobody, somebody, or someone are used,	the verb and the possessive pronoun are singular.	Everyone has his own plans.
18. THE WORD NUMBER IS THE SUBJECT	(a) it is used with a,	(a) the verb and possessive pronoun are plural.	(a) A number of men are making their own plans.
	(b) it is used with the,	(b) the verb and possessive pronoun are singular.	(b) The number of men making its plans is growing.

SITUATION	IF	THEN	EXAMPLE
19. A COLLECTIVE NOUN LIKE <u>TEAM</u> IS THE SUBJECT	(a) it represents a single unit,	(a) the verb and possessive pronoun are singular.	(a) The group has voted its own interests.
	(b) it represents separate individuals,	(b) the verb and possessive pronoun are plural.	(b) The class are divided in their views.

See if you can interpret these entries. Two examples of agreement situations are given here. WRITE the identifying number (or number and letter) of the THEN column that it exemplifies:

_____ (1) The team is going to win today.
_____ (2) Nobody here likes to do his own work.

- - - - - - - - - - - - - - - - - - - -

19a (1) 17 (2)

9. CHOOSE the right verb (or part of the verb), the right possessive pronoun, or both. USE Chart 2 whenever necessary.

(1) The number of colleges we had to investigate (was, were) considerable.
(2) One of his classmates who (has, have) recently married (has, have) decided to run for Congress.
(3) Nobody from our group (is, are) expected to do (her, their) own typing.
(4) The number of students who (wants, want) to go to Harvard (increases, increase) every year.
(5) The team has already elected (its, their) player representative.
(6) None of the older students (agrees, agree) with that principle.
(7) Everybody here (has, have) decided to adopt (his, their) own plan.
(8) A number of students (was, were) cited for participating in the demonstrations.
(9) When health fails, nothing else (seems, seem) worthwhile.
(10) None of the students who (is, are) here (has, have) been militant.

- - - - - - - - - - - - - - - - - -

(1) (<u>was</u>, were) (18e)
(2) (has, <u>have</u>) (<u>has</u>, have) (16)

(3) (is, are) (her, their) (17)
(4) (wants, want) (increases, increase) (18b)
(5) (its, their) (19a)
(6) (agrees, agree) (17)
(7) (has, have) (his, their) (17)
(8) (was, were) (18a)
(9) (seems, seem) (17)
(10) (is, are) (has, have) (17)

USING PRONOUNS TO AVOID NOT

10. This chapter has given you new raw materials that you can use to improve your sentences. Pronouns like nothing, nobody, and none also offer alternative ways of making negative statements to avoid using not. (As you'll see in Chapter 10, a positive approach is usually more effective.)

As an illustration, notice how the use of each and none in sample (b) was able to improve the set of short, choppy sentences in sample (a):

(a) The books are all novels. They are also about a woman. But these books are not mysteries.
(b) Each book is a novel about a woman, but none is a mystery.

Sample (a) is just another example of the use of three sentences to express one main idea. The word all is the tip-off that a single pronoun would cover everything in the first two sentences. And with none to cover the third sentence, both parts of sample (b) can be positive.

Here is a similar example. See if you can combine the two sentences into a single sentence, with each part a positive statement. First, decide which sentence carries the main idea, and build on that.

All the people have agreed to take their vacations in August. They don't want to be in town during the miserably hot weather.

\- - - - - - - - - - - - - - - - - -

Suggestions

~~All the people have~~ Everyone has agreed to take ~~their~~ his vacation~~s~~ in August, since no one ~~They don't~~ wants to be in town during the miserably hot weather.

COLLECTIVE NOUNS

11. You can also make a general statement by using a collective noun. Often this is a more concise form of expression.

(a) The students on the school governing board have voted to strike. It was an unprecedented move. The reason for the strike was to protest the Kent State shootings.

(b) In an unprecedented move, the student governing board has voted to strike to protest the Kent State shootings.

Note that the words the students on the school governing board can be replaced by the words student governing board.

Try this one yourself. Hint: Pick the sentence that carries the main idea and build around it.

The people on the jury voted to acquit the man. This surprised all the members of the press. The people outside the courtroom thought he was guilty, though.

- - - - - - - - - - - - - - - - - - -

Suggestions

To the surprise of the press,

~~The people on~~ the jury voted to acquit the man, although ~~This surprised all the members of the press.~~ ~~The~~ the public ~~people outside the courtroom~~ thought he was guilty. ~~though.~~

COMBINING SENTENCES

12. Again combine each set of sentences into one general, positive sentence:

(1) All the people are busy. They have to prepare a large report.

They won't do other work until this report is finished.

(2) The men and women listening to her gave her a standing ovation. Her performance was magnificent. She would not sing other songs, though.

- - - - - - - - - - - - - - - - - -

Suggestions

(1) ~~All the people are~~ [Everyone is so] busy ~~. They have to~~ prepar~~e~~[ing] a large report ~~.~~ [that nothing else will be done] ~~They won't do other work~~ until ~~this report~~ [it] is finished.

(2) The ~~men and women listening to her~~ [audience] gave her a standing ovation ~~.~~ [for] ~~H~~[h]er [magnificent] performance ~~was magnificent.~~ [But] ~~S~~[s]he would ~~not~~ sing ~~other songs, though.~~ [nothing more.]

Now do the review of Chapter 7.

REVIEW

1. In each of these sentences UNDERLINE the right verb or the right possessive pronoun and the right verb:

(a) Nothing (goes, go) unless I see it first.
(b) Each of us (is, are) doing (her, their) part to make the party a success.
(c) One of the best things about the house (is, are) its newness.
(d) One of the teachers who (lives, live) out there (has, have) agreed to tutor him.
(e) The class (has, have) voted to skip its reunion this year.
(f) We're voting on issues that no one (admits, admit) are problems.
(g) The number of sports fans here (grows, grow) every year.
(h) The legislature (has, have) voted unanimously to raise salaries.
(i) A number of books on ecology (is, are) already on the market.
(j) One of the key issues (is, are) pollution.

(k) Everyone here (asks, ask) for a raise (his, their) first year.

(l) The committee (is, are) divided in their ideas about how to run the school.

(m) One of the more difficult records to beat (is, are) Matzdorf's 7 feet 6 1/4 inches on the high jump.

(n) The large number of fires in diners around here (is, are) suspicious.

(0) One of the students who (is, are) on the team (was, were) suspended.

2. Try to combine each set of sentences into a single sentence without using the word <u>not</u>:

(a) All the students in the senior class have decided to go to Washington for their senior trip. One reason is that not a single person has been there before. Also, Washington is a fascinating city.

(b) All the people in the store were asked to take vacations in July and August. This is when all customers take vacations. They are not buying.

<u>Suggested Answers</u>

1. (a) <u>goes</u>, go
(b) <u>is</u>, are <u>her</u>, their
(c) <u>is</u>, are
(d) lives, <u>live</u> <u>has</u>, have
(e) <u>has</u>, have
(f) <u>admits</u>, admit
(g) <u>grows</u>, grow
(h) <u>has</u>, have
(i) is, <u>are</u>
(j) <u>is</u>, are
(k) <u>asks</u>, ask <u>his</u>, their
(l) is, <u>are</u>
(m) <u>is</u>, are
(n) <u>is</u>, are
(o) is, <u>are</u> <u>was</u>, were

2. (a) ~~All the students in~~ the senior class ~~have~~ decided to go to Washington for ~~their~~ senior trip. ~~One reason is that not a single person~~ has been there before. ~~Also, Washington~~ is a fascinating city.

(b) ~~All the people~~ in the store ~~were~~ asked to take vacations in July and August. ~~This is~~ when ~~all customers~~ take vacations. ~~They are not~~ buying.

In the REVIEW column of the Self-Evaluation Record for Chapter 7 (page 156) put a check beside questions you answered satisfactorily. If you are marking the entries in Chart 2 that you are likely to need most, check entry 16 if you missed sentence c, d, j, m, or o in question 1; check entry 17 if you missed sentences a, b, f, or k in this question; check entry 18 if you missed sentence i, g, or n; and check entry 19 if you missed sentence e, h, or l. Then go on to Chapter 8.

CHAPTER EIGHT

Speaking Directly

Chapter 7 dealt with problems of agreement—occasions when the writer doesn't follow the standards of grammatical English because he's not sure what they are.

But not all agreement problems are the result of faulty grammar. Sometimes they are accidental, as here:

(a) The year 1935 saw Frank Stanton come to New York in a Model A Ford. He had spent his first night in a Y.M.C.A. And quickly a reputation was earned by him as the boy wonder of broadcasting, later becoming president of C.B.S.

We would write something like sample (a) only because we're so busy thinking about <u>what</u> to say that we don't pay enough attention to <u>how</u> we say it. And, for a first draft, this is fine. But sample (a) jumps around so much that it loses its impact and is hard to follow. Mainly, we can't tell immediately that Frank Stanton is the star of this paragraph. We can also become confused about when the action took place.

Some simple copyediting can fix up sample (a), however:

(b) The year [was] 1935 [when] ~~saw~~ Frank Stanton c~~o~~[a]me to New York in a Model A Ford. He ~~had~~ spent his first night in a Y.M.C.A. And quickly [he earned] a reputation ~~was earned by him~~ as the boy wonder of broadcasting, later becoming president of C.B.S.

What an improvement! And all we did was to make sure that everyone knows that the paragraph is about Frank Stanton—also, when everything happened.

This chapter is about shifts in point of view, in time, or in word order that are confusing, occasionally foolish, and sometimes awkward.

Once in a while, shifts are humorous too. As an example, look at this sentence. Does it strike you as funny?

(c) Today's telephone operator in Manhattan is about 95 percent black.

What about the other 5 percent? From the subject of this sentence, we expect to read about a representative operator. Instead, we read about operators as a group of individuals.

A collective noun can represent either the group as a whole or representative individuals. But if operator is considered as a representative individual in this sentence, the idea of "racial purity" is introduced. And this has nothing whatever to do with it! Obviously the writer didn't think about this second meaning.

But before considering shifts and how to correct them, do the preview of Chapter 8.

PREVIEW

1. COPYEDIT this passage so that it is consistent in both time and point of view:

   Until the turn of the century, an "apothecary shop" sold only medicines. And that is the way it still is in England, except that they call it the "chemist's." But we have had a complete revolution: Now we have been calling it the drug store, and you may think that medicines are its least important product. Today we can buy drugs, scrambled eggs, books, and even radios in the corner drug store.

   However, in terms of language we are completely reversed. You know of course that the term drug store implies drugs alone. Apothecary shop, on the other hand, meant a warehouse dispensing a variety of wares.

2. Insert the word only or just in each sentence so that the meaning will be the one specified:

   (a) He read the book.
   (Use just to mean he finished reading a short time ago.)

   (b) He is the teenager who passed.
   (Use only to mean no one else passed.)

   (c) Sports cars are my vice.
   (Use only to mean I have no other vice.)

(d) Spring water is colder.

(Use only to mean nothing except spring water is colder.)

(e) He wrote one book.

(Use just to mean he wrote one and no other book.)

3. Put a check mark beside each passive sentence. Then change the passive sentence to an active form, provided you can keep the exact meaning. Don't change it if you need to add more information.

_____ (a) Theater goers enjoy intermissions.

_____ (b) Many Independents can be counted with the Democrats this year.

_____ (c) Intermissions are appreciated by many actors.

_____ (d) Scott Nearing and his wife have planted their own cabbage, kale, and broccoli.

_____ (e) Many deer were killed by hunters last November.

_____ (f) The novel Birds of America was written by Mary McCarthy.

_____ (g) He was fired by the University because of his socialistic views.

_____ (h) The performing arts are enjoyed by most people.

_____ (i) Neither one has smoked for the last five years.

_____ (j) A sex pamphlet is given to all Yale students.

Suggested Answers

1. Until the turn of the century, an "apothecary shop" sold only medicines. And that is the way it still is in England, except that ~~they~~ it is call[ed] ~~it~~ the "chemist's." But ~~we have had~~ there has been a complete revolution in this country: Now ~~we have been calling it~~ the apothecary shop is called the drug store, and ~~you may think that~~ medicines are its least important product. Today the corner drug store sells ~~we can buy~~ drugs, scrambled eggs, books, and even radios~~in the corner drug store~~.

However, in terms of language, we are completely reversed. You know of course that the term drug store implies drugs alone. Apothecary shop, on the other hand, meant a warehouse dispensing a variety of wares.

2. (a) He read the book.
   (b) He is the teenager who passed.
   (c) Sports cars are my vice.
   (d) Spring water is colder.
   (e) He wrote one book.

3. _____ (a) NO CHANGE
   _____ (b) NO CHANGE
   _____ (c) Intermissions are appreciated by many actors.
   _____ (d) NO CHANGE
   _____ (e) Many deer were killed by hunters last November.
   _____ (f) The novel Birds of America was written by Mary McCarthy.
   _____ (g) He was fired by the University because of his socialistic views.
   _____ (h) The performing arts are enjoyed by most people.
   _____ (i) NO CHANGE
   _____ (j) NO CHANGE

If you answered all the questions satisfactorily, you may review the chapter lightly before continuing to Chapter 9. Otherwise mark the Self-Evaluation Record for Chapter 8, and proceed as usual.

SELF-EVALUATION RECORD FOR CHAPTER 8

	PREVIEW	FRAMES	REVIEW
Question 1		1 through 6; also 9	
Question 2		7 through 9	
Question 3		10 through 17	

A SHIFT IN VIEWPOINT OR IN TIME

1. The most confusing shifts for the reader to deal with are in viewpoint (subjects) or in time (verbs).

Although some shifts in viewpoint are plausible, you must prepare your reader for them. Any sudden, unexpected change can throw him. For example, if the writer has been describing his topic impersonally and then suddenly addresses the reader personally, the reader may become confused.

There are actually four different viewpoints that you can write from. These are reflected in the subjects of the sentences:

(a) The pronoun I always represents the writer's personal viewpoint: I love people. (Writers often avoid I because they prefer to be anonymous.)

(b) The pronoun you always represents the reader's personal viewpoint: You love people. (Writers like to use the you because it is informal and sounds friendly.)

(c) The pronoun we always represents a personal viewpoint that reader and writer share: We love people. (Writers also like to use the we; they often use it when they really mean I. We call it the "editorial we.")

(d) A noun subject (or its pronoun replacement) represents the impersonal viewpoint of the topic: The Andersons love people. They love people. (This is more formal than the others.)

However, you don't have to stick to one subject throughout if you have a reason for changing it. For example, in instructional materials like these three viewpoints are commonly used: the impersonal, the you, and the we. The impersonal viewpoint is handy for describing the topic; the you is useful for giving directions; and the we is good for discussions of common situations.

You must decide when a shift in viewpoint is appropriate, but you must very carefully show each action in its proper time. Has everything already happened? Is it happening right now? Will it happen at another time? The reader must know, and the writer tells him by the form of his verbs. We call this form the tense.

(a) The past tense shows that something has already happened.
(b) The present tense shows that something is happening now.
(c) The future tense shows that something will happen but hasn't yet.

Of course, there are finer, more subtle differences too, such as things that must happen; but these three tenses are the main ones.

We'll consider some examples of these shifts in viewpoint and time.

2. Remember that the writer has to keep his subjects and verbs straight if he wants to keep his reader.

Look over sample (a). Can you detect the shifts in person (subject) and time?

(a) Some teachers grade a student on his behavior. When he hasn't turned in a paper on time, they gave him a lower grade. In fact, they lowered the grade by one letter for each week he was late. But you should really grade a student on his achievement.

The passage begins impersonally with a description of general teacher behavior. The next two sentences continue impersonally, but with a shift from present to past tense. Then the last sentence winds up with a personal appeal to the reader.

You can copyedit this passage easily, however, by picking one point of view and one point in time and sticking to them. (There really isn't a reason to change viewpoint here.) Sample (b) illustrates:

(b) Some teachers grade a student on his behavior. When he hasn't turned in a paper on time, they give him a lower grade. In fact, they lower the grade by one letter for each week he is late. But they should really grade a student on his achievement.

ANSWER these questions:

(1) When does all the action take place? ______________________.

(2) Who is doing it? ______________________.

- - - - - - - - - - - - - - - - - -

(1) In the present
(2) The teachers

3. Unfortunately there is no simple way of recognizing shifts in time or point of view except to look carefully when you copyedit. You should be able to avoid most of them by deciding on a single point of time beforehand, and also on a single point of view, unless you have a particular reason for switching.

Some practice in correcting these shifts is useful, however. We'll take them one at a time, shifts in viewpoint first.

Samples (a) and (b) below are identical and have a sudden switch in viewpoint. This means that you have to look for a change in the subject. COPYEDIT sample (a) so that it is written from the point of view of both writer and reader (<u>we</u>). Then COPYEDIT sample (b) so that it addresses only the reader (<u>you</u>).

(a) Nowadays, many movies don't have heroes as you used to know them. In a movie like <u>Joe</u>, for example, who are we supposed to identify with: Joe, the hippies, or the advertising man? When the movie ends, you feel that everyone is bad.

(b) Nowadays, many movies don't have heroes as you used to know them. In a movie like <u>Joe</u>, for example, who are we supposed to identify with: Joe, the hippies, or the advertising man? When the movie ends, you feel that everyone is bad.

- - - - - - - - - - - - - - - - - -

(a) Nowadays, many movies don't have heroes as we used to know them. In a movie like Joe, for example, who are we supposed to identify with: Joe, the hippies, or the advertising man? When the movie ends, we feel that everyone is bad.

(b) Nowadays, many movies don't have heroes as you used to know them. In a movie like Joe, for example, who are you supposed to identify with: Joe, the hippies, or the advertising man? When the movie ends, you feel that everyone is bad.

4. Samples (a) and (b) are identical, except that two viewpoints are presented. COPYEDIT (a) from the impersonal point of view, and (b), from the you point of view.

(a) The American voter tends to vote his pocketbook. When times are bad, you vote against those in office. Any change would be an improvement, or so he thinks. Many times you are right to do so because those in office are really the problem. At other times you aren't right: The times are bad and not the people in office.

(b) The American voter tends to vote his pocketbook. When times are bad, you vote against those in office. Any change would be an improvement, or so he thinks. Many times you are right to do so because those in office are really the problem. At other times you aren't right: The times are bad and not the people in office.

- - - - - - - - - - - - - - - - - -

Suggestions

(a) The American voter tends to vote his pocketbook. When times are bad, he votes against those in office. Any change would be an improvement, or so he thinks. Many times he is right to do so because those in office are really the problem. At other times you aren't right: The times are bad and not the people in office.

(b) The American voter tends to vote his pocketbook. When times are bad, you vote against those in office. Any change would be an improvement, or so he thinks. Many times you are right to do so because those in office are really the problem. At other times you aren't right: The times are bad and not the people in office.

(Instead of "As an American voter" in sentence 1, you might have said "You the American voter," or also "You American voters.")

5. Now let's consider shifts in time. See if you can COPYEDIT each sentence so that the reader is always confident he knows when the action takes place. You can follow this example:

After I had planned the party for a convenient hour, I will expect more people to accept the invitation.

(1) When he lectures, he had a bad habit of coughing nervously.

(2) Occasionally the congressmen tested their popularity by having made public appearances in their home states.

(3) Before lecturing to his students, Professor Harris decides to dismiss his class early.

(4) One student wins two awards, both of which he refused.

(5) After typing the report, I have edited it.

\- - - - - - - - - - - - - - - - - -

Suggestions

(1) When he lectures, he ~~had~~ has a bad habit of coughing nervously.

(2) Occasionally the congressmen tested their popularity by ~~having made~~ making public appearances in their home states.

(3) Before lecturing to his students, Professor Harris ~~decides~~ decided to dismiss his class early.

(4) One student ~~wins~~ won two awards, both of which he refused.

(5) After typing the report, I ~~have~~ edited it.

6. COPYEDIT this passage so that it is consistent in time and point of view:

(1) Modern warfare is perhaps the biggest ecological menace.
(2) As an example, the test explosions of nuclear weapons have already spread radioactivity into every ecological system. (3) They have also deposited radioactive isotopes in human bodies and caused potential health hazards that will still not be fully known. (4) We have used massive amounts of herbicides in Vietnam on the advice that effects have been short-lived. (5) Unfortunately, we won't see mangrove swamps recovering for twenty years.

\- - - - - - - - - - - - - - - - - -

Suggestions

(1) Modern warfare is perhaps the biggest ecological menace.
(2) As an example, the test explosions of nuclear weapons have already spread radioactivity into every ecological system. (3) They have also deposited radioactive isotopes in human bodies and caused potential

health hazards that will still not be fully known. (4) We have used massive amounts of herbicides in Vietnam on the advice that effects have been short-lived. (5) Unfortunately, we won't see mangrove swamps recovering for twenty years.

In sentence 4 you might have said "The U.S. forces have used" instead of "We have used."

THE WORD ONLY OR JUST

7. Shifts in word order can often cause shifts in meaning. As we saw in Chapter 2, when phrases attach themselves to unsuitable subjects, the result can be awkward, misleading, or ridiculous!

Now let's consider another kind of shift in word order—this time, shifts in meaning involving the words only and just. Read these sentences and note how meaning changes according to the position of the word only:

(a) Only Tom wrote the book.
(b) Tom only wrote the book.
(c) Tom wrote the only book.

Sample (a) means that Tom didn't have a coauthor; sample (b) means that Tom wrote the book and did nothing more on it; and sample (c) means that no one else wrote a book except Tom.

The word only (just does this too) attaches itself to a word close by—usually the next one—and limits its meaning. You should always read over a sentence with only or just very carefully to make sure it carries the meaning you intended.

As an example, suppose you wanted to let a friend know that you liked M*A*S*H and no other movie that year, but you wrote this:

That year only the movie I liked was M*A*S*H.

(1) What did you actually tell your friend?

____

(2) Where should the word only go to get your meaning across?

____

- - - - - - - - - - - - - - - - - - - -

(1) It didn't happen any other year.
(2) Before movie.

8. Note how the meaning of our example in the last frame changes when just is moved around:

(a) Just Tom wrote the book.
(b) Tom just wrote the book.
(c) Tom wrote just the book.

Samples (a) and (c) with just have the same meaning they had with only. Sample (c) could have another meaning too—that Tom wrote the most suitable book. And note that sample (b) might also mean that Tom finished the book a short time ago.

Just one small point.... Suppose you wanted to say that Joe needs one more point to win and no more. Which do you think is a better way to say this, sample (d) or sample (e)?

(d) Joe needs just (only) one more point to win.
(e) Joe just (only) needs one more point to win.

Sample (d) is slightly better because it is more direct. Joe needs the point; only or just should be as close to the word point as possible.

INSERT the word only (or just) in each sentence so that the meaning is the one specified:

(1) This is the house you should buy.

(Use only to mean that he shouldn't buy any other house.)

(2) This is the house you should buy.

(Use only to mean no one else should buy the house.)

(3) Cortobez won an ear in the bullfight today.

(Use just to mean he didn't win anything else.)

(4) Cortobez won an ear in the bullfight today.

(Use just to mean no other bullfighter won an ear.)

\- - - - - - - - - - - - - - - - -

(1) This is the house you should buy.

(2) This is the house you should buy.

(3) Cortobez won an ear in the bullfight today.

(4) Cortobez won an ear in the bullfight today.

USING CHART 2

9. Before we continue to still another shift, note how those we've looked at so far were summarized in Chart 2:

SITUATION	IF	THEN	EXAMPLE
20. A SHIFT IN VIEWPOINT OR IN TIME	(a) it is a shift in viewpoint,	(a) keep to one viewpoint unless there is reason to change. The subject is a pronoun for a personal view-point: <u>you</u>, the reader's; <u>I</u>, the writer's; <u>we,</u> the writer's and reader's. The subject is a noun (or pro-noun replacement) for an impersonal viewpoint des-cribing the topic.	(a) You expect to see a change. I expect to see a change. We expect to see a change. The change (it) will be apparent.
	(b) it is a shift in time,	(b) keep the verb to one time: the past tense for something that has happened; the present for something that is happening; and the future for something that will happen.	(b) I expected this to happen. You expect this to happen. We will expect you at once.

SITUATION	IF	THEN	EXAMPLE
21. THE WORD <u>ONLY</u> OR <u>JUST</u>		put it as close as possible to the word you want it to limit.	(a) She was the only daughter. (This means he didn't have any other daughters.) (b) She just bought a car. (This means she bought a car a short time ago.)

FOLLOW the directions in each example:

(1) Insert <u>only</u> so that the sentence means that no one else waved to the winner except his mother.

His mother waved to the winner.

(2) Change this sentence to an impersonal viewpoint, in past time:

We saw a deer standing still in the path.

- - - - - - - - - - - - - - - - - - - -

<u>Suggestions</u>

(1) Only ~~H~~is mother waved to the winner.

(2) ~~We saw~~ A deer stood ~~standing~~ still in the path.

You might have said <u>was standing</u> instead of <u>stood</u>.

A PASSIVE SENTENCE

10. Now let's look at examples of shifts in word order that either make the entire sentence sound awkward or focus attention on the wrong subject. Compare these sentences, for example:

(a) Couples was written by John Updike.
(b) John Updike wrote Couples.

In sample (a) the subject is Couples, which is not actively carrying out the action. John Updike actually does the writing, and Couples—the book he wrote—just passively experiences it. We say this kind of word order is passive. In sample (b) the real doer of the action—John Updike—is mentioned first. This sentence arrangement is called active.

In some passives the true actor isn't stated at all.

(c) The passengers were asked for identification.

Notice that the passengers didn't do the asking. Whoever did it—probably the authorities—weren't important enough to be mentioned. Passives like these are common.

See if you can recognize the passives that follow. PUT A CHECK MARK beside each one. (The test is who is doing the acting.)

_____ (1) John Mitchell was assigned to patrol duty.
_____ (2) He was arrested for speeding.
_____ (3) Mary did some research on marketing.
_____ (4) Clever people do unclever things sometimes.
_____ (5) He was told about the meeting by the other students.

- - - - - - - - - - - - - - - - - - - -

✓ (1) ✓ (2) ✓ (5)

11. Read this brief passage. Does any sentence sound awkward to you?

Johnny isn't doing well in algebra. He failed the last two weekly quizzes, and he hasn't turned in his homework for days. A tutor is thought to be necessary by his teacher.

Some people would find the last sentence awkward because it sounds so much more formal than the other sentences. As you can see, it's passive, whereas the first two sentences are active.

Notice too that the passage starts off emphasizing Johnny, but we have to read carefully to realize that the third sentence has anything to do with him. What happened was that the word order in that sentence switched the emphasis too abruptly.

You should write both active and passive sentences. However, you should avoid two kinds of passives: those that sound awkward and those that unexpectedly shift the emphasis in a paragraph.

You'll see how to recognize these awkward passives.

12. Back in Chapter 2 you learned that the most common word order for a sentence is subject (doer of the action), verb, and any supporting material. This order describes an active sentence.

A passive arrangement, however, is often useful too. In fact, whenever the doer of the action is either obvious or fairly unimportant, he doesn't need to be mentioned; the passive may be better than the active counterpart.

Sample (a) for example is passive:

(a) Richard Nixon was elected president in 1968.

The writer doesn't need to say <u>who</u> elected Richard Nixon because the reader already knows it was the American voters.

Because the passive is not the most common arrangement, it may sound more formal than you want to be. It is also less direct because it often doesn't name the doer of the action until the very end of the sentence. You can keep your prose more forceful by using active sentences most of the time and passives only when you <u>don't</u> have to name the real doer of the action.

In other words, try to avoid a passive in which the doer of the action is mentioned after the verb and is introduced by the word <u>by</u>, as in sample (b):

(b) All students are assumed to be radical <u>by</u> <u>the</u> <u>over-thirty</u> <u>crowd</u>.

You should also avoid a passive if it shifts the emphasis of the paragraph abruptly.

We'll examine these <u>awkward passives</u> in more detail.

13. Remember that a passive sentence may be awkward if it has this characteristic:

The real doer of the action is named after the verb and is introduced by the word <u>by</u>.

PUT A CHECK MARK beside each sentence that you think may be an awkward passive:

_____ (1) The novel was read by us.
_____ (2) Shoes aren't worn by babies who don't walk.
_____ (3) That test paper was marked wrong.
_____ (4) Mice are chased by cats.
_____ (5) His shirts are washed and ironed by his mother.
_____ (6) Successful communes have been established all across the country.
_____ (7) We were told that the conservatives are in favor of that bill.
_____ (8) My schedule was arranged yesterday.
_____ (9) We were driven around the park.
_____ (10) The pain will be relieved by this medicine.

- - - - - - - - - - - - - - - - - - -

✓ (1) ✓ (2) ✓ (4) ✓ (5) ✓ (10)

14. A passive may also be awkward if it shifts the emphasis of the passage abruptly.

(1) The modern husband leaves his suburban home at eight. (2) All day a hostile world is encountered. (3) He returns home at eight, weary and wilted. (4) He is defeated. (5) No wonder his wife will probably outlive him!

Notice that sentence 2 is an awkward use of the passive because it interrupts the mood. Sentence 4 is not awkward, although it is a passive, since it maintains the emphasis on the husband. READ over this set of brief sentences and UNDERLINE any that you think is awkward because it shifts the emphasis.

(1) The best time for you to find shells along the Carolina beach is at low tide after a storm or heavy blow. (2) Many interesting varieties are to be found. (3) You will probably prize the sand dollar just as most casual collectors do. (4) But you will also enjoy the common coquina because it is so colorful.

- - - - - - - - - - - - - - - - - - -

...storm or heavy blow. (2) Many interesting varieties are to be found. (3) You will probably...

15. How do you correct an awkward passive? When the doer of the action is mentioned after the verb and is introduced by the word by, you rearrange the words so that the subject comes first.

(a) A policy of open admissions has been adopted by New York City colleges.

(b) New York City colleges have adopted a policy of open admissions.

Notice that both sentences are exactly alike in meaning. But a simple rearrangement turned the awkward one (a) into an active sentence.

If a passive is awkward only because it shifts the emphasis abruptly away from the real doer of the action, again you need to turn the sentence around and mention the real subject first. As an example, note how the awkward sentence you identified in frame 14 can be repaired:

(c) You may find ~~Many~~ many interesting varieties. ~~are to be found.~~

TRY some yourself. Assume that the first five passives are awkward. You have already identified the last five as awkward (in frame 13). COPY-EDIT to make them active.

(1) Undergraduate sports are not supported.

(Emphasis of the paragraph should be on the doer—"the graduate students.")

(2) Class was dismissed by the dean today.

(3) Fashions are followed slavishly by unliberated women.

(4) Teenagers are not understood by parents.

(5) Parents are not understood by teenagers.

(Emphasis of the paragraph should be on the doer "teenagers.")

(6) The novel was read by us.

(7) Shoes aren't worn by babies who don't walk.

(8) Mice are chased by cats.

(9) His shirts are washed and ironed by his mother.

(10) The pain will be relieved by this medicine.

- - - - - - - - - - - - - - - - - - - -

Suggestions

(1) Undergraduate sports are not supported.

(2) Class was dismissed by the dean today.

(3) Fashions are followed slavishly by unliberated women.

(4) Teenagers are not understood by parents.

(5) Parents are not understood by teenagers.

(6) The novel was ready by us.

(7) Shoes aren't worn by babies who don't walk.

(8) Mice are chased by cats.

(9) His shirts are washed and ironed by his mother.

(10) The pain will be relieved by this medicine.

USING CHART 2

16. The entry in Chart 2 on passives is included here. Study it:

SITUATION	IF	THEN	EXAMPLE
22. A PASSIVE SENTENCE	(a) the real doer of the action is not mentioned, either because it is obvious or relatively unimportant,	(a) maintain the passive. (Change to active only if passive switches emphasis away from the doer too abruptly.)	(a) He was greeted warmly. He was escorted to his seat. (If emphasis was shifted too abruptly: Mary escorted him to his seat.)
	(b) the real doer of the action is mentioned after the verb and introduced by the word by,	(b) make it active: Start with the real doer of the action.	(b) He was bitten by a rabid dog.

COPYEDIT these passives. (Assume each one is awkward.)

(1) Birds trapped in the oil slicks were cleaned by volunteers in San Francisco.

(2) Life in the dormitory is believed to be unsatisfactory.

(Emphasis in the paragraph should be on real doer, "the students.")

(3) Polluted air is expected by New Yorkers every day.

(4) Their own supplies were bought by the students.

(5) Books and clothing were collected by the Women's Auxiliary League.

(6) Capital punishment is forbidden by state law.

(7) A good report was written last semester by Mary Brown.

- - - - - - - - - - - - - - - - - - - -

Suggestions

(1) Birds trapped in the oil slicks were cleaned by volunteers in San Francisco.

(2) Life in the dormitory is believed to be unsatisfactory.

(3) Polluted air is expected by New Yorkers every day.

(4) Their own supplies were bought by the students.

(5) Books and clothing were collected by the Women's Auxiliary League.

(6) Capital punishment is forbidden by state law.

(7) A good report was written last semester by Mary Brown.

17. COPYEDIT this passage to rid it of any passives that you feel are awkward:

(1) Written messages can now be sent anywhere in the United States by New Yorkers. (2) They will be delivered by mailmen on the next business day. (3) A joint undertaking by Western Union and the post office, this new service is called Mailgram. (4) It works this way. (5) A customer

calls Western Union by telephone. (6) Or a major branch office is visited and a direct call is placed. (7) The rest is then handled by a high-speed computer. (8) The cost is $1.60 for the first hundred words and 80 cents for each additional hundred-word block. (9) So Mailgram is faster than regular mail and cheaper than the telephone.

- -

Suggestions

(1) Written messages can now be sent anywhere in the United States by New Yorkers. (2) They will be delivered by mailmen on the next business day. (3) A joint undertaking by Western Union and the post office, this new service is called Mailgram. (4) It works this way. (5) A customer calls Western Union by telephone. (6) Or a major branch office is visited and a direct call is placed. (7) The rest is then handled by a high-speed computer. (8) The cost is $1.60 for the first hundred words and 80 cents for each additional hundred-word block. (9) So Mailgram is faster than regular mail and cheaper than the telephone.

(Note: Sentence 3 is passive but not awkward. Sentence 6, however, is passive and also awkward.)

Now do the review of Chapter 8.

REVIEW

1. Copyedit this passage to make it consistent in time and point of view.

You might have thought that a man tied to "apron strings" must be tied to his mother. But we haven't always meant "mother" when we were talking about apron strings. As an example, when the Alabama laws prohibited George Wallace from succeeding himself as governor for another term, he was making a bid for "apron-string tenure." We meant by this the right to hold property or office because of one's wife. And Governor Wallace has been careful to tell us that he was intending to continue to hold his authority through his wife.

2. Insert the word only or just in each sentence so that the meaning will be the one specified.

(a) A cat is the pet we have.

(Use only to mean we have no other pet.)

(b) He needs three more credits to graduate.

(Use just to mean no more than three credits.)

(c) The course to give him trouble was math.

(Use only to mean he didn't have any trouble with any of the other courses.)

(d) He finished the exam.

(Use just to mean he finished the exam a short time ago.)

(e) He wants to retire young.

(Use only to mean nobody else wants to retire young.)

3. Put a check mark beside each passive sentence. Then change the passive sentence to its active form, provided you can keep the exact meaning. (Don't change it if you have to add more information.)

_______ (a) Real art is appreciated by most people.

_______ (b) He was elected president of the senior class.

_______ (c) Graduate students often want to teach in universities after they get their degrees.

_______ (d) I was referred to the Personnel Department by the editor.

_______ (e) He was asked to resign by the Board.

_______ (f) Canonero II was expected to win the Belmont Stakes and the Triple Crown.

________ (g) Most people enjoy watching fireworks on the Fourth of July.

________ (h) Fireworks are felt to be dangerous by many states.

________ (i) Compulsive gamblers are believed to be first-rate suckers.

________ (j) These farms have been abandoned by their owners.

Suggested Answers

1. You might have thought that a man tied to "apron strings" must be tied to his mother. But we haven't always mean "mother" when we were talking about apron strings. As an example, when the Alabama laws prohibited George Wallace from succeeding himself as governor for another term, he was making a bid for "apron-string tenure." We meant by this the right to hold property or office because of one's wife. And Governor Wallace had been careful to tell us that he was intending to continue to hold his authority through his wife.

2. (a) A cat is the pet we have.
   (b) He needs three more credits to graduate.
   (c) The course to give him trouble was math.
   (d) He finished the exam.
   (e) He wants to retire young.

3. ________ (a) Real art is appreciated by most people.
   ________ (b) NO CHANGE
   ________ (c) NO CHANGE

(d) I was referred to the Personnel Department by the editor.

(e) He was asked to resign by the Board.

(f) NO CHANGE

(g) NO CHANGE

(h) Fireworks are felt to be dangerous by many states.

(i) NO CHANGE

(j) These farms have been abandoned by their owners.

If you answered each question satisfactorily, put checks in the REVIEW column of the Self-Evaluation Record for Chapter 8 (page 174). If you didn't answer question 1 satisfactorily, put a check beside entry 20 in Chart 2; if you had any difficulty with question 2, check entry 21; and if question 3 was a problem, check entry 22. Then go on to Chapter 9.

CHAPTER NINE

Paring the Words to Spare the Paragraph

Suppose you have your choice of two books. Both have the same facts and the same format, but one has more words than the other. Which would you read?

You would pick the shorter one, of course. Why read extra words that don't tell you anything more? You could go to extremes and write in telegram style, as if each word cost money. This kind of economy isn't necessary. But in most of your writing—the shorter the better, provided you cover all the information.

So far in this book, brevity has been just a by-product of other revisions. As an example, when you changed an awkward passive to the active, you made the sentence more direct, but you also used fewer words. Compare these:

(a) The artist Andrew Wyeth is appreciated by most Americans.
(b) Most Americans appreciate the artist Andrew Wyeth.

Sample (b) was shorter by two words.

When we reduce a clause to a two-word description, we make the sentence livelier and again we use fewer words.

(c) She wore a sweater that fitted her form.
(d) She wore a form-fitting sweater.

Sample (d) was also shorter by two words.

Norman Mailer once wrote a sentence that was better than a thousand words. That sentence was "So."

This chapter will give you lots more practice in being brief when just being brief is better. Primarily, you'll take out over-long words and phrases; and you'll try to reduce clauses to phrases and phrases to a few words—or even a single word.

In theory, if you follow all the suggestions in this book, you won't have any "deadwood"—any unnecessary words—to weed out of your own writing. But somehow these wordy expressions do sneak into writing anyway, and you need to be on the lookout for them when you copyedit.

First, however, turn to the preview of Chapter 9.

PREVIEW

1. In these sentences eliminate <u>there</u> or <u>it</u> if it is unnecessary. Then revise the rest of the sentence (or sentences) to keep the meaning.

   (a) It is probable that Lou Alcindor is the best professional basketball player.

   (b) There are many repairs to be made on that house.

   (c) There are two reasons for taking a winter vacation.

   (d) It is necessary for middle-income people to save all year for a one-week vacation.

   (e) There was a recession in 1970.

   (f) She wore a loose-fitting sweater. In fact, it was so loose that no one could tell whether she was fat or thin.

   (g) She said it was possible that they might go to Europe.

   (h) It was suspected that canned soup caused botulism, a severe food poisoning.

   (i) Next summer there will be two interesting art courses given at the studio.

   (j) A teacher has to remember so many faces that it is important for her to have a good memory.

2. Reduce these sentences by simplifying the wordy expressions.

   (a) He lives in the vicinity of Pittsfield, Massachusetts.

   (b) Owing to the fact that he was a native, he was excused.

   (c) Madame Curie was a person who had a scientist's curiosity.

   (d) They spoke to him in regard to his grades.

   (e) This room is used for study purposes.

3. Delete any repetitious words in these sentences.

   (a) The material is too coarse in texture.

   (b) Each and every student voted to strike in protest.

(c) He enjoys field events, such as the pole vault, the high jump, etc.

(d) I personally have never forgiven him.

(e) You should refer back to the tables.

Suggested Answers

1. (a) ~~It is probable that~~ Lou Alcindor is *probably* the best professional basketball player.

   (b) ~~There are~~ many repairs *need* to be made on that house.

   (c) NO CHANGE

   (d) ~~It is necessary for~~ middle-income people ~~to~~ *must* save all year for a one-week vacation.

   (e) NO CHANGE

   (f) NO CHANGE

   (g) She said ~~it was possible~~ that they might *possibly* go to Europe.

   (h) ~~It was suspected that~~ canned soup *was suspected of causing* ~~caused~~ botulism, a severe food poisoning.

   (i) Next summer ~~there will be~~ two interesting art courses *will be* given at the studio.

   (j) A teacher has to remember so many faces that ~~it is important for her to~~ *she should* have a good memory.

2. (a) He lives ~~in the vicinity of~~ *near* Pittsfield, Massachusetts.

   (b) ~~Owing to the fact that~~ *Because* he was a native, he was excused.

   (c) Madame Curie ~~was a person who~~ had a scientist's curiosity.

   (d) They spoke to him ~~in regard to~~ *about* his grades.

   (e) This room is used for study ~~purposes~~.

3. (a) The material is too coarse ~~in texture~~.

   (b) ~~Each and~~ every student voted to strike in protest.

(c) He enjoys field events, such as the pole vault, the high jump, ~~etc.~~ and

(d) I ~~personally~~ have never forgiven him.

(e) You should refer ~~back~~ to the tables.

If you did particularly well on all the questions, you can just skim over this chapter. Otherwise you should mark the Self-Evaluation Record for Chapter 9 and proceed as you usually do.

SELF-EVALUATION RECORD FOR CHAPTER 9

	PREVIEW	FRAMES	REVIEW
Question 1		1 through 5	
Question 2		6 through 8 and 13 and 14	
Question 3		9 through 14	

THE WORD THERE

1. The hunt for unnecessary words is easier than you might think if you follow the right clues. One clue may be the word there.

When the writer hasn't really decided who should carry the action of the sentence, he often lets there do it, as here:

(a) There are many national issues that interest college students.
(b) Many national issues interest college students.

Notice how we lopped off the first two words—and one more too—without any ill effects. In fact, the sentence sounds stronger without the deadwood. Sample (a) already had a subject (national issues) and there didn't do anything except hide it.

The "there" construction is grammatical, though, and often useful:

(c) How many Great Lakes are there? There are five.

Here, there is actually the subject. You could rewrite the sentence another way without there, but you would probably need more words.

Starting off with there is a habit many writers have. (It's comparable to the speech habit of starting every sentence with "you know.") Use there occasionally as the subject of the sentence, but try not to use it if the subject is already in the sentence.

LOOK OVER these sentences and decide which there constructions are probably necessary. COPYEDIT the others and make any necessary revisions.

(1) There are any of at least six other men who could do this job better.

(2) There are many reasons to celebrate Martin Luther King's birthday.

(3) There are twenty-five students in the usual composition class.

(4) There are several courses in ecology listed in the catalogue.

(5) There is nothing more to say about it.

- - - - - - - - - - - - - - - - - - - -

Suggestions

(1) ~~There are~~ any of at least six other men ~~who~~ could do this job better.

(2) CORRECT

(3) ~~There are~~ twenty-five students ^are in the usual composition class.

(4) ~~There are~~ several courses in ecology ^are listed in the catalogue.

(5) CORRECT

THE WORD IT AS THE SUBJECT

2. Here is another clue to deadwood.

The word it is an appropriate subject of a clause or a sentence if the it represents something definite. Otherwise you should always replace the it as indirect and wordy.

COMPARE samples (a) and (b). In one sample the it is not definite. In the other it is. Can you tell which is which?

(a) John is failing algebra. It is obvious that he should be tutored.
(b) John is failing algebra. It is a difficult subject for him to grasp.

If you look carefully at sample (a), you'll see that the it doesn't stand for anything; but in sample (b) the it represents the word algebra.

A favorite trick of writers is to let it carry the action when they don't want to assign responsibility to a subject. They often use the passive then, too, as here:

(c) It is felt that the Orioles will win the pennant.

Who felt it? The writer didn't want to say. This is another example of an indefinite it that ought to be replaced—unless you're a politician who deliberately wants to obscure responsibility for an action. The samples show some possible revisions:

(d) The Orioles will win the pennant.
(e) Most fans feel that the Orioles will win the pennant.
(f) The Orioles will probably win the pennant.

Which the writer should choose depends on how definite he wants to be.

See if you can RECOGNIZE an indefinite it. PUT A CHECK MARK beside a sentence if you think it has one.

_____ (1) That sentence is strong and direct: It has no extras.
_____ (2) That game is fun to play—it is certain to be a bestseller.
_____ (3) The Yankees are good this year. It is probable that they will make a good showing.
_____ (4) The school year is short. It is over in June.
_____ (5) The team has many new players this year. It is hard to recognize all of them.
_____ (6) It is thought that the construction of the house is sound.

- - - - - - - - - - - - - - - - - -

✓ (3) ✓ (5) ✓ (6)

3. You can easily correct an indefinite it by recasting the sentence so that the subject does the acting. Sample (a) illustrates one possible revision:

(a) Since John is failing algebra, ~~. It is obvious that~~ he obviously should be tutored.

Notice that once we eliminate the it expression here we have two short, choppy sentences that are more effective if they are combined.

Sample (b) illustrates an indefinite it that is harder to correct:

(b) The team has so many new players this year. It is hard to recognize them.

Again, the short sentences were combined for a smoother effect.

COPYEDIT each sentence with an indefinite it:

(1) The snow fell so hard all night. It is certain that classes will be dismissed today.

(2) I saw the Colts work out. It is probable that they will win.

(3) The team has to catch up. It is necessary for it to win every game from now on.

(4) The movie is rated "X." I hear it has several violent scenes.

(5) She is such a nice person. It is easy to like her.

- -

Suggestions

(1) The snow fell so hard all night. It is certain that classes will be dismissed today.

The snow fell so hard all night. It is certain that classes will be dismissed today.

(2) I saw the Colts work out. It is probable that they will win.

(3) The team has to catch up. It is necessary for it to win every game from now on.

(4) CORRECT

(5) She is such a nice person. It is easy to like her.

4. In the sentences so far you could eliminate the indefinite it without changing the meaning in any way. When you choose to assign responsibility, however, you of course change the meaning. For example, compare samples (a), (b), and (c).

(a) It is suspected that a few students are stirring up all the trouble.

(b) ~~It is suspected that~~ a few students are suspected of stirring up all the trouble.

(c) ~~It is~~ The college administrators suspected that a few students are stirring up all the trouble.

Note that sample (b) maintains the original meaning, but it does not assign any subject to the action. Sample (c) assigns responsibility and also changes the meaning. As the writer, you have to decide how definite you want to be in sentences such as these.

COPYEDIT these sentences to rid them of the indefinite it. In (a) try to maintain the original meaning; in (b) assign the responsibility.

(a) It is supposed that children are ready to read by age six.

(b) It is supposed that children are ready to read by age six.

(a) Unfortunately it is considered unpleasant in the library.

(b) Unfortunately it is considered unpleasant in the library.

- - - - - - - - - - - - - - - - - -

Suggestions

(a) ~~It is supposed that~~ children are supposidly ready to read by age six.

(b) ~~It is~~ Educators supposed that children are ready to read by age six.

(a) Unfortunately ~~it~~ is considered unpleasant ~~in~~ the library.

(b) Unfortunately many students consider ~~it is considered unpleasant in~~ the library unpleasant.

USING CHART 2

5. Here are the entries from Chart 2:

SITUATION	IF	THEN	EXAMPLE
23. THE WORD THERE	(a) there is the subject,	(a) there is a suitable subject unless it is overused.	(a) There are actually two choices.

SITUATION	IF	THEN	EXAMPLE
23. THE WORD THERE (Continued)	(b) the sentence already has a subject concealed by there is or are,	(b) take out the useless there and revise as necessary.	(b) ~~There are~~ too many students are enrolled in this course.
24. THE WORD IT AS THE SUBJECT	(a) the it represents something,	(a) don't change it if it's clear.	(a) This candy isn't good. It is too sweet.
	(b) the it doesn't represent anything,	(b) take out the it and recast the sentence as necessary: Decide how definite you want to be.	(b) ~~It is necessary for~~ a pitcher ~~to~~ must conserve his energy. ~~It is believed~~ grades believed to be in school are punishing. ~~It is~~ The teachers believed that grades in school are punishing.

USE these entries to help you COPYEDIT these sentences. Combine any short, choppy ones.

(1) There are several words misspelled in that article.

(2) The book is good, and it is on all the bestseller lists.

(3) An actor has to remember many lines. It is necessary for him to have a good memory.

(4) There are only two considerations: the location and the price.

(5) It is believed that cyclamates are dangerous.

- - - - - - - - - - - - - - - - - - -

Suggestions

(1) ~~There are~~ several words are misspelled in that article.

(2) CORRECT

(3) An actor has to remember many lines. It is necessary for him to have a good memory.

(4) CORRECT

(5) It is believed that cyclamates are dangerous.

It is believed that cyclamates are dangerous.

AVOIDING WORDY EXPRESSIONS

6. The words there and it are clues that you may be able to cut out words. Since you can't recognize other examples of wordiness so easily, you won't eliminate all vague, useless words; but you can sensitize yourself to the problem of wordiness.

When you copyedit, you should be on the lookout for words that merely take up space. The solution is to cut them out altogether; or, if that isn't possible, to replace them with a more economical or more meaningful expression. Try to reduce a clause to a phrase, or even a few words; and a phrase to a one- or two-word expression.

You have already learned how to reduce many over-long expressions, such as a clause introduced by who is or which is. (See Chapter 4, page 88.) The table below lists the common wordy expressions and possible ways to reduce them. STUDY this table carefully:

COMMON WORDY EXPRESSIONS	NUMBER OF WORDS		POSSIBLE REDUCTIONS
1. Owing to the fact that	5	1	1. Because, since
2. The fact that he could not be found	8	2	2. His disappearance
3. She is a person who	5	1	3. She
4. Used for study purposes	4	3	4. Used for study
5. In the vicinity of	4	1	5. Near
6. Call to your attention	4	2	6. Remind you
7. In regard to	3	1	7. About
8. Question as to whether	4	1, 2	8. Whether, question whether
9. In a defensive manner	4	1	9. Defensively
10. Cornwallis, who was the general at Yorktown,	7	5	10. Cornwallis, the general at Yorktown,

7. The table in frame 6 was used to copyedit these examples. STUDY them:

(a) He stopped the car ~~in an~~ abrupt*ly* ~~manner~~.

(b) ~~Owing to the fact that~~ *Because* he belongs to a minority group, he feels he must work harder than other people.

(c) He lived in Battle Creek, ~~which is in~~ Michigan.

(d) He lives ~~in the neighborhood of~~ *near* the ball park.

Single words like fashion, nature, and thing are often used unnecessarily too, as here:

(e) His actions are ~~of a~~ mysterious~~.~~ ~~nature~~.

Try some yourself. LOOK for vague words and expressions that you can either eliminate entirely or reduce. Of course, refer to the table in frame 6 whenever you need to.

(1) Due to the fact that he turned his term paper in late, he flunked the course.

(2) This room is reserved for purposes of play.

(3) She is a person who studies hard to make good grades.

(4) They inquired at the hospital in regard to his condition.

(5) The thing is that corn is native to this country.

(6) Owing to the fact that school is still in session, the speed limit is low.

(7) They spoke in a private fashion.

(8) Campers can buy many food supplies in the village owing to the fact that it is close by.

(9) The only thing I can think of is that he is unlucky in love.

(10) Mr. Jenkins still hasn't decided the question as to whether he should fail the star football player.

- - - - - - - - - - - - - - - - - - - -

Suggestions

(1) ~~Due to the fact that~~ Since he turned his term paper in late, he flunked the course.

(2) This room is reserved for ~~purposes of~~ play.

(3) She ~~is a person who~~ studies hard to make good grades.

(4) They inquired at the hospital about ~~in regard to~~ his condition.

(5) ~~The thing is that~~ corn is native to this country.

(6) ~~Owing to the fact that~~ Since school is still in session, the speed limit is low.

(7) They spoke ~~in a~~ private ly ~~fashion~~.

(8) Campers can buy many food supplies in the village ~~owing to the fact that it is~~ close by.

(9) ~~The only thing~~ I guess ~~can think of it that~~ he is unlucky in love.

(10) Mr. Jenkins still hasn't decided ~~the question as to~~ whether he should fail the star football player.

8. For extra practice, try editing any vague and wordy expressions in these sentences:

(1) The fact is that I can't decide what role suits him best.

(2) He walked in a hesitant manner after the cast was first taken off.

(3) They spoke in regard to politics and the election.

(4) Due to the fact that money is tight, we can't afford to go out so often.

(5) She is the girl who is wearing the yellow coat.

(6) I was born in the city of Newark, which is located in the state of New Jersey.

(7) They ran in a fearful way.

(8) The deal is that I can get only first-class seats.

(9) These are the clothes I wear for housework purposes.

(10) They discussed the question as to whether the United States should interfere in the affairs of other nations.

- - - - - - - - - - - - - - - - - - -

Suggestions

(1) ~~The fact is that~~ I can't decide what role suits him best.

(2) He walked ~~in a~~ hesitant*ly* ~~manner~~ after the cast was first taken off.

(3) They spoke ~~in regard to~~ *about* politics and the election.

(4) ~~Due to the fact that~~ *Because* money is tight, we can't afford to go out so often.

(5) She is the girl ~~who is wearing~~ *in* the yellow coat.

(6) I was born in ~~the city of~~ Newark, ~~which is located in the state of~~ New Jersey.

(7) They ran ~~in a~~ fearful*ly.* ~~way~~

(8) ~~The deal is that~~ I can get only first-class seats.

(9) These are the clothes I wear for housework~~ purposes~~.

(10) They discussed ~~the question as to~~ whether the United States should interfere in the affairs of other nations.

AVOIDING REPETITIONS

9. Repetitions, or partial repetitions, are another offender to look for in your economy drive in sentences. They are hard to spot, though, because many of them are expressions that we use so often we imagine they must be right. Hasn't everyone said and written "each and every one of us" at least once—to be emphatic?

Perhaps you can never rid your writing of all repetitions, just because you won't always realize you are being repetitious. But you can be on the alert for common ones.

Let's look at some examples. Expressions whose meanings are partly alike are underlined:

(a) Bobby Kennedy was equally as bright as President Kennedy.
(b) The solution is to rewrite the sentence in different words.
(c) The South was rich in natural resources such as sunshine and beaches, etc.

You can't take your pick of the underlined expressions to use here because they're only partly repetitious. Only one expression makes sense in each example. WRITE it below:

(a) ____________________
(b) ____________________
(c) ____________________

- - - - - - - - - - - - - - - - - - - -

(a) as bright as
(b) rewrite
(c) such as

10. The right way to handle a repetition is always to delete the less desirable word or words. Usually the choice is obvious. Suppose you had written this sentence:

(a) His distress was evident to the eye.

Anything that is "evident" is something the eye can see or the ear can hear. So either evident or to the eye must go. It will have to be to the eye because the sentence would be nonsense without the word evident.

Sometimes the choice isn't so clear, as here:

(b) Relations between them will probably continue to remain strained.

The possibilities are as follows:

(c) Relations between them will probably continue strained.
(d) Relations between them will probably remain strained.

If you read both sentences aloud, you will probably agree that sample (c) sounds better—at least, out of context. But sample (d) isn't wrong. It's far better than the original sentence, and in some contexts it may be better than sample (c).

This is a very common example of repetition. Notice the treatment:

(e) The job also includes such duties as proofreading, and typing, ~~etc.~~

Remember (from Chapter 6) that such as introduces an incomplete list. This means that adding etc., the short form of "and others," is repetitious.

Try COPYEDITING these sentences:

(1) I have never in my life experienced such poor service.

(2) This movie is restricted just to adults.

- - - - - - - - - - - - - - - - - - -

Suggestions

(1) I have never ~~in my life~~ experienced such poor service.

(2) This movie is restricted ~~just~~ to adults.

11. CROSS OUT the unnecessary word or expression. Follow this example:

The river looks muddy. ~~in appearance.~~

(1) Its fur is smooth in texture.

(2) History repeats itself over again.

(3) Personally, I suspect that political parties are to blame.

(4) The Pine Barrens in New Jersey is much bigger in size than the Rocky Mountain National Park.

(5) Each and every voter should attend this meeting.

(6) In the fall the leaves are red in color.

(7) Cats may be more preferable for apartment dwellers.

(8) The physician lectured about drug abuse while at the same time becoming addicted himself.

(9) He enjoys winter sports, such as skating, skiing, etc.

(10) The food here is equally as good as that at the Student Union.

- - - - - - - - - - - - - - - - - - -

STUDY any of these you missed:

(1) Its fur is smooth. ~~in texture.~~

(2) History repeats itself over again.

(3) Personally, I suspect that political parties are to blame.

(4) The Pine Barrens in New Jersey is much bigger in size than the Rocky Mountain National Park.

(5) Each and every voter should attend this meeting. (You could also delete every and leave in each.)

(6) In the fall the leaves are red in color.

(7) Cats may be more preferable for apartment dwellers.

(8) The physician lectured about drug abuse while at the same time becoming addicted himself.

(9) He enjoys winter sports such as skating, skiing, etc.

(10) The food here is equally as good as that at the Student Union.

12. The best way to accustom yourself to eliminating repetitious or partially repetitious expressions is to practice finding them.

COPYEDIT each sentence to rid it of the less effective expression:

(1) This alternative apparently seems sensible.

(2) Relations between them will probably continue to remain unpleasant.

(3) The grass is the color green.

(4) I personally have never cheated in class.

(5) The report is so late that I will accept it in any shape or form.

(6) The tabloid is much smaller in size than the regular newspaper.

(7) You should rewrite the composition again.

(8) His is quite sensitive in feeling.

(9) You must write a note to thank each and every contributor.

(10) He needs basic tools, such as reading, writing, math, etc.

- - - - - - - - - - - - - - - - - -

(1) This alternative apparently seems sensible.

(2) Relations between them will probably continue to remain unpleasant.

(3) The grass is the color green.

(4) I personally have never cheated in class.

(5) The report is so late that I will accept it in any shape. ~~or form.~~

(6) The tabloid is much smaller ~~in size~~ than the regular newspaper. (Sometimes we would purposely add "in size" so that it wouldn't be taken in another sense—"in circulation," for example.)

(7) You should rewrite the composition. ~~again.~~

(8) His is quite sensitive. ~~in feelings.~~

(9) You must write a notice to thank each ~~and every~~ contributor.

(10) He needs basic tools, such as reading, writing, and math. ~~etc.~~

REDUCING PARAGRAPHS

13. This time, edit out both repetitious and wordy expressions:

I heard of him at that time when he campaigned in New Jersey, which is my home state. Owing to the fact that he was a bachelor, however, he wasn't convincing on such issues as sex education, drug addiction, etc. Parents felt that his views had to be shallow in depth because of the fact that he personally hadn't any children of his own.

As far as I was concerned, I didn't think the question as to whether he was qualified to discuss family matters was a relevant one. Does a cook have to lay an egg before he can make an omelet? Perhaps a bachelor is better qualified to talk in regard to the positive merits of sex education and the negative dangers of drug addiction, despite the fact that he hasn't any children of his own. At least, he can look over the problems in an objective manner.

Not each and every voter agreed with me. But apparently the vast majority seemed to think he was the more preferable man: He was elected.

- - - - - - - - - - - - - - - - - - -

Suggestions

I heard of him ~~at that time~~ when he campaigned in New Jersey, ~~which is~~ my home state. ~~Owing to the fact that~~ *Because* he was a bachelor, however, he wasn't convincing on such issues as sex education*, and* drug addiction~~, etc~~. Parents felt that his views had to be shallow ~~in depth because of the fact that~~ *since* he ~~personally hadn't~~ *didn't have* any children~~ of his own~~.

~~As far as I was concerned~~, I didn't think the question ~~as to~~ whether he was qualified to discuss family matters was ~~a~~ relevant~~ one~~. Does a cook have to lay an egg before he can make an omelet? Perhaps a bachelor is better qualified to talk ~~in regard to~~ *about* the ~~positive~~ merits of sex education and the ~~negative~~ dangers of drug addiction, ~~despite the fact that~~ *even though* he ~~hasn't~~ *doesn't have* any children~~ of his own~~. At least, he can look over the problems ~~in an~~ objective*ly*~~ manner~~.

Not ~~each and~~ every voter agreed with me. But ~~apparently~~ the ~~vast~~ majority seemed to think he was ~~the more~~ preferable~~ man~~. He was elected.

14. TRY TO REDUCE this paragraph without changing the meaning. Use your dictionary, of course.

(1) Many laboratories here in this country and in other countries abroad are trying to develop techniques for culturing embryos. (2) The goal they are working for is not particularly so much to produce test-tube babies as to understand what factors there are that are involved in control of the gestation process. (3) It is probable this information would help to explain what sometimes goes wrong and in some cases leads to individuals who are born with birth defects. (4) It would also allow researchers to test what effects certain drugs and food additives have on the development of unborn embryos and if they lead eventually to birth defects. (5) Up to now the major obstacle that stood in the way of full laboratory gestation has been the step in which the unborn embryo attaches itself to the wall of the

womb. (6) However, Dr. Yu-Chih Hou, who is of the Johns Hopkins University School of Hygiene and Public Health, in the state of Maryland, recently overcame this obstacle by developing unborn embryos to the stage when their hearts are beating. (7) According to specialists who are experts in this field, this was a significant step. (8) It is now possible that mammals—including human beings—can now be developed in the laboratory and outside the body.

- -

Suggestions

(1) Many laboratories ~~here~~ in this country and ~~in other countries~~ abroad are trying to develop techniques for culturing embryos. (2) The its goal ~~they are working for~~ is not ~~particularly~~ so much to produce test-tube babies as to understand what factors ~~there are that are involved in~~ control ~~of the~~ gestation. ~~process~~. (3) ~~It is probable~~ this information would probably help to explain what sometimes goes wrong and ~~in some cases~~ leads to ~~individuals who are born with~~ birth defects. (4) It would also allow researchers to test ~~what~~ the effects of certain drugs and food additives ~~have~~ on ~~the~~ embryo development. ~~of unborn embryos and if they lead eventually to birth defects~~. (5) ~~Up to now~~ the major obstacle to ~~that stood in the way of~~ full laboratory gestation has been the step in which the ~~unborn~~ embryo attaches itself to the wall of the womb. (6) However, Dr. Yu-Chih Hou~~, who is~~ of ~~the~~ Maryland's Johns Hopkins University School of Hygiene and Public Health~~, in the state of Maryland,~~ recently overcame this obstacle by developing ~~unborn~~ embryos to the heart-beating stage. ~~when their hearts are beating~~. (7) According to specialists~~ who are experts in this field~~, this was a significant step. (8) ~~It is now~~ possibly, ~~that~~ mammals—including human beings—can now be developed in the laboratory. ~~and outside the body~~.

Now turn to the review of Chapter 9.

REVIEW

1. In these sentences eliminate any unnecessary there or it. Then revise the rest of the sentence to keep the meaning.

   (a) It is expected that the Knicks will finish high—if not first.

   (b) She did read a book this semester, but it wasn't the book she was told to read.

   (c) There were two chemistry classes conducted in the laboratory.

   (d) It is probable that the fish will return once antipollution measures are adopted.

   (e) There is only one rule given.

   (f) It is possible that tennis is getting more popular.

   (g) There are two reasons for the recession.

   (h) When you want to see a baseball game in New York, it is necessary for you to get tickets well in advance.

   (i) In the private schools it is expected that the boys will keep their hair short.

   (j) It is believed that Lindsay is a Democrat at heart.

2. Reduce these sentences by simplifying the wordy expressions:

   (a) He wants in the neighborhood of a thousand dollars for that table.

   (b) Due to the fact that he is a Republican, he couldn't vote in the interesting primary races.

   (c) He spoke in a hesitant manner.

   (d) Margaret Mitchell wrote Gone with the Wind, which is probably the best-selling novel of all time.

   (e) He spoke to him in regard to a job in his factory.

3. Delete any repetitious words in these sentences:

(a) That girl is beautiful in appearance.

(b) You should repeat the course over again.

(c) She sang while playing the piano at the same time.

(d) Mr. Gould has been in such movies as M*A*S*H*, Getting Straight, etc.

(e) I personally wish the riot had never taken place.

Suggested Answers

1. (a) ~~It is expected that~~ the Knicks ~~will~~ [are expected to] finish high—if not first.

(b) NO CHANGE

(c) ~~There were~~ two chemistry classes [were] conducted in the laboratory.

(d) ~~It is probable that~~ the fish will [probably] return once antipollution measures are adopted.

(e) ~~There is~~ only one rule [is] given.

(f) ~~It is possible that~~ tennis is [possibly] getting more popular.

(g) NO CHANGE

(h) When you want to see a baseball game in New York, ~~it is necessary for~~ you [must] ~~to~~ get tickets well in advance.

(i) In the private schools ~~it is expected that~~ the boys ~~will~~ [are expected to] keep their hair short.

(j) ~~It is believed that~~ Lindsay is [believed to be] a Democrat at heart.

2. (a) He wants ~~in the neighborhood of~~ [almost] a thousand dollars for that table.

(b) ~~Due to the fact that~~ [Because] he is a Republican, he couldn't vote in the interesting primary races.

(c) He spoke ~~in a~~ hesitant[ly.] ~~manner.~~

(d) Margaret Mitchell wrote Gone with the Wind, which is probably the best-selling novel of all time.

(e) He spoke to him in regard to a job in his factory.

3. (a) That girl is beautiful in appearance.

(b) You should repeat the course over again.

(c) She sang while playing the piano at the same time.

(d) Mr. Gould has been in such movies as M*A*S*H*, Getting Straight, etc.

(e) I personally wish the riot had never taken place.

If you answered all the questions satisfactorily, put checks in the REVIEW column of the Self-Evaluation Record for Chapter 9 (page 197). If you missed parts of question 1, check to see whether your problem was with there or it. Check entry 23 on Chart 2 if you need more help with there and entry 24 if you need more help with it. If you missed questions 2 or 3, make a note on Chart 2 (under the last entry—OTHERS) that you need to check your work for wordiness. Then go on to Chapter 10 .

CHAPTER TEN

Being Specific

Even at this stage, when we've covered so many of the important ways to produce clear prose, we could easily lapse into this kind of trap:

(a) The status of the telephone operator has declined because of competition from more glamorous jobs allowing for visual contacts.

Almost every word is gobbledygook. In "translation" the meaning is that being an operator nowadays isn't so popular because girls can get jobs where people can see them.... But why does such a simple message need to be translated?

On the other hand, plainness can be carried too far. How would the start of Lincoln's Gettysburg address sound in everyday words? The art of "four score and seven years ago" would become an uninspired "eighty-seven years ago."

Sample (b) shows an appropriate revision of sample (a).

(b) Being an invisible operator is not so appealing to a girl nowadays, with so many more glamorous jobs to choose from.

Most of the words in the revision are plain, with <u>invisible</u> the only unusual expression. Although we all know that an operator isn't actually invisible, we aren't troubled by the use of this word here because all the other words mean exactly what they say.

Knowing which words work best is something you can learn from reading a lot of good writing and from a lot of practice in writing. But you can start right now to apply some "do's" and "don'ts" to help you find the right words for whatever you want to say. If this chapter has a message, it is in the title: Be Specific.

Before you begin, however, turn to the preview of Chapter 10.

PREVIEW

1. Make each sentence as specific as possible.

   (a) She tried to find the right words to express herself.

   (b) He shook because he was afraid.

   (c) He reads a news magazine once a week.

   (d) He walked back and forth in the room.

   (e) He bought some things today.

2. In these sentences get rid of not unless it is used in contrast; replace a hedge word with a more specific word or delete the hedge.

   (a) He doesn't pay attention to his garden.

   (b) My favorite foods are plain, not rich.

   (c) He didn't pass the eighth grade.

   (d) He has a very infrequently occurring disease.

   (e) That is an awfully odd circumstance.

3. COPYEDIT this passage to rid it of cliches and overly pretentious words:

Do you know the Yiddish word chutzpah, pronounced HUTZ-PAH (as if you were clearing your throat)? A person with chutzpah possesses audacity in all his endeavors, and he also possesses unmitigated nerve so far as satisfying his innermost desires are concerned. When all is said and done, he does his own thing, whether anyone else or anything else will suffer thereby. A well-known definition of chutzpah runs something along these lines: A boy with real chutzpah is one who would kill both his parents and then demand leniency of the court on the grounds that he is an orphan. In today's world chutzpah is not a necessary ingredient for making it. But it helps.

Suggested Answers

1. (a) She tried to find the right words to express herself.
   (b) He shook because he was afraid.
   (c) He reads a news magazine once a week.
   (d) He walked back and forth in the room.
   (e) He bought some things today.

2. (a) He doesn't pay attention to his garden.
   (b) NO CHANGE
   (c) He didn't pass the eighth grade.
   (d) He has a very infrequently occurring disease.
   (e) That is an awfully odd circumstance.

3. Do you know the Yiddish word chutzpah, pronounced HUTZ-PAH (as if you are clearing your throat) ? A person with chutzpah possesses audacity in all his endeavors, and he also possesses unmitigated nerve so far as satisfying his innermost desires are concerned. When all is said and done, he does his own thing, whether anyone else or anything else will suffer thereby. A well-known definition of chutzpah runs something alone these lines: A boy with real chutzpah is one who would kill both his parents and then demand leniency of the court on the grounds that he is an orphan. In today's world chutzpah is not a necessary ingredient for making it. But it helps.

If you answered each question satisfactorily, review the chapter lightly and then continue to Chapter 11. Otherwise mark the Self-Evaluation Record for Chapter 10 and proceed as usual.

SELF-EVALUATION RECORD FOR CHAPTER 10

	PREVIEW	FRAMES	REVIEW
Question 1		1 through 5	
Question 2		6 through 9	
Question 3		10 through 21	

USING SPECIFIC VERBS

1. One principle of good writing is to use a specific action verb instead of a general verb with a lot of phrases. Compare these:

(a) He glared at the child.
(b) He looked at the child with anger in his eyes.
(c) He looked at the child glaringly.

Sample (a) brings a clear image to mind with just the single word glared. Notice that the general verb looked in sample (b) needed five additional words before it could give us the same meaning. Sample (c) doesn't work because glaringly is awkward, though correct. So, finding a specific verb will rid the sentence of useless clutter and make it more effective.

You often have to work hard to think of the right word. A reference book like a dictionary or a thesaurus will be helpful, provided you don't go overboard and use a bunch of inappropriate words. (Don't create another problem while avoiding the first!) COMPARE the two sentences in each set and PUT A CHECK MARK beside the one that seems better. Then UNDERLINE the over-long general expression in the one sentence and the specific replacement for it in the other:

_______ (1a) The fire was so bad that it went out of control.
_______ (1b) The fire raged out of control.
_______ (2a) The women chattered over coffee for hours.
_______ (2b) The women talked on and on over coffee for hours.

- - - - - - - - - - - - - - - - - -

_______ (1a) The fire was so bad that it went out of control.
___✓___ (1b) The fire raged out of control.
___✓___ (2a) The women chattered over coffee for hours.
_______ (2b) The women talked on and on over coffee for hours.

2. In your first draft you want to get the ideas down on paper—"get black on white." But, when you revise this first draft, get into the habit of searching for specific verbs. Everyone who writes needs practice on this.

Here is a brief list of specific alternatives to the general verb to eat when it means "putting food into one's mouth":

lunch	mouthe	taste	devour	peck at
breakfast	dine	nibble	gorge	pick at
swallow	chew	consume	feed	slurp

We haven't exhausted the possibilities, but notice that each word would be more interesting and give more information than the general word to eat.

Most of the time, you should use a dictionary or a thesaurus. Just this once, without looking at either one, see if you can WRITE three specific verbs that the following general verbs make you think of:

(1) To make noise: __________, __________, __________

(2) To talk: __________, __________, __________

(3) To walk: __________, __________, __________

(4) To lie: __________, __________, __________

(5) To drink: __________, __________, __________

- -

Suggestions

(1) clatter, clang, crash, roar, scream, whistle
(2) chatter, gossip, drone, report, converse, mumble, whisper
(3) amble, stroll, promenade, saunter, hide, sashay
(4) deceive, feign, sham, pretend, fib or repose, recline, languish, locate, remain
(5) sip, guzzle, quaff, tipple, imbibe, absorb, chug, swallow

3. Try to COPYEDIT these sentences to make them more specific. Look for an imaginative verb that can carry the description all by itself. FOLLOW this example:

He ~~walked~~ dashed to the office ~~in a hurried manner~~.

(1) The earthquake was a great surprise to the experts.

(2) He spoke to the child soothingly and made him feel better.

(3) The car came to a stop with a screeching noise.

(4) He ate his lunch rapidly.

(5) He spoke in a hushed voice.

(6) The umbrella was in the corner dripping.

(7) When she laughed in a silly way, he laughed in a silly way too.

(8) He looked over that book long and hard.

(9) He walked lamely.

(10) He felt worshipful of the speaker.

Suggestions

Keep in mind that the aim is to use a more precise word. This means you might substitute any number of specific words for the general verb, and your revision will probably be different from those suggested here.

(1) The earthquake was a great surprise to the experts.

(2) He spoke to the child soothingly and made him feel better.

(3) The car came to a stop with a screeching noise.

(4) He ate his lunch rapidly.

(5) He spoke in a hushed voice.

(6) The umbrella was in the corner dripping.

(7) When she laughed in a silly way, he laughed in a silly way too.

(8) He looked over that book long and hard.

(9) He walked lamely.

(10) He felt worshipful of the speaker.

USING SPECIFIC NOUNS

4. You will also make your writing more interesting if you use specific nouns instead of general ones; for example, names instead of general descriptions.

(a) I read a <u>book</u> last night.
(b) I read <u>Catcher in the Rye</u> last night.

Sample (b) doesn't leave anything for the reader to wonder about. Unless you have a special reason for <u>not</u> being specific, you will usually make your writing more meaningful if you share what you know with your reader. Say "pine bench" rather than "piece of furniture"; say "painting," not "work of art," and say "new ski boots," not "some things."

Try COPYEDITING these sentences to make them more specific. You'll have to be inventive, as in this example:

He borrowed ~~money~~ ten dollars from me.

(1) The doctor said to be more active.

(2) He earned a letter in two sports.

(3) She wore the latest fashion to the party.

(4) They read two magazines.

(5) They read a newspaper every day.

<u>Suggestions</u>

(1) The doctor said to ~~be more active~~ swim as often as possible and to walk a mile a day.

(2) He earned a letter in ~~two sports~~ basketball and in track.

(3) She wore ~~the latest fashion~~ hot pants to the party.

(4) They read ~~two magazines~~ Saturday Review and Newsweek.

(5) They read ~~a newspaper~~ The Indianapolis Star every day.

5. COPYEDIT this paragraph to make it more specific:

(1) Are you a pencil chewer? (2) If so, you have a right to have a worry. (3) New York City's Health Department said in an announcement that perhaps one-third of the pencils sold in New York City had a coating of leaded paint. (4) In some pencils, in fact, the lead content is as high as 30 percent. (5) Ironically, the Health Department had always given people the assurance that the lead in pencils didn't have anything to do with lead poisoning. (6) Now the people in the Health Department made the finding that the bad effects came from the coating.

- - - - - - - - - - - - - - - - - -

Suggestions

(1) Are you a pencil chewer? (2) If so, you ~~have a right~~ to ~~have a worry~~. (3) New York City's Health Department ~~said in an announcement~~ that perhaps one-third of the pencils sold in New York City ~~had a~~ coat~~ing~~ ~~of~~ leaded paint. (4) In some pencils, in fact, the lead content is as high as 30 percent. (5) Ironically, the Health Department had always ~~given~~ people ~~the assurance~~ that the lead in pencils didn't ~~have anything to do with~~ lead poisoning. (6) Now ~~the people in the Health Department made the findings~~ that the bad effects came from the coating.

THE WORD NOT

6. A second important principle of good writing is to avoid the word not whenever possible, unless you want to emphasize a contrast.

(a) He was not encouraged when he saw the team work out.
(b) He was discouraged when he saw the team work out.

Nobody needs to be "Reader's Digest cheerful" all the time. Sometimes, there are negative things to say. But your writing will always be stronger if you say what someone is (discouraged) rather than what he is not (not encouraged).

One occasion when you do want to use not is to emphasize a contrast between positive and negative.

(c) He needs guidance, not punishment.

By reserving not for such contrasts, your writing will have greater impact than if you used not for all negative situations. (Your writing will have more variety too.)

Sometimes words to use that will avoid not are hard to think of. See what you can do with these. To start you off, the first two are done for you:

(1) everybody nobody

(2) trust mistrust

(3) important __________

(4) classified __________

(5) desirable __________

(6) guilty __________

(7) skilled __________

(8) normal __________

(9) everyone __________

(10) clear __________

- -

Suggestions

(3) unimportant
(4) unclassified
(5) undesirable
(6) innocent
(7) unskilled
(8) abnormal
(9) no one, nobody
(10) hazy, cloudy, muddy, mixed up, confused, unclear

7. COPYEDIT these negative statements by using a word that will keep the meaning yet avoid not. However, KEEP the negative not for a contrast. You can follow the example:

He ~~didn't pay any attention to~~ ignored the rules.

(Use your thesaurus here!)

(1) His remarks were not relevant.

(2) This criticism isn't important.

(3) There isn't any way.

(4) The women are not asking for a privilege, but a right.

(5) He is not generous.

(6) The Black Panthers don't have confidence in White America.

(7) Her boss was not satisfied with her work.

(8) She is not interested in school.

(9) The teacher's remarks were not constructive, but overcritical.

(10) Some of the boys are not afraid of getting caught.

- - - - - - - - - - - - - - - - - - -

Suggestions

(1) His remarks were ~~not~~ irrelevant.

(2) This criticism ~~isn't important~~ is unimportant.

(3) There ~~isn't any~~ is no way.

(4) NO CHANGE

(5) He is ~~not generous~~ stingy.

(6) The Black Panthers ~~don't have~~ lack confidence in White America. (or mistrust.)

(7) Her boss was ~~not satisfied~~ dissatisfied with her work.

(8) She is ~~not~~ uninterested in school.

(9) NO CHANGE

(10) Some of the boys are ~~not~~ unafraid of getting caught.

A WORD LIKE RATHER OR PRETTY

8. Certain words can be signals that the writer is hedging or that he should be more specific. These words include *rather*, *very*, *pretty*, or *little*. Notice the effect that *pretty* has on *tired*:

(a) He is pretty tired of his job.

The meaning is that he is not *completely* tired, but just "somewhat."

You can strengthen your writing by eliminating the hedge altogether (if you can be that definite); or you can soften your message with a more appropriate word, such as *slightly* or *somewhat*.

Two possibilities for revising sample (a) are as follows:

(b) He is tired of his job.
(c) He is somewhat tired of his job.

Another possibility is to think of a more specific word that really describes the degree of fatigue, as here:

(d) He is bored with his job.

COPYEDIT these sentences to make them more specific. Either delete the hedge or try to think of a more specific word to replace it.

(1) I was pretty happy to see him.

(2) I was rather unhappy with my small raise.

(3) The Orioles are very good this year.

(4) Circus performers are a little odd.

(5) His grades are usually pretty high.

- - - - - - - - - - - - - - - - - -

Suggestions

(1) I was ~~pretty happy~~ delighted to see him.

(2) I was ~~rather unhappy~~ disappointed with my small raise.

(3) The Orioles are ~~very~~ good this year.

(4) Circus performers are ~~a little odd.~~ *eccentric.*

(5) His grades are usually ~~pretty~~ high.

USING CHART 2

9. Here are the entries in Chart 2:

SITUATION	IF	THEN	EXAMPLE
25. THE WORD <u>NOT</u>	(a) you want to emphasize the negative or the contrast between a positive and a negative,	(a) keep <u>not</u>.	(a) He is not guilty. He is thirty, not forty.
	(b) there is no special reason to emphasize the negative,	(b) replace with a word with the same meaning that does not require <u>not</u>.	(b) Your boss ~~did not~~ *dis*obey*ed* the rules.
26. A HEDGE LIKE <u>RATHER</u> OR <u>PRETTY</u>	(a) other examples: <u>a little</u>, <u>a bit</u>, <u>very</u>, <u>awfully</u>,	(a) if possible, replace the hedge and the word it affects with a more specific word; or delete the hedge to be more definite.	(a) Your boss is *angry.* ~~pretty upset.~~ The children are ~~rather~~ restless.

USE these entries to help you COPYEDIT these sentences. Get rid of a not unless it is used in a contrast; replace a hedge with a more specific word or delete it.

(1) This is a rather unusual situation.

(2) He isn't an honest employee.

(3) He is rich, not poor.

(4) He wouldn't vote for president.

(5) I don't agree with his policies.

Suggestions

(1) This is ~~a rather~~ an unusual situation.

(2) He is~~n't an~~ a dishonest employee.

(3) NO CHANGE

(4) He ~~wouldn't~~ refused to vote for president.

(5) I ~~don't agree~~ disagree with his policies.

CLICHÉS

10. Now let's look at a perfectly correct paragraph. What do you think of it?

I used to think that school was a waste of time, and I quit. I was going to have the time of my life. So I sallied forth, looking for a job, but I couldn't get one. All I saw was the seamy side of life. At long last I returned to this seat of learning, a sadder but wiser person.

Does everything sound familiar? You've heard it a thousand times—so often, in fact, that if you hear the first few words of any of these underlined expressions, you can supply the rest.

Expressions that are used so often are grammatically correct but dull. Sometimes they sound a bit insincere, even though they express important ideas. These too familiar expressions, called clichés, are hard to weed out of your writing altogether. But you should be able to get rid of the worst ones.

In today's world, everybody is hung up, freaks out, and makes revolutions; and everybody who is anybody has to do his own thing. That's the name of the game. But when you come right down to the nitty gritty, maybe there is nothing new under the sun anyway. And that's where it's at . . . .

11. Try this experiment. Each blank represents a word. SEE if you can FILL IN the missing words to complete one of these overused expressions or clichés.

(1) After all is said ________ ________

(2) A good time was had ________ ________

(3) Age before ________

(4) The best laid plans of mice ________ ________

(5) A sight for ________ ________

(6) I saw my whole life pass before ________ ________

(7) Circumstances over which I have ________ ________

(8) All good things must come to ________ ________

(9) A fate worse ________ ________

(10) It isn't the heat, it's ________ ________

Even if you weren't able to complete all the expressions, you will probably recognize them once you see the answers.

- - - - - - - - - - - - - - - - - -

(1) After all is said and Done.
(2) A good time was had by all.
(3) Age before beauty
(4) The best laid plans of mice And men
(5) A sight for sore eyes
(6) I saw my whole life pass before my eyes.
(7) Circumstances over which I have no Control
(8) All good things must come to an end.
(9) A fate worse than Death
(10) It isn't the heat, it's the humidity.

12. You wouldn't use a cliché if you realized it was so worn out. The problem is to recognize that the life has run out of it.

LOOK OVER the next sentence: Can you recognize the cliché? Parents want to be sure that the school will prepare their children for today's world.

In today's world, so many people say "today's world" that we no longer pay attention to it. Although an expression like this was once fresh and witty, it has become "the worse for wear."

The clue that words are probably worn out is if they occur to us too easily—if they come "trippingly to the tongue."

See if you can RECOGNIZE the cliché in each sentence below, and then UNDERLINE it. The way to proceed is to read the sentence through once. Then search for an expression of two or more words that sounds familiar—"has a familiar ring."

(1) John is popular with members of the opposite sex.
(2) By and large the comma is the punctuation mark that causes the most problems.

- - - - - - - - - - - - - - - - - -

(1) members of the opposite sex
(2) By and large

13. Each sentence has at least one cliché. UNDERLINE any you find.
REMEMBER: Read the sentence through first; then examine closely any expression that sounds familiar.

(1) If worse comes to worse, at least we will have the weekend off.
(2) People in small towns seem to lead quiet lives, but often they have skeletons hidden in the closets.
(3) First, I saw only a sea of faces, and then I heard a round of applause.
(4) You have given me much food for thought.
(5) I have done a lot of work along these lines.
(6) We saw the church steeple silhouetted against the sky.
(7) He fell to the ground with a dull, sickening thud.
(8) The detective suspected foul play as soon as he saw her fragile form.
(9) It goes without saying that the fond parents praised the baby to the skies.
(10) On this gala occasion I want to point out someone in our midst who needs no introduction.

- - - - - - - - - - - - - - - - - -

(1) If worse comes to worse
(2) skeletons hidden in the closets
(3) sea of faces   round of applause

(4) food for thought
(5) along these lines
(6) silhouetted against the sky
(7) dull, sickening thud
(8) foul play fragile form
(9) It goes without saying fond parents to the skies
(10) On this gala occasion in our midst who needs no introduction

14. Again UNDERLINE each cliché you find. All the sentences have at least one.

(1) A blanket of snow covered Chicago.
(2) Since I have returned to school, I feel like a different person.
(3) As soon as the detective arrived on the scene, the kids beat a hasty retreat.
(4) We should give our friends the benefit of the doubt.
(5) The children seemed to grow by leaps and bounds, almost before our eyes.
(6) I wish you luck in all of your endeavors.
(7) As luck would have it, his vacation didn't coincide with mine.
(8) Earlier this summer she had been the picture of health.
(9) We fought to the bitter end.
(10) Let's have a beer and chase the blues away.

- - - - - - - - - - - - - - - - -

(1) a blanket of snow
(2) I feel like a different person
(3) arrived on the scene beat a hasty retreat
(4) the benefit of the doubt
(5) leaps and bounds, almost before our eyes.
(6) all of your endeavors.
(7) As luck would have it,
(8) picture of health
(9) to the bitter end
(10) chase the blues away

15. COMPARE these sentences:

(a) The old man was none the worse for wear, even after the long trip.
(b) The old man looked fresh, even after the long trip.

Sample (a) makes a general statement and lets us guess what it really means, but sample (b) adequately describes the old man.

We use clichés mainly because they're so much easier to think of than something more specific. But if we want to keep the reader's interest, we should be on the lookout for fresh, interesting ways to speak to him.

No general rule will help. Remember, however, that a cliché is a general statement that you should always replace. Ask yourself questions: Why did I say that? What did I really want to say? Maybe this kind of probing will produce the specific you're looking for.

See if you can COPYEDIT these two sentences so that they are more specific and therefore more interesting:

(1) He is interested in the weaker sex.

(2) Mr. Smith introduced us to his better half.

- - - - - - - - - - - - - - - - - - -

Suggestions

(1) He is interested in ~~the weaker sex~~ girls.

(2) Mr. Smith introduced us to his ~~better half~~ wife Mamie.

16. The sentences here are choked with clichés. COPYEDIT by replacing each dull expression with a more specific statement:

(1) I am assuming that this paper will meet your satisfaction.

(2) After three hours of driving, we reached our destination—Boston.

(3) Now that I'm older, I enjoy the finer things of life.

(4) He looked none the worse for his experience.

(5) He has been rude on more than one occasion.

(6) Politicians in this day and age must look good on television.

(7) It dawned on me that he would learn better from experience.

(8) Gas stations in the desert are few and far between.

(9) Our guests did ample justice to the meal.

(10) Marriage saved me from a fate worse than death: a job.

\- - - - - - - - - - - - - - - - - -

Suggestions

(1) I am assuming that this paper will *satisfy you.* ~~meet with your satisfaction.~~

(2) After three hours of driving, we reached ~~our destination,~~ Boston.

(3) Now that I'm older, I enjoy *luxuries.* ~~the finer things of life.~~

(4) He looked *unharmed by* ~~none the worse for~~ his experience.

(5) He has *often* been rude ~~on more than one occasion.~~ *(Occasionally)*

(6) Politicians *today* ~~in this day and age~~ must look good on television.

(7) ~~It dawned on me~~ *I realized* that he would learn better from experience.

(8) Gas stations in the desert are *scarce.* ~~few and far between.~~

(9) Our guests *relished* ~~did ample justice to~~ the meal.

(10) Marriage save*d* me from ~~a fate~~ *something* worse: ~~than death:~~ a job.

17. COPYEDIT these paragraphs by replacing clichés with more specific statements. Try to retain the same meaning.

When I graduated from high school, I held the cherished belief that I was a budding genius. My fond parents and my other ardent admirers (members of the weaker sex) agreed. Everything was clear as crystal: College would be as easy for me as rolling off a log, although not enjoyable. Enjoyment would come later, when I would enter the business world and become a successful captain of industry.

And then I came to State and saw the light of day. I am not breezing through. I have found that each and every course is just plain hard work. For all the trials and tribulations of meeting rigid schedules and standards, however, I have also discovered that learning itself can satisfy the inner me, and not just the almighty dollar. In fact, I don't have to wait for the finer things of life: I already have them.

- - - - - - - - - - - - - - - - - - - -

Suggestions

When I graduated from high school, I ~~held the cherished belief~~ believed that I was a ~~budding~~ genius. My ~~fond~~ parents and my ~~other ardent admirers (members of the weaker sex)~~ girlfriend agreed. Everything was clear~~, as crystal:~~. College would be ~~as~~ easy ~~for me as rolling off a log,~~ although not enjoyable. Enjoyment would come later, when I would enter the business world and become a successful captain of industry.

And then I came to State~~, and saw the light of day~~. I am not breezing through; I ~~have found that each and~~ every course is ~~just plain~~ hard work. ~~For all the trials and tribulations of meeting~~ Despite the rigid schedules and standards, however, I have also discovered ~~that~~ satisfaction in learning itself. ~~can satisfy the inner me, and not just the almighty dollar.~~ In fact, I don't have to wait for the finer things of life: I already have them.

Note that in this case sentences in these paragraphs were left untouched, despite the clichés, to achieve a humorous effect. The clichés include "captain of industry," "breezing through," and "finer things of life."

BEING SPECIFIC

18. COPYEDIT this passage. Keep in mind that there are many ways to revise, depending on your intention. Each writer will create his own style and will use what seems appropriate to him. The important point is that he knows he is in control and that he knows what techniques (and effects) are available.

In today's world we hear a lot of things about the generation gap. The age factor is supposedly responsible for the course of recent strained events between parents and children. The young assume that their parents are of a hostile character due to the fact that they are over thirty. The parents assume that their children are of an irresponsible character due to the fact that they are under thirty.

Among the Taos Indians in New Mexico, however, the generation gap is small. The Taos are not a part of the main stream of American life, of course. The fact is that young and old together still cling to a culture of a religious nature that gets its strength from the land.

\- - - - - - - - - - - - - - - - - - - -

Suggestions

In today's ~~world~~ we hear ~~a lot of things~~ *many stories* about the generation gap. ~~The~~ age ~~factor~~ is supposedly responsible for ~~the course of~~ recent strained *relationships* ~~events~~ between parents and children. The young assume that their parents are ~~of a~~ hostile ~~character due to the fact that~~ *because* they are over thirty. The parents assume that their children are ~~of an~~ irresponsible *because* ~~character due to the fact that~~ they are under thirty.

Among the Taos Indians in New Mexico, however, the generation gap is small. The Taos *live apart from other Americans,* ~~are not a part of the main stream of American life, of course.~~ ~~The fact is that~~ *And* young and old together still cling to a *religious* culture ~~of a religious nature~~ that ~~gets~~ *draws* its strength from the land.

USING PLAIN WORDS

19. This example illustrates another consideration. Suppose you are driving your car, heading toward an intersection, when the back-seat driver with you notices something in the road. If he wants to warn you

in a hurry, which would be more effective—sample (a) or sample (b)?

(a) Decrease your velocity!
(b) Slow down!

The answer is obvious. Yet many writers make similar errors. They choose their words to impress their readers rather than to express their meaning. To be clearly understood, choose the simpler word or expression. However, remember that you should always use one precise word in place of many vague words. Sometimes the long word is the most effective, as in this example in which pretentious replaces eight shorter words

(c) His writing sounds as if he is trying to impress someone.
(d) His writing sounds pretentious.

You have to use your judgment, of course. As a guiding principle, use just one word wherever possible and make that word the simplest available. The aim, as always, is for precision and clarity.

20. Many "fancy" words come to English straight from Latin. (If you had Latin in high school, you can easily spot them.)

But you don't need to be a Latin scholar to love Latinized words. A word is "fancy" if you can replace it with a shorter, plainer word without changing the meaning.

(a) They utilize their schooling on the job.
(b) They use their schooling on the job.

No two words in English mean exactly the same thing. But there are synonyms, or words that have similar meanings. The words use and utilize are examples. Use is generally better because it is shorter and plainer.

Assume that the underlined words are inappropriately fancy. COPY-EDIT these sentences by replacing the fancy words with shorter, plainer ones:

(1) Students here possess high standards.

(2) The dance committee convened twice this month.

(3) He informed me how I should accomplish this operation.

(4) The majority of the meat was spoiled.

(5) They desire that you purchase your edibles there.

- - - - - - - - - - - - - - - - - -

Suggestions

(1) Students here have ~~possess~~ high standards.

(2) The dance committee met ~~convened~~ twice this month.

(3) He told ~~informed~~ me how I should do ~~accomplish~~ this work. ~~operation~~

(4). Most ~~The majority~~ of the meat was spoiled.

(5) They want ~~desire that~~ you to buy ~~purchase~~ your food ~~edibles~~ there.

21. COPYEDIT this passage to make it readable. Use short, simple words wherever possible.

Unfortunately, students seek inappropriate rewards for their endeavors in the pursuit of academic knowledge. They desire high grades because these are indicative of scholastic success. However, they are unaware that they have attained the pinnacle of success if they have acquired a skill. They are unaware that the reward is the knowledge itself and not the academic evaluation.

But the faculty members have performed in a manner to provoke the students' appraisals. They have strengthened the relationship between high academic achievement and high academic evaluations. They don't strengthen the relationship between academic knowledge and satisfaction in its acquisition.

- - - - - - - - - - - - - - - - - -

Suggestions

Unfortunately, students seek inappropriate rewards for their efforts ~~endeavors~~ in school. ~~the pursuit of academic knowledge~~ They want ~~desire~~ high grades because these ~~are~~ indicate ~~indicative of scholastic~~ success. However, they are unaware that they have succeeded ~~attained the pinnacle of success~~ if they have acquired a skill. They are unaware that the reward is the knowledge itself and not the academic evaluation.

But the faculty members have performed in a manner to provoke the students' appraisals. They have strengthened the relationship between high academic achievement and high academic evaluations. They don't strengthen the relationship between academic knowledge and satisfaction in its acquisition.

Now do the review of Chapter 10.

REVIEW

1. Make each sentence as specific as possible.

   (a) She waited for a bit before talking about it.

   (b) She shook because she was angry.

   (c) She didn't do her duties.

   (d) I saw a play last night.

   (e) I take some exercise every day.

2. In these sentences get rid of not unless it is used in contrast; replace a hedge word with a more specific word or delete the hedge.

   (a) He didn't take the nomination.

   (b) He is a bit anxious about his grades.

   (c) They are pretty bothered by problems.

   (d) That county is dry, not wet.

   (e) He wasn't satisfied with his grades.

3. COPYEDIT this passage to rid it of clichés and overly pretentious words. (Don't copyedit the quoted sentence, however.)

Bureaucratic language is probably here to stay. Some call it "governmentese"; some say it is "officialese." Whatever it is named, we can go whole hog and say it is gobbledygook. As an example, a U.S. Public Health Service report on the Cutter polio vaccine investigation utilized this pretentious vehicle: "The cause of the trouble was inadequate inactivation coupled with failure of the safety test to demonstrate the presence of the virus."

Getting down to the nitty gritty, the report meant in essence that the laboratory had failed to kill all the live virus. But why is such language deemed essential?

Those who employ such language do so with the intent of impressing their fellow employees and particularly those superiors who control the purse strings. Unfortunately they fail to impress because no one possesses the power to comprehend what they are attempting to express.

Suggested Answers

1. (a) She waited for a bit before talking about it.
   (b) She shook because she was angry.
   (c) She didn't do her duties.
   (d) I saw a play last night.
   (e) I take some exercise every day.

2. (a) He didn't take the nomination.
   (b) He is a bit anxious about his grades.
   (c) They are pretty bothered by problems.
   (d) NO CHANGE
   (e) He wasn't satisfied with his grades.

3. Bureaucratic language is probably here to stay. Some call it "governmentese"; some say it is "officialese." Whatever it is

name, we can ~~go whole hog and~~ say it is gobbledygook. ~~As an example,~~ A U.S. Public Health Service report on the Cutter polio vaccine investigation *is an example:* ~~utilized this pretentious vehicle~~: "The cause of the trouble was inadequate inactivation coupled with failure of the safety test to demonstrate the presence of the virus."

~~Getting down to the nitty gritty, the~~ *What this* report meant ~~in essence~~ *was* that the laboratory had failed to kill all the live virus. But why ~~is~~ *does* such language ~~deemed essential?~~ *seem necessary?*

Those who ~~employ such language~~ *use it* ~~do so with the intent of~~ *try to* impress~~ing~~ their fellow ~~employees~~ *workers* and particularly ~~those~~ *their* superiors ~~who control the purse strings~~. Unfortunately they fail to impress because no one ~~possesses the power to comprehend~~ *can understand* what they are ~~attempting~~ *trying* to ~~express.~~ *say.*

How did you do? If you answered each question satisfactorily, mark the Self-Evaluation Record for Chapter 10 (page 219) Then go on to Chapter 11. If you feel you could use more practice on finding and correcting clichés and other nonspecific language, indicate this on your copy of Chart 2 under OTHER in the SITUATION column. Also check entry 25 or 26, whichever is appropriate, if you missed parts of question 2.

CHAPTER ELEVEN

Odds and Ends

At this point you have covered all the important principles and practices of good writing. This chapter is just what the title suggests—odds and ends. Mainly, it is about capital letters and other marks that you can use to distinguish certain words and show that they represent particular things.

As an example, notice that the words in samples (a) and (b) are identical. But what a difference the capital letters and the quotation marks make!

(a) I want to read a story about a dog.
(b) I want to read "A Story About a Dog."

Any story will do in sample (a). But the quote marks and the capital letters in sample (b) mean a particular story, and this story is so special that it is the only one like it in the world.

This chapter will also cover two minor situations that bother students when they write: where to put punctuation like a comma or a period with a closing parenthesis, and when to spell out a number and when to use the figure. Some of the practices you will be advised to follow in handling these situations are not the only possibilities. But they are convenient,* and they help you to be consistent.

The virtue of such consistency is that you can then give your full attention to expressing your ideas, instead of wasting a lot of time wondering how to handle trivial matters.

You may decide that you want to study only parts of this chapter now and defer other parts to a later time. In that case you should do only relevant parts of the preview of Chapter 11:

---

*They are also the practices recommended in The Chicago Manual of Style.

(1) Do question 1 if you want to study the capitalization and punctuation of the title of any publication.
(2) Do question 2 if you want to find out about other capitalization matters.
(3) Do question 3 if you want to find out how to deal with punctuation at the end of a quotation.
(4) Do question 4 if you want to learn how to express numbers.

Now turn to the preview of Chapter 11; however, if you plan to skip the entire chapter at this time, turn to page 263.

PREVIEW

1. In the following titles of a publication, insert any distinguishing marks such as underlines or quotations and draw the slash line through any letter that should be a small one:

(a) the book Of Mice And Men
(b) the song Let It Be
(c) the TV show The Dating Game
(d) the movie Making It
(e) the book A Long Row Of Candles
(f) the song Love The One You're With

2. Capitalize the following, as necessary:

(a) bayer's aspirin
(b) the fourth of july
(c) the spring season
(d) Go east on dodd street.
(e) senator jacob javits
(f) the empire state building
(g) sophomore class
(h) aunt may
(i) the delaware river

3. Punctuate the titles in these sentences:

(a) I read the article Prisoner of Sex, and I thought Norman Mailer had some good points.

(b) My favorite song is Treat Her Like a Lady; however, I may have a new favorite by tomorrow.

(c) Did you like the song Moon River?

(d) That is the song Hey Jude.

(e) This is the title song Jesus Christ Superstar: It's from the rock opera.

4. Express the numbers in these sentences correctly:

(a) The graduating class consists of 50 boys and 20 girls.

(b) 2 girls dropped out last semester.

(c) The class consists of 103 French majors and 67 Spanish majors.

(d) It was 10 degrees below 0 last night.

(e) That happened 2,000,000 years ago.

(f) The reference is on page 25.

(g) He grew 3/4 inch.

Suggested Answers

1 (a) the book Of Mice And Men
(b) the song "Let It Be"
(c) the T.V. show "The Dating Game"
(d) the movie Making It
(e) the book A Long Row Of Candles
(f) the song "Love The One You're With"

2. (a) bayer's aspirin
(b) the fourth of july
(c) CORRECT
(d) Go east on dodd street.
(e) senator jacob javits
(f) the empire state building
(g) CORRECT
(h) aunt may
(i) the delaware river

3. (a) I read the article "Prisoner of Sex," and I

(b) My favorite song is "Treat Her Like a Lady"; however,

(c) Did you like the song "Moon River?"

(d) That is the song "Hey Jude."

(e) This is the title song "Jesus Christ Superstar." It's from the rock opera.

4. (a) Of ~~50~~ fifty boys and ~~20~~ twenty girls

(b) ~~2~~ Two girls

(c) CORRECT

(d) ~~10~~ ten degrees below ~~0~~ zero last

(e) ~~2,000,000~~ 2 million years ago.

(f) CORRECT

(g) CORRECT

As usual, if you answered all the questions correctly, you may review the chapter lightly. Otherwise mark your Self-Evaluation Record for Chapter 11 and continue.

SELF-EVALUATION RECORD FOR CHAPTER 11

	PREVIEW	FRAMES	REVIEW
Question 1		1 through 5	
Question 2		6 through 9	
Question 3		10 through 12	
Question 4		13 and 14	

THE TITLE OF ANY PUBLICATION

1. The title of any publication is always a special name—whether it's a poem, book, newspaper, magazine article, movie, or television show. This means it deserves some attention-getting marks like quotation marks or underlines (italics in printed matter); it also deserves some attention-getting capital letters. Let's consider the appropriate capital letters first.

As you probably know, the first and last words of every title of a book or other publication are capitalized, to mark where the title begins and ends. However, all the other words in the middle of the title are capitalized too, except for the short, common words in these groups:

(a) An article: a, an, or the.
(b) The words and, but, or, or nor.
(c) Any preposition, no matter how long it is.
(d) The to in the infinitive

Certain words in the titles below are not capitalized. Below each of them WRITE the letter of the rule that explains why, as here:

The Coming of the New Deal
(c) (a)

As you can see, of is a preposition and therefore belongs to group (c); the is an article and therefore belongs to group (a).

(1) "The Lady Is a Tramp"

____

(2) The Decline and Fall of the Third Reich

____

(3) She Stoops to Conquer

____

(4) Gone with the Wind

____

(5) All about Eve

____

- -

1.	a	2.	and	of	the	3.	to
	(a)		(b)	(c)	(a)		(d)
4.	with	the		5.	about		
	(c)	(a)			(c)		

2. Note that the first letter of every word in the ten titles below is capitalized. COPYEDIT by indicating which capital letters need to be a small, or lower-case, letter. Remember that the copyediting symbol to indicate that a capital letter should be a lower-case letter is this: /

(1) Dictionary Of Modern English Usage
(2) Arms And The Man
(3) Prufrock And Other Observations
(4) "What To Listen For"
(5) "The Love Song Of J. Alfred Prufrock"
(6) The History Of The Separation
(7) The Years With Ross
(8) No Man Is An Island
(9) A Man For All Seasons
(10) A Manual Of Style

- -

(1) /Of
(2) /And /The
(3) /And
(4) /To
(5) /Of
(6) /Of /The
(7) /With
(8) /An
(9) /For
(10) /Of

3. When you refer to the title of any publication, follow these general rules:

(a) Use underlines (italics replace underlines in printed materials) for a book or any long feature that is a book or could be a book by itself. (Examples: a movie; a book; a newspaper; a long musical work such as a symphony or an opera; a painting or drawing; and a poem long enough to be a book.)

(b) Use quote marks for a shorter feature that is, or could be, a part of a book rather than a separate book by itself. (Examples: a song, poem, and radio or television show.)

There are exceptions. As an example, sometimes sonatas and symphonies are mentioned by number; Piano Sonata No. 2, or a key may be given. Since Piano Sonata No. 2 is not actually the title, it is capitalized but not italicized or quoted.

STUDY these examples:

(a) the song "Yankee Doodle"
(b) the book The Good Earth
(c) the television show "Bonanza"

COPYEDIT the following five titles by inserting quotation marks or underlines, whichever is appropriate:

(1) the article Maternal Behavior and Attitudes
(2) the book The Old Curiosity Shop
(3) the newspaper The New York Times
(4) the book The Rise of the West
(5) the song The Star-Spangled Banner

- - - - - - - - - - - - - - - - - -

(1) the article "Maternal Behavior and Attitudes"
(2) the book The Old Curiosity Shop
(3) the newspaper The New York Times
(4) the book The Rise of the West
(5) the song "The Star-Spangled Banner"

Note: Both words in the hyphenation are capitalized.

4. The entry in Chart 2 for the title of a book or any other publication is divided into capitalization (A) and punctuation (B). STUDY it and note that it summarizes the rules you applied earlier:

SITUATION	IF	THEN	EXAMPLE
27. THE TITLE OF ANY PUBLICATION A. Capitalization	(a) it is the first or last word and any word in the middle with the exception of those in 27(b),	(a) capitalize. (Capitalize both words that are hyphenated.)	(a) In Cold Blood; The Holy Roman Empire
	(b) it is a word in the middle and is an article; a linking adverb like and, but, or, nor; a preposition; or the to in the infinitive;	(b) don't capitalize.	(b) Gone with the Wind; Ends and Means; or She Stoops to Conquer
B. Punctuation	(a) it is a book, movie, newspaper, magazine, opera, or long enough to be a book,	(a) underline (italicize) it.	(a) Paradise Lost
	(b) it is only part of a book or is not long enough to be a book by itself,	(b) put quote marks around it.	(b) the T.V. show "Bonanza"

Now punctuate these five titles and make capital letters lower case (small) wherever necessary. By all means refer to the entry.

(1) the movie Love Story
(2) the play Arms And The Man
(3) the article A Defense Of Shelley's Poetry
(4) the novel Of Human Bondage
(5) the magazine New Yorker

- - - - - - - - - - - - - - - - - -

(1) Love Story
(2) Arms And The Man
(3) A Defense Of Shelley's Poetry
(4) Of Human Bondage
(5) New Yorker

5. Now use Chart 2 to help you punctuate these titles correctly and to indicate which letters that are capitalized here should actually be lower case:

(1) the book Russia At War
(2) the Book The Quest For Arthur's Britain
(3) the article The Prisoner of Sex
(4) the show The Tonight Show
(5) the poem Miniver Cheevy
(6) the magazine Ebony
(7) the opera La Traviata
(8) the article Country Full Of Swedes
(9) the movie Oliver
(10) the song America The Beautiful

- - - - - - - - - - - - - - - - - -

(1) Russia At War
(2) The Quest For Arthur's Britain
(3) "The Prisoner Of Sex"
(4) "The Tonight Show"
(5) "Miniver Cheevy"
(6) Ebony
(7) La Traviata
(8) "Country Full Of Swedes"
(9) Oliver
(10) "America The Beautiful"

OTHER CAPITALIZATION

6. As you know, many other names are capitalized besides the titles of publications. Here is the general rule:

CAPITALIZE any word that is a special name or any part of that name. But DON'T capitalize a word that is just a general reference to the special name.

If you remember this general rule, you won't need to learn a dozen particular ones. However, Chart 3 on capitalization lists some common situations that might be confusing.

Look at Chart 3 now (page 332) and note that it is set up much like Chart 2. First you must recognize your word as an example of a general situation. Then you can read across that row to find out which feature makes the difference—which one determines whether the word is capitalized.

Let's take an example. Suppose you wanted to write this:

"I asked mother if she. . . ." But now you wonder, should I capitalize mother?

Since mother is a special person to you, you may think that she rates a capital letter. On the other hand, you also realize that she isn't special to everyone else. To find out how to handle this, you look down the column headed by SITUATION and find FAMILY MEMBER. Reading across this row, you find that your use of mother is an example of 6a because mother in your sentence represents a particular person. Following across, you see that you should capitalize mother here.

Try one yourself.

Which situation would you refer to in Chart 3 if you wanted to find out whether to capitalize the word state in the expression "the state of Wisconsin?"

- - - - - - - - - - - - - - - - - - - -

9. GEOGRAPHICAL PLACE

7. Of course, you must understand the situations and also recognize examples of them if you hope to make good use of Chart 3. But, first, make sure you know what all these situations mean. Without referring to Chart 3, give an example of each situation:

________________ (1) BUILDING, STREET, OR OTHER PUBLIC PLACE

________________ (2) TRADE NAME

________________ (3) HIGH SCHOOL OR COLLEGE CLASS OR CLASS MEMBER

________________ (4) DAY OF THE WEEK, MONTH, OR SEASON

________________ (5) HOLIDAY

________________ (6) FAMILY MEMBER

________________ (7) INSTITUTION, COMPANY, CLUB, OR OTHER ORGANIZATION

________________ (8) OFFICIAL TITLE

________________ (9) GEOGRAPHICAL PLACE

________________ (10) LANGUAGE OR RACE OR CULTURAL GROUP

- - - - - - - - - - - - - - - - - -

(1) the World Trade Building, Washington
(2) Kellogg's corn flakes
(3) senior class
(4) Monday, May, fall
(5) Fourth of July
(6) Uncle Joe
(7) Atlantic and Pacific Company
(8) Dr. Jones or Governor Rockefeller
(9) the Montana hills
(10) English, Negro, black

8. This time, try to IDENTIFY each example of a situation in Chart 3. WRITE the name of the situation on the blank. You don't need to write the name of the entire situation—just the part that applies.

____

______________	(1)	the summer
______________	(2)	the Empire State Building
______________	(3)	Aunt Mary
______________	(4)	Breck's shampoo
______________	(5)	the freshman class
______________	(6)	Greeks
______________	(7)	Christmas Eve
______________	(8)	Columbia University
______________	(9)	the Far East
______________	(10)	the sergeant, Private Peters

- - - - - - - - - - - - - - - - - - - -

(1) Season
(2) Building
(3) Family member
(4) Trade name
(5) High school or College class
(6) Group (cultural)
(7) Holiday
(8) Institution
(9) Geographical place
(10) Official title

9. COPYEDIT each title below by capitalizing when necessary. Also refer to Chart 3 and WRITE the number and letter (if there is a letter) from the IF column that applies. FOLLOW this example:

1a harvard square

________	(1)	thursday
________	(2)	my mother's house
________	(3)	Go west for three blocks.
________	(4)	congress
________	(5)	the spring term
________	(6)	the senior class
________	(7)	washington square

________ (8) the black people

________ (9) He is a representative.

________ (10) hotel standards

- - - - - - - - - - - - - - - - - -

4a (1) thursday

6b (2) my mother's house

9b (3) Go west for three blocks.

7a (4) congress

4b (5) the spring term

3a (6) the senior class

1a (7) washington square

10b (8) the black people

8b (9) a representative

1b (10) hotel standards

OTHER PUNCTUATION AT THE END OF A QUOTATION

10. When you write, you get credit for every word. If you use what other people say (and it's no crime!), you must tell the reader in some way so that you don't take credit for what someone else did. In this respect the rules of punctuation are like all other morals: "Thou shalt not steal."

You know that quotation marks go around everything you write that someone else actually said first, whether it has been said once or many times. You also capitalize the first word of a quotation. These are not new notions. But you may wonder where to put the closing quote if you have to use other punctuation marks with it. Entry 28 from Chart 2 gives the few simple rules.

SITUATION	IF	THEN	EXAMPLE
28. OTHER PUNCTUATION AT THE END OF A QUOTATION	(a) the quotation ends in a comma or a period,	(a) put the comma or period INSIDE the closing quote mark.	(a) I saw the show "Bonanza." I read the poem "Trees," and I loved it.
	(b) the quotation ends with a colon or a semicolon,	(b) put the colon or the semicolon OUTSIDE the closing quote mark.	(b) He said, "I do not choose to run"; however, nobody believed him. "I do not choose to run": Calvin Coolidge.
	(c) the whole sentence is a question or an exclamation,	(c) the ? or ! goes OUTSIDE the closing quote.	(c) Who said "I do not choose to run"? That's "Trees"!
	(d) the quotation is a question or an exclamation,	(d) the ? or ! goes INSIDE the closing quote.	(d) He said, "Why not!" He asked,"Why not?"
	(e) a quotation is within a quotation,	(e) use single quotes around a quotation within a quotation.	(e) I asked, "Did you like 'Trees'"?

Let's make sure you can interpret the chart and recognize examples of the special situation in the IF column. WRITE the appropriate letter for each example:

_______ (1) Do you use the expression "nitty gritty"?
_______ (2) He always uses the expression "nitty gritty."
_______ (3) He often uses the expression "nitty gritty"; however, he doesn't realize it.
_______ (4) He repeated, "Nitty gritty!"

- - - - - - - - - - - - - - - - - - -

___c___ (1) ___a___ (2) ___b___ (3) ___d___ (4)

11. Use Chart 2 to help you insert quote marks in the following sentences.

(1) He wrote Gentle on My Mind.
(2) She was on Girl Talk, but I didn't see her then.
(3) Who said, Give me liberty or give me death?
(4) She screamed, Help!
(5) He saw The Tonight Show: It was superb.
(6) I have heard many comments about the article Prisoner of Sex; however, I haven't read it yet.
(7) I read Auden's poem Talking to Dogs.
(8) How many students remember the radio show Gangbusters?
(9) The band played Dixie, and I knew I was home.
(10) We read the poem By All Means; it was nice.

- - - - - - - - - - - - - - - - - - - -

(1) "Gentle on My Mind."
(2) "Girl Talk,"
(3) "Give me liberty or give me death"?
(4) "Help!"
(5) "The Tonight Show":
(6) "Prisoner of Sex";
(7) "Talking to Dogs."
(8) "Gangbusters"?
(9) "Dixie,"
(10) "By All Means";

12. Now use Charts 2 and 3 to help you punctuate these sentences. You can assume that all punctuation except quotation marks, underlines, and capitalization of titles is correct.

(1) Francis Scott Key wrote the star-spangled banner, which later became our national anthem.
(2) You want to know what I thought of the article how to discipline a child?
(3) I heard him scream, Save me!
(4) I just read the article called to use or not to use the pill; I don't think it presented all the facts.
(5) Have you ever seen the television show sesame street?
(6) My favorite poem is the love song of j. alfred prufrock.
(7) Bert Bacharach wrote the song gentle on my mind, didn't he?
(8) He read Norman Mailer's article the prisoner of sex, which is one male's response to women's lib.
(9) Nancy Mitford took several years to write the book zelda; however, she also produced two children during that time.
(10) The first words ever spoken on the moon were, That's one small step for man, but one giant step for mankind.

- - - - - - - - - - - - - - - - - -

(1) the star-spangled banner, which
(2) how to discipline a child?
(3) scream, Save me!
(4) to use or not to use the pill;
(5) sesame street?
(6) the love song of j. alfred prufrock.
(7) gentle on my mind,
(8) the prisoner of sex,
(9) zelda
(10) That's one small step for man, but one giant step for mankind.

NUMBERS

13. One trivial matter that can cost you time, if you don't know how to handle it, is whether to spell out a number or to use the figure.

Numbers are so common in scientific writing that you wouldn't want to spell them all out. They also need to be emphasized, and the best way to emphasize a number is to use the figure instead of the words. In general nonscientific writing, however, numbers are not so common and usually don't need to be emphasized. The handiest rule (though there are others) is the following:

SPELL OUT any whole number that is less than 100; USE THE FIGURE for 100 and any whole number that is higher than 100--also for numbers like scores.

Also, you must include the hyphen between the two words of any number from twenty-one through ninety-nine.

Now APPLY this general rule to these numbers:

(1) It was 20 degrees below zero last night.

(2) We have 34 children in the class.

(3) The graduating class consists of 103 girls.

(4) I applied to 11 schools before being accepted by 1.

(5) He ranks 25th in his class.

- - - - - - - - - - - - - - - - - - - -

(1) 20 degrees below zero

(2) 34 children

(3) NO CHANGE

(4) 11 schools 1

(5) 25th

14. Like a lot of general rules, the rule for expressing numbers has exceptions. These are given in Chart 4 (page 334).

You probably won't have any difficulty interpreting this chart—except for the first and last entries. Let's look at the first exception.

One reason for spelling out a number beginning a new sentence is to prevent any possible confusion with the period in the preceding sentence.

Look at this example:

(a) I will ask him tomorrow. 198 people have applied so far.

With tight spacing, you could imagine that the period in the first sentence plus the 198 made a decimal figure.

The second reason for spelling out an initial number is that a figure is really an abbreviation, and a new sentence never begins with any kind of abbreviation—even in scientific writing, which has more figures and more abbreviations than other kinds of writing.

The last exception depends on the meaning of the word category. Two numbers used with the same unit are in the same category:

(b) Three men and two women are in the classroom. The notebook is twelve inches by eight inches.

The three men and two women are in the same category and so are the twelve inches and eight inches.

TEST yourself to see if you can interpret Chart 4. Each example is expressed correctly. Write the identifying number (and letter if there is one) of the exception it illustrates.

______ (1) They lost $2 million in 1970.
______ (2) This rose by 60 percent.
______ (3) This happened on July 21, 1969.
______ (4) Look at page 25, in Chapter 9.
______ (5) One hundred fifty years ago they agreed to disagree.
______ (6) Probably more than forty-five thousand people were trapped.
______ (7) That company used to have 15 machines; now it has 350 of the same machines.

- - - - - - - - - - - - - - - - - -

2c (1) 5 (2) 3 (3) 4 (4)
1 (5) 2a (6) 6 (7)

REVIEW

1. Insert any distinguishing marks such as underlines or quotations in the following titles, and draw the slash line through any letter that should be small.

   (a) the book Birds In Our Lives

   (b) the song I Want To Hold Your Hand

(c) the T. V. show The Tonight Show

(d) the movie Five Easy Pieces

(e) the book The Manufacture Of Madness

(f) the article The Secret History Of The War

2. Capitalize the following, as necessary.

(a) the woolworth building

(b) morton's salt

(c) her mother's farm

(d) the winter season

(e) thanksgiving day

(f) secretary of state rogers

(g) the rotary club

(h) the junior play

(i) saranac lake

3. Punctuate the titles in these sentences.

(a) I heard the song Layla, but I didn't enjoy it.

(b) I like the song Give Peace a Chance.

(c) I like the song Thirteen Questions: It's my favorite by the Sea Train.

(d) Do you like the song Monkberry Moon Delight?

(e) He asked, "Do you know the song Brown Sugar?"

4. Express the numbers in these sentences correctly:

(a) 3 boys were drafted this week.

(b) That costs $2,000,000,000.

(c) About 80 percent of the students live on campus.

(d) Only 93 girls graduated and 105 boys.

(e) The group consisted of 60 people.

(f) I knew him about 20 years ago.

(g) He grew 3 inches.

Suggested Answers

1. (a) the book Birds In Our Lives

(b) the Song I want To Hold Your Hand

(c) the T. V. show The Tonight Show

(d) the movie Five Easy Pieces

(e) the book The Manufacture Of Madness

(f) the article The Secret History Of The War

2. (a) the woolworth building

(b) morton's salt

(c) CORRECT

(d) CORRECT

(e) thanksgiving day

(f) secretary of state rogers

(g) the rotary club

(h) CORRECT

(i) saranac lake

3. (a) I heard the song Layla, but

(b) I like the song Give Peace a Chance.

(c) I like the song Thirteen Questions: It's my favorite by the Sea Train.

(d) Do you like the song Monkberry Moon Delight?

(e) He asked, "Do you know the song Brown Sugar?"

4. (a) 3 boys

(b) $2,000,000,000

(c) CORRECT

(d) CORRECT

(e) ~~60~~ sixty people

(f) ~~20~~ twenty years ago

(g) ~~3~~ three inches

How did you do? If you answered the questions correctly, you can check them off in the REVIEW column of the Self-Evaluation Record for Chapter 11 (page 244). But, if you missed any questions, you may want to mark your own copy of Chart 2. If you missed parts of question 1, you can check entry 27; if you missed parts of question 3, check entry 28. And if you felt shaky about expressing numbers or capitalization, you can note it under entry 29 (OTHER).

Closing Remarks

Chapter 11 concludes the program. You have learned all the important ways to turn a first draft into good, effective English and have applied them.

Of course, you won't remember everything even if you do a great deal of writing. But that is why the charts were prepared—and particularly Chart 2. If you can recognize a situation that may need some attention, you can then consult Chart 2 to find out how to handle it.

You may feel you also need practice or reminders on some of the points that you might forget. Remember the practice exercises in the Appendix and also A Concise Guide to Clear Writing, in which writing principles are summarized with examples. Before you start on a big writing project, you may want to read these principles over to remind yourself of key points.

Other editorial matters will crop up—things that aren't covered in this book. An excellent reference to use is the revised edition of Words Into Type, by Marjorie E. Skillin, Robert M. Gay, and other authorities, published by Appleton-Century-Crofts in 1964.

All the aids are at hand. With practice you can become the writer you want to be.

Appendix

Practice Exercises

CHAPTER 1

1. Read the passage below, and put a paragraphing symbol beside each sentence that you think should start a new paragraph.

(1) Although all boats were once reserved for only the very rich, ordinary Americans are now discovering the pleasures of the houseboat. (2) The Boat Owners Council of the U.S.A. reports a tremendous surge in the number of houseboats sold in the last few years. (3) On the average, most houseboats are owned by a fellow in his early forties, who earns between $15,000 and $20,000 a year. (4) He probably bought his thirty-five-foot boat for $15,000. (5) There are several reasons for the growth in houseboat sales. (6) First, houseboats are much less expensive and much more spacious than cabin cruisers. (7) They can also be used more months of the year. (8) They're perfect for parties, leisurely trips, and escape from daily city living. (9) Women like them; they like being topside with the other passengers and the scenery, instead of below the decks doing the kitchen work. (10) As one member of the boat industry said, "There is a large measure of Huckleberry Finn in a lot of people who like to drift down the river in a lot more comfort than Finn did." (11) But all is not completely well. (12) Many claim that the owners of these floating cottages, while exercising their squatters' rights, are also usurping hundreds of acres of public waters. (13) They pay no property tax, they block the view, and they pollute the waters. (14) On the other hand, the owners and guests on cabin cruisers have committed the same offense for years, yet no one complains. (15) But perhaps that's the next step for the houseboat: to become the status symbol that the cabin cruiser already is.

\- - - - - - - - - - - - - - - - -

Suggestions

(a) The first paragraph, sentences 1 through 4, gives the surprising facts about the houseboats.

(b) The second paragraph, sentences 5 through 10, explains the reasons for this popularity.

(c) The third paragraph, sentences 11 through 15, explains the problems.

You could also make sentence 11 a paragraph by itself to serve as a transition. Another possibility is to start a new paragraph with sentence 14 to dramatize the special privileges of the owners of cabin cruisers.

2. Now read the next passage and again put a paragraphing symbol beside each sentence that you think should start a new paragraph.

(1) Vitamin A was one of the first essential food elements that could be associated with physical symptoms. (2) Yet today some physicians don't even recognize the symptoms of a vitamin A deficiency. (3) And, even more surprising, scientists still don't know how much vitamin A we need or what is the best way to get it. (4) The most dramatic symptom of vitamin A deficiency is night blindness and other eyesight disabilities. (5) However, in a recent study conducted on prisoner volunteers, doctors discovered other effects much before any serious eye defects appeared. (6) The men developed skin rashes that looked like adolescent-type acne. (7) They also suffered from dizziness. (8) The most common food sources of vitamin A are liver and kidneys. (9) Leafy vegetables and yellow vegetables also provide beta-carotine that the body converts to vitamin A. (10) Yet, according to a health expert in Guatemala, these foods have only limited use. (11) He suggests that vitamin A should be administered in another food instead. (12) In prosperous countries it could be in margerine and in milk; in poorer ones wheat could be fortified, since even the poorest people eat it. (13) Surprisingly, he chose sugar as ideal in Latin American countries for vitamin A fortification. (14) What does it all mean? (15) Chances are that the doctors wouldn't recognize early symptoms of a vitamin A deficiency. (16) No one seems to know how much vitamin A we need or how we can get it. (17) But there is agreement about one thing: According to all the experts, there is a correlation between the amount of vitamin A we get and resistance to infection. (18) So, while they're making up their minds about all the other things about vitamin A, you'd better see that you get plenty of it.

- - - - - - - - - - - - - - - - - - - -

Suggestions

(a) The first paragraph, sentences 1 through 3, introduces the topics to be discussed.

(b) The second paragraph, sentences 4 through 7, explains the symptoms of vitamin A deficiency.

(c) The third paragraph, sentences 8 through 13, explains possible sources of vitamin A.

(d) The fourth paragraph, sentences 14 through 18, is a summary.

(e) Another possibility is for sentence 14 to stand by itself as a single-sentence paragraph, for a dramatic effect.

3. Read this passage through to see if you think you could improve it if you shifted one of the sentences. Then check the suggestions following the paragraph to see if you agree.

(1) The Labor Department conducted an interesting study based on statistics taken from the 1970 national census. (2) The Labor Department didn't attempt to draw any conclusions from these statistics. (3) According to this study, the number of families headed by a woman and living in poverty was the same in 1970 as it was in 1959. (4) But of poor families headed by a man, only half of those living in poverty in 1959 were still poor in 1970. (5) The Labor Department noted that, although women headed only 11 percent of all poor families in 1970, they accounted for 37 percent of all poor families. (6) The proportion of poor Negro families headed by a woman that year was even greater: 57 percent.

- - - - - - - - - - - - - - - - -

Suggestions

(a) Sentence 2 is misplaced and would be more appropriate after sentence 6 or between sentences 3 and 4.

4. The following paragraph is arranged in a completely haphazard fashion. Decide on a logical order, and number the sentences accordingly.

_______ (a) As a cultural figure, Dr. Spock is extremely conservative. _______ (b) The implications of his life's work, in fact, are deeply hostile to the rationale underlying the movement of women's lib. _______ (c) Dr. Spock may have adopted radical politics, but his politics weren't of interest to delegates to the National Women's Political Caucus. _______ (d) He has criticized working mothers of preschool children if they are not economically compelled to work. _______ (e) They booed him and labeled him a "sexist," since they perceived him in a cultural rather than a political role. _______ (f) He has also written that even the best day-care center is no substitute for the one-to-one relationship of a devoted mother to her child.

- - - - - - - - - - - - - - - - - -

Suggestions

1. 3 (a) 4 (d) OR 3 (a) 5 (d)
6 (b) 2 (e) 4 (b) 2 (e)
1 (c) 5 (f) 1 (c) 6 (f)

5. Read the passage below to see if you could improve it by deleting any sentences that are repetitious.

(1) How do we measure productivity in industry? (2) Usually, it is in terms of the sensible yardstick of inputs against outputs. (3) We put so many of our resources in, and we get this much of a product out. (4) It's just a matter of what we get for what we invest. (5) In most industries input and output have grown at the same rate since the thirties. (6) But, when the input-output yardstick was recently applied to higher education, the findings were quite different. (7) According to a study that measured the cost of producing a credit hour of instruction from 1930 to 1970, the cost of college rose a little more than 3 percent a year. (8) Yet students are not getting 3 percent more out of their instruction each year. (9) In short, the students are not getting their money's worth.

- - - - - - - - - - - - - - - - - -

Suggestions

(a) Sentence 4 can be deleted, since it repeats the idea of sentence 3.
(b) Sentence 6 can be deleted (it merely says generally what sentences 7 and 8 say in detail), and possibly sentence 9 (since it is a summary of sentences 7 and 8).

6. Delete any sentence in the paragraph below that you think is merely repetitious and interferes with the sense.

(1) In Manhattan these days you don't need to do all of your shopping indoors. (2) You can buy many beautiful things right on the streets—leather belts, sheepskin rugs, homemade candles, jewelry, and even tacos and organic food. (3) There are many restrictions on those who peddle their wares, of course. (4) First, they are required to be licensed by New York City's Department of Consumer Affairs. (5) They are also forbidden to sell within five hundred feet of a retail store. (6) But the peddlers pay little attention to these laws. (7) They find peddling too profitable. (8) Young peddlers can make as much as $60 to $90 a day in profits. (9) Obviously, peddling pays off.

- -

Suggestions

Since sentences 7 and 9 carry the same message, one or the other of these sentences can be deleted.

CHAPTER 2

1. Each blank marks the beginning of a supporting clause. Supply an appropriate starter:

   (a) The economy of Vermont, __________ is not a coastal state, depends heavily on the tourists, __________ mostly come to ski.
   (b) The children __________ we saw playing in the yard were a group of disadvantaged children.

(c) They found some stores ________ did not comply with the price freeze.
(d) ________ all the votes were counted, Harry Truman was still President.
(e) Most people work ________ they need the money.
(f) Burt Lancaster is in the movie at the Bijou ______ we saw last night.

2. Punctuate these sentences:

(a) Busing as everyone knows is not a new issue.
(b) Although the people used to flock into California that trend is now beginning to reverse.
(c) Doris Day who used to sing with Les Brown's band knows how to belt out a song.
(d) Everyone was stunned when the Mets became the World Champions in 1969.
(e) After registering for the two courses that I wanted to take I left school for the day.

3. See if you can write each set of three short sentences as one sentence, with one main idea.

(a) Once only the wealthy could afford the large Long Island estates. Now high taxes make them too expensive even for the wealthy. These estates are being divided and sold.
(b) The Saturday Evening Post folded a few years ago. Most people were surprised. The Saturday Evening Post seemed almost like an institution.

- - - - - - - - - - - - - - - - - -

Suggestions

1. (a) which; who (d) After, or When, or Once
(b) whom or that (e) because
(c) that (f) that

2. (a) Busing, as everyone knows, is
(b) California, that trend
(c) Day, who used to sing with Les Brown's band, knows
(d) CORRECT
(e) After registering for the two courses that I wanted to take, I

3. (a) The large Long Island estates, which once only the wealthy could afford, are being divided and sold because now they are too expensive even for the rich.

(b) Most people were surprised when The Saturday Evening Post folded a few years ago, since it had seemed almost like an institution.

CHAPTER 3

1. Punctuate these sentences:

(a) Although I was very tired I continued to work late again however I think the project is worthwhile.

(b) I enjoyed two of his books especially Bech: A B ook and Rabbit, Run.

(c) In high school he was first in his class nevertheless he couldn't get into Harvard.

(d) If I had to choose one book that I wouldn't want to do without I'd pick Words into Type but many people are not enthusiastic about it.

(e) High school sports are very popular in New Jersey but in New York they are less so.

2. See if you can unify this passage by combining short sentences and by inserting words or expressions that will tie it together.

(1) One way to motivate workers is through the work itself. (2) Many exit interviews with telephone operators reveal that telephone operators feel they are taken for granted. (3) Telephone operators don't get enough attention or recognition. (4) The philosophy of motivation through work itself is that workers must become more satisfied with their jobs. (5) They will if workers have more responsibility for themselves. (6) They must also have more responsibilities for planning and controlling their jobs. (7) They must be able to handle this responsibility.

- - - - - - - - - - - - - - - - -

Suggestions

1. (a) Although I was very tired I continued to work late again however I think the project is worthwhile.

   (b) I enjoyed two of his books especially Bech: A Book and Rabbit, Run.

   (c) In high school he was first in his class nevertheless he couldn't get into Harvard.

   (d) If I had to choose one book that I wouldn't want to do without, I'd pick Words into Type but many people are not as enthusiastic about it.

   (e) High school sports are very popular in New Jersey but in New York they are less so.

2. Examine the following:

   (1) One way to motivate workers is through the work itself.

   (2) Many exit interviews with telephone operators reveal that telephone operators feel they are taken for granted. (3) Telephone operators don't get enough attention or recognition. (4) The philosophy of motivation through work itself is that workers must become more satisfied with their jobs. (5) They will if workers have more responsibility for themselves. (6) They must also have more responsibilities for planning and controlling their jobs. (7) They must be able to handle this responsibility.

CHAPTER 4

1. Punctuate these sentences:

   (a) Whitney Young a black civil rights leader died tragically of a heart attack.

   (b) We hope you will be able to use the guide in the Appendix to Clear Writing A Concise Guide to Clear Writing as a permanent reference.

   (c) The musical Fiddler on the Roof was one of the most popular ever to play on Broadway.

(d) Julie Nixon Eisenhower President Nixon's younger daughter broke her foot.

(e) I believe in the expression "The squeaky wheel gets the grease."

2. Insert the description "a great actor" appropriately into each of these three sentences. Punctuate the first sentence so you will emphasize the description; the second so you de-emphasize the description; and the third as it would normally be punctuated.

(a) Clark Gable played Rhett Butler.

(b) Clark Gable played Rhett Butler.

(c) Clark Gable played Rhett Butler.

3. Reduce these sentences and punctuate them correctly.

(a) That dish is seasoned with paprika the other dish is seasoned with just salt.

(b) She was born in Newark in the state of New Jersey on January 4 in the year 1897.

(c) I need to borrow the pen that belongs to Charles.

\- - - - - - - - - - - - - - - - - -

Suggestions

1. (a) Young, a black civil rights leader, died
   (b) Writing: A Concise Guide to Clear Writing, as
   (c) CORRECT
   (d) Eisenhower, President Nixon's younger daughter, broke
   (e) CORRECT

2. (a) Clark Gable -- a great actor -- played Rhett Butler.
   (b) Clark Gable (a great actor) played Rhett Butler.
   (c) Clark Gable, a great actor, played Rhett Butler

3. (a) That dish is seasoned with paprika; the other, ~~dish is seasoned~~ with just salt.

(b) She was born in Newark, ~~in the state of~~ New Jersey, on January 4 ~~in the year~~, 1897.

(c) I need to borrow ~~the~~ Charles's pen ~~that belongs to Charles~~.

CHAPTER 5

1. Punctuate these sentences:

   (a) They use high pressure sales techniques.
   (b) He wore a gray loose fitting jacket.
   (c) They have decidedly different attitudes.
   (d) He wrote a short brilliant statement in his own defense.
   (e) He expects to write two or three scientific papers this year.
   (f) He went to a distinguished prep school first.
   (g) They bought two strikingly good water colors.
   (h) It depends on whether you make short or long range plans.
   (i) They showed her the three new length skirts.
   (j) He bought two new earth science books.

2. Reduce each sentence by using a two-word description instead of a longer phrase or clause.

   (a) Television writers must imagine that only people who are undemanding and mentally asleep listen to those programs.
   (b) After listening to his principles that sounded so important, I decided he was just a phony who talked fast.

\- - - - - - - - - - - - - - - - - - -

Suggestions

1. (a) They use high-pressure sales techniques.
   (b) He wore a gray, loose-fitting jacket.
   (c) CORRECT
   (d) He wrote a short, brilliant statement in his own defense.
   (e) CORRECT
   (f) CORRECT
   (g) CORRECT

(h) It depends on whether you make short or long range plans.
(i) They showed her the three new length skirts.
(j) CORRECT

2. (a) Television writers must imagine that only people who are undemanding and mentally asleep listen to those programs.
(b) After listening to his principles that sounded so important I decided he was just a phony who talked fast.

CHAPTER 6

1. Copyedit these sentences so that each item in a list is in the same form as the other items. Punctuate each list correctly.

(a) My interests are playing the guitar tending a garden and the horses.

(b) Her students are young eager and they have a lot of respect for her.

(c) He expects the following that we recognize his rights around the house he needs spending money and his privacy.

(d) He spent three days at home one to relax one to write a term paper and one for shopping.

(e) He borrowed a large sum of money to buy a house for a trip and to pay back his debts.

2. Turn this set of facts into a regular, complete list:

Very soon this country will probably convert to the metric system. This system has advantages. Every other country now uses it. It is based on the decimal system. The decimal system is simple and efficient. It will also be more convenient to apply.

\- - - - - - - - - - - - - - - - - - -

Suggestions

1 (a) My interests are playing the guitar, tending a garden, and the horses.

(b) Her students are young, eager, and they have a lot of respect for her.

(c) He expects the following: that we recognize his rights around the house, he needs spending money, and his privacy.

(d) He spent three days at home: one to relax, one to write a term paper, and one for shopping.

(e) He borrowed a large sum of money to buy a house, for a trip, and to pay back his debts.

2\. Very soon this country will probably convert to the metric system. This system has advantages. Every other country now uses it. It is based on the decimal system. The decimal system is simple and efficient. It will also be more convenient to apply.

CHAPTER 7

In each sentence UNDERLINE the correct verb or possessive pronoun:

(a) One of the movies I'd like to see again (is, are) Gone with the Wind.
(b) Everybody (has, have) (his, their) own problems to worry about.
(c) A number of students in the senior class (has, have) decided to have a peace march next Saturday.
(d) The jury (was, were) undecided most of the afternoon.
(e) The number of women who (is, are) executives in the company (is, are) fairly small.
(f) Everybody (asks, ask) for (his, their) raise despite the freeze.
(g) The club (has, have) voted to drop the June meeting.
(h) Anybody who (wants, want) to get his grades early (has, have) to leave (his, their) name in the office.
(i) One of the senators who voted against it (was, were) a Democrat.
(j) A number of June graduates (stays, stay) on campus all summer.

(a) is, are

(b) has, have his, their

(c) has, have

(d) was, were

(e) is, are is, are

(f) asks, ask his, their

(g) has, have

(h) wants, want has, have his, their

(i) was, were

(j) stays, stay

CHAPTER 8

Change each of the following passive sentences to actives without changing the meaning.

(a) Public nudity is prohibited by law in all fifty states.

(b) However, nudity has been accepted casually by many teenagers in the United States.

(c) He was invited by his colleagues to prepare a special address.

(d) T. S. Eliot was urged by his parents to return to the States with his wife to pursue a university career.

(e) Many of these ideas have been suggested before by overly ambitious students.

(f) These songs have been sung by Columbia undergraduates for as long as I can remember.

(g) Many chaperones have been invited to the class dances by the students, but the French teacher is their favorite.

(h) Wigs are worn by many fashionable women nowadays.

(i) Pot is smoked by so many students that the laws are not enforced by the school authorities.

(j) Paris was once considered the capital of the fashion industry by American women.

- - - - - - - - - - - - - - - - - -

Suggestions

(a) Public nudity is prohibited by law in all fifty states.

(b) However, nudity has been accepted casually by many teenagers in the United States.

(c) He was invited by his colleagues to prepare a special address.

(d) T. S. Eliot was urged by his parents to return to the States with his wife to pursue a university career.

(e) Many of these ideas have been suggested before by overly ambitious students.

(f) These songs have been sung by Columbia undergraduates for as long as I can remember.

(g) Many chaperones have been invited to the class dances by the students, but the French teacher is their favorite.

(h) Wigs are worn by many fashionable women nowadays.

(i) Pot is smoked by so many students that the laws are not enforced by the school authorities.

(j) Paris was once considered the capital of the fashion industry by American women.

CHAPTER 9

1. Try to pare this passage so it is economical yet smooth:

(a) It is probable that each and every American Indian living in New York City suffers from a sense of isolation. (b) Although there were only 4,366 Indians counted in New York in the 1960 census, that number has increased considerably in size. (c) There were more than 10,000 counted in 1970. (d) But due to the fact that they are scattered throughout the five boroughs, many Indians believe that they are alone. (e) One young woman, Suzan Shown, said that she and her husband felt lucky to meet two Indian actresses when they first arrived here. (f) For the most part, the vast majority of Indians came largely to escape the poverty of the reservations. (g) Others, such as Suzan Shown, her husband, etc., came to pursue careers. (h) All left family ties behind. (i) But there are signs apparent to the eye that Indians in New York City are becoming more aware of one another. (j) They have organized a Community House for Indians, for example. (k) However, there is one interesting requirement they have in regard to membership: The organization is not for all Indians; it is only for the full-blooded ones!

\- - - - - - - - - - - - - - - - -

Suggestions

(a) ~~It is probable that each and~~ every American Indian living in New York City *probably* suffers from a sense of isolation. (b) Although ~~there were~~ only 4,366 Indians *were* counted in New York in the 1960 census, that number has increased considerably ~~in size~~. (c) ~~There were~~ more than 10,000 *were* counted in 1970. (d) But *because* ~~due to the fact that~~ they are scattered throughout the five boroughs, many Indians believe that they are alone. (e) One young woman, Suzan Shown, said that she and her husband felt lucky to meet two Indian actresses when they first arrived here. (f) ~~For the most part,~~ the ~~vast~~ majority of Indians came largely to escape the poverty of the reservations. (g) Others, such as Suzan Shown *and* her husband, ~~etc.,~~ came to pursue careers. (h) All left family ties behind. (i) But there are signs ~~apparent to the eye~~ that Indians in New York City are becoming more aware of one another. (j) They have organized a Community House for Indians, for example. (k) However, *they have* ~~there is~~

one interesting requirement ~~they have in regard to~~ membership: The organization is not for all Indians; it is only for the full-blooded ones!

2. If you would like more paring practice, try out your techniques on this passage:

(a) Can you venture a guess as to whether the greatest cook in history ate gourmet dinners himself ? (b) You may be surprised to know that Escoffier's evening meal was almost always the same in content: It was a bowl of soup, with a little rice, and some fresh fruit. (c) And, due to the fact that he wanted to keep his sense of taste and smell as keen in sensitivity as possible, he neither smoked nor drank. (d) Yet there is no doubt in regard to the fact that he changed the eating habits of fashionable Englishmen. (e) Just before 1900 the Prince of Wales and several friends, dining at the most posh hotel there was in London at the time, ordered a dish called <u>Cuisses de Nymphes a l' aurore</u>, or "nymphs' thighs at dawn." (f) It was so good that they demanded to know what they were eating. (g) And they got the word: The "nymphs' thighs" were really in fact frogs' legs, which Englishmen had always disdained. (h) Then from that moment on frogs' legs became the favorite food of English society. (i) It was Escoffier who was the magician who transformed the frogs' legs and changed them into nymphs' thighs.

\- - - - - - - - - - - - - - - - - - -

<u>Suggestions</u>

(a) Can you ~~venture a~~ guess ~~as to~~ whether the greatest cook in history ate gourmet dinners himself? (b) You may be surprised to know that Escoffier's evening meal was almost always the same ~~in content:~~ It

~~was~~ a bowl of soup, with a little rice, and some fresh fruit. (c) And, *because* ~~due to the fact that~~ he wanted to keep his sense of taste and smell as keen ~~in sensitivity~~ as possible, he neither smoked nor drank. (d) Yet ~~there is no doubt in regard to the fact that~~ he *undoubtedly* changed the eating habits of fashionable Englishmen. (e) Just before 1900 the Prince of Wales and several friends, dining at ~~the~~ *London's* most posh hotel ~~there was in London at the time~~, ordered a dish called Cuisses de Nymphes a l' aurore, or "nymphs' thighs at dawn." (f) It was so good that they demanded to know what they were eating. (g) And they got the word: The "nymphs' thighs" were really ~~in fact~~ frogs' legs, which Englishmen had always distained. (h) ~~Then~~ From *then* ~~that moment~~ on, frogs' legs became the favorite food of English society. (i) ~~It was~~ Escoffier ~~who~~ was the magician who *made nymphs' thighs from* ~~transformed the~~ frogs' legs. ~~and changed it into nymphs' thighs.~~

CHAPTER 10

1. Apply everything you learned in Chapter 10 to strengthen this passage by making it as positive and specific as possible.

(a) Black people have played various roles in the history of our nation from its inception. (b) Their inclusion in American history as it is taught in today's classroom is not representative of a concession to current black aspirations, but is a better-late-than-never acknowledgment of the veracity of the facts. (c) Crispus Attucks, a black man, participated in the Boston Massacre of 1770. (d) When he expired because of his wounds, he became one of the first martyrs to American independence. (e) Black men made explorations of the West with Fremont and also with Lewis and Clark. (f) In other fields of endeavor, the emancipated slave Phyllis Wheatley was an accomplished creator of poetry. (g) And a black physician developed the blood bank system that was put into operation during World War II. (h) Yet until the late 1960's the all-white orientation of American society didn't make any recognition of the existence and contributions of black Americans.

- - - - - - - - - - - - - - - - - - - -

<u>Suggestions</u>

(a) Black people have played various roles in the history of our nation from its inception. (b) Their inclusion in American history as it is taught in today's classroom is not representative of a concession to current black aspirations, but is a better-late-than-never acknowledgment of the veracity of the facts. (c) Crispus Attucks, a black man, participated in the Boston Massacre of 1770. (d) When he expired because of his wounds, he became one of the first martyrs to American independence. (e) Black men made explorations of the West with Fremont and also with Lewis and Clark. (f) In other fields of endeavor the emancipated slave Phyllis Wheatley was an accomplished creator of poetry. (g) And a black physician developed the blood bank system that was put into operation during World War II. (h) Yet until the late 1960's the all-white orientation of American society didn't make any recognition of the existence and contributions of black Americans.

2. Again, see if you can apply the techniques of Chapter 10 to make this passage positive and specific.

(a) One of life's most memorable experiences is the distinctive aroma of a new automobile. (b) Now we are informed that it is a potential candidate for a hazard to life and limb. (c) According to <u>Environment,</u> a magazine published by the Committee on Environmental Information, the new-car aroma is the toxic result of chemicals evaporating from the plastic inside the automobile. (d) The author of the article, Kevin

Shea, cited recent disclosures of the toxic effects of these PVC plastics components. (e) First, mercury was determined to be in tuna fish and also in swordfish. (f) In fact, swordfish may not be in our diets again. (g) Next, the low-calorie drinks were deemed hazardous. (h) And then we faced similar difficulties with some canned soups. (i) Isn't anything sacred in today's world?

\- - - - - - - - - - - - - - - - - - -

Suggestions

(a) One of life's most memorable experiences is the distinctive aroma of a new automobile. (b) Now we are informed that it is a potential candidate for a hazard to life and limb. (c) According to Environment, a magazine published by the Committee on Environmental Information, the new-car aroma is the toxic result of chemicals evaporating from the plastic inside the automobile. (d) The author of the article, Kevin Shea, cited recent disclosures of the toxic effects of these PVC plastics components. (e) First, mercury was determined to be in tuna fish and also in swordfish. (f) In fact, swordfish will not be in our diets again. (g) Next, the low-calorie drinks were deemed hazardous. (h) And then we faced similar difficulties with some canned soups. (i) Isn't anything sacred in today's world?

CHAPTER 11

1. Insert such distinguishing marks as capitals, quotation marks, or underlines as they are needed.

   (a) We saw the television show the name of the game.
   (b) The movie revolt in the big house is playing at the olympia.
   (c) He enjoys the cereal alphabits for breakfast.
   (d) Who wrote the song born free?

(e) The fall season in the northeast is sensational.
(f) I used to like the song maggie may, but now I'm getting tired of it.
(g) She said, "My favorite song is still stardust."
(h) I loved the poem blue girl; however, my students had never even heard of it.
(i) On the fourth of july we always sing yankee doodle: my father's and uncle joe's favorite.
(j) The magazine parents will publish my article one to grow on in december.

2. Express the numbers in these sentences correctly.

(a) 5 men were drafted last week.
(b) The class was reading page 50.
(c) I saw 2 small children holding hands.
(d) There were 110 students in the graduating class.
(e) He needed assurance from the 105 seniors and 83 juniors.
(f) The thermometer dropped to 30 degrees.

- - - - - - - - - - - - - - - - - - -

1. (a) We saw the television show the name of the game.
(b) The movie revolt in the big house is playing at the olympia.
(c) He enjoys the cereal alphabits for breakfast.
(d) Who wrote the song born free?
(e) The fall season in the northeast is sensational.
(f) I used to like the song maggie may, but now I'm getting tired of it.
(g) She said, "My favorite song is still stardust."
(h) I loved the poem blue girl; however, my students had never even heard of it.
(i) On the fourth of july we always sing yankee doodle: my father's and uncle joe's favorite.
(j) The magazine parents will publish my article one to grow on in december.

2. (a) ~~5~~ five men were drafted last week.

   (b) CORRECT

   (c) I saw ~~2~~ two small children holding hands.

   (d) CORRECT

   (e) CORRECT

   (f) The thermometer dropped to ~~30~~ thirty degrees.

A Concise Guide to Clear Writing

This Guide is your permanent reference; it contains the main principles and techniques you will need to apply whenever you write.

WRITE A "WORKING" DRAFT

First write down, somewhere, your goal and a list of the main points you should cover to satisfy that goal. Next decide on an effective way to present these points and number them in sequence. Then you are ready to write. You may expand each main point into a paragraph, or perhaps you'll need several paragraphs to develop one idea. It depends on what you want to say. At this stage, however, don't agonize over punctuation, the poetic phrase, the perfect word, or even the right spelling. Your only concern is to develop your ideas fully.

SET THE FIRST DRAFT ASIDE FOR AS LONG AS POSSIBLE

Anyone who does a lot of writing expects to do a lot of revising. Ideally, you could ask a professional editor to look at your work with his cold, fresh eye and to revise it for you. But few of us are so fortunate: We must divorce ourselves from our own writing so that we can be extremely critical of it, and revise it ourselves. The best way to do this is to put as much time as possible between writing the working draft and revising it. But even a five-minute break or a walk around the block will help.

COMPARE YOUR WORKING DRAFT WITH YOUR GOAL AND LIST OF MAIN POINTS.

Check to make sure you have covered all the points on your list, that you have developed each idea appropriately, and that you have satisfied your goal. Then you're ready to revise. If possible, try to imagine that you are really the reader and not the writer; try to make changes that will improve the writing from the reader's standpoint. You can simplify your revision by using standard copyediting marks (see Chart 1). Then you won't need to rewrite until you're ready to type up another complete draft.

As you revise, use the checklist following. Each point includes a brief discussion and example; chapter or chart references are given for further explanation.

1. Read the draft to make sure it is paragraphed effectively. (Chapter 1)

There are no fixed rules about when to start a new paragraph. The "average paragraph" has four or five sentences, each related to a central thought. Yet a paragraph may also be a single sentence, serving as a bridge or transition between paragraphs.

Some common reasons for starting a new paragraph are

(1) to show a shift from one idea to another;
(2) to dramatize an idea;
(3) to break up a long paragraph to make it easier to read;
(4) to show, with quotations, that someone different from the preceding speaker has started to speak.

This passage could be paragraphed in various ways; some suggestions follow.

(1) To celebrate the fifty years his family had been in business, a New York theater owner, Donald Rugoff, spent a whole day giving away free movie admissions to ninety-nine feature showings. (2) He opened the doors of fourteen movie houses to tens of thousands of young people. (3) And, since the wait could be as long as four hours, he served iced cola drinks and cups of hot popcorn to make it more pleasant. (4) Mr. Rugoff estimated the cost at about $25,000, including the loss of normal admissions. (5) But the total value of what he gave away—60,000 free admissions, worth $2 to $3 each—would run closer to $130,000! (6) And did everyone appreciate Mr. Rugoff's generosity? (7) Well, many did. (8) One school teacher was so appreciative that she brought her entire class. (9) But you can't please everyone. (10) A woman scolded a theater manager severely because of the behavior of the audience. (11) And young people trying to crash into an already filled theater became violent, flying at Mr. Rugoff in a rage when he told them to move back into line. (12) Two of them scored, in fact, with blows to his face. (13) The question we wonder about now is, How will Mr. Rugoff celebrate the anniversary of his next ten or twenty years in business?

Suggestions

(a) The first paragraph would consist of sentences 1 through 5, describing the gift. However, to dramatize the cost of this gift, we could put sentences 4 and 5 in a separate paragraph.
(b) Sentence 6 would start a new paragraph consisting of sentences 6 through 12, describing the appreciation of the gift. However,

sentence 6 could serve as a transition between the two descriptions (of the gift and its appreciation). In that case, sentence 7 would introduce the paragraph describing the appreciation.

(c) Sentence 13 would start a new paragraph for an abrupt but dramatic ending.

2. Check to see that all the sentences are in the most logical or effective order. (Chapter 1)

Your first draft may seem completely logical while you're writing it. But when you reread it later, you may find that a sentence isn't in a sensible place or would be more effective elsewhere.

You could improve this passage by shifting a sentence or two; suggestions follow.

(1) David Stein has been exhibiting again. (2) He's the famous art forger who made hundreds of thousands of dollars by unloading his "masterpieces" on unsuspecting art lovers. (3) Perhaps David Stein would never have been caught if Chagall hadn't come face to face with a Stein creation signed as a Chagall. (4) He imitated the style of such artists as Picasso, Chagall, Miro, and Matisse so successfully that he fooled all the experts. (5) Public exposure followed, and then deportation to France and a prison sentence. (6) The sales at exhibitions of his jail works were interesting. (7) In jail, Stein continued to paint, sometimes "in-the-style-of" but signed "Stein, d" (for David), and sometimes in his own style. (8) Nobody seemed to want paintings in the style of Stein, which were gloomy prison interiors. (9) But Stein's "in-the-style-of" paintings sold like hot cakes.

Suggestions

(a) Sentence 4 logically belongs after sentence 2. Then sentence 5 will follow sentence 3, as it does logically: Exposure follows the catch.

(b) Sentence 6 would be more effective after sentence 7, to set the stage for the descriptions in sentences 8 and 9.

3. Check to see that you have not repeated an idea unintentionally. (Chapter 1)

Often we are so busy making sure we have expressed all of our ideas that we fail to notice when we have repeated an idea, perhaps with slightly different words. Repetitions are not only boring, but they also muddy up the message and make it hard to follow.

The sentences enclosed in brackets in this passage are merely repetitious: Sentence 5 is just a rehash of sentence 2, and sentence 9 doesn't say anything that sentence 6 hadn't already said and better. Read the passage with and without the two unnecessary sentences, and note how much clearer it is without them.

(1) The state of Israel was supposed to be a haven where Jews could live and worship freely. (2) How odd, then, that religion has become such a sore point there. (3) Recently, some hoodlums in Jerusalem beat up a rabbi and shaved off his beard. (4) Other rowdies set upon a group of religious students. [(5) There is no unanimous feeling toward Judaism in Israel.] (6) On the other side, to many nonreligious Israeli, the Orthodox represent a dictatorial strain. (7) They force shops to close on Saturday and all public institutions to maintain kosher kitchens. (8) And students at Orthodox schools are exempt from military duty. [(9) Some even say the Orthodox are like the fascists.] (10) No one can make any guess about the outcome. (11) But what is happening certainly seems to be a good argument for keeping religion out of government.

4. <u>Make sure you have used a main clause for an idea you want to emphasize</u>. (Chapter 2)

The two main units of a sentence are the <u>main clause</u> and the <u>supporting clause.</u> The difference is, a main clause can stand alone as a sentence and a supporting clause cannot. This means that you should use a main clause to carry your main thought and a supporting clause for an idea that supports it.

In the table following, note how the form of the clause can change the emphasis. (Each main clause has been underlined to distinguish it from a supporting clause.)

	SAMPLE	EMPHASIS
1.	College students are protesting less, although they are no more content with present conditions in the schools.	The more important idea is that students are protesting less.
2.	College students are no more content with present conditions in the schools, although they are protesting less.	The more important idea is that there has been no change in student satisfaction.
3.	College students are protesting less. But they are no more content with present conditions in the schools.	These sentences sound like two equally important ideas, neither one depending on the other.

5. Make sure you have started each supporting clause with a word that expresses the meaning precisely. (Chapter 2)

Here are some common starters, listed according to their meaning:

ON THIS CONDITION	AT THIS TIME	FOR THIS REASON	FOR THIS PURPOSE	IN SPITE OF THIS
if, provided, providing, when, once	while, as, before, when, after, until, once, since, as soon as	because, since	so that, in order that	even if, although, even though

In this table note the different implications that different starters can give, although the other words in the sentences are identical:

	Washington baseball fans will be bitter	IMPLICATION
(1)	if the Senators go to Dallas next year.	The condition for the bitterness of the fans is the departure of the Senators.
(2)	after the Senators go to Dallas next year.	The occasion or time for the bitterness will be the departure of the Senators.
(3)	because the Senators go to Dallas next year.	The reason for the bitterness is the departure of the Senators.
(4)	so that the Senators go to Dallas next year.	The purpose of the bitterness is to send the Senators off to Dallas.
(5)	although the Senators go to Dallas next year.	The departure of the Senators will not prevent the bitterness.

6. Make certain that each adjective or adverb you use makes the meaning of the sentence more precise. (Chapter 2)

You should try to pack as much of the sentence's meaning as possible into the subject and the verb. The verb expresses the action and the subject is the person or thing that carries it out. However, sometimes you need to develop a sentence and make the meaning more specific by using adjectives and adverbs. The table following illustrates:

		EXAMPLE	DESCRIBES
(1)	Without an adjective or adverb:	The man walked .	what a man was doing.
(2)	With an adjective:	The blind man walked .	what a particular man was doing.
(3)	With an adverb:	The blind man walked cautiously.	what a particular man was doing and how.

7. <u>Make the meaning more precise by using prepositional phrases to specify where or when the action occurs.</u> (Chapter 2)

A prepositional phrase is a sentence unit that starts with a word called a <u>preposition</u> (like <u>in</u>, <u>by</u>, or <u>with</u>) and has no verb.

		EXAMPLE	DESCRIBES
(1)	Without any prepositional phrases:	They found the body .	what they found.
(2)	With one prepositional phrase:	They found the body near the river.	what they found and where.
(3)	With two prepositional phrases:	In the morning they found the body near the river.	what they found, where they found it, and when.

8. <u>Be sure you have put a supporting clause where it will be most effective.</u> (Chapter 2)

There aren't any rules about where the supporting clause goes—just some general guidelines: The clause will be most conspicuous in the middle of the sentence or at the beginning and least conspicuous at the end. However, the main question is how the sentence fits in with the other sentences in the paragraph.

Note how the first sentence in the paragraph below fits in with the others and how the emphasis changes as the supporting clause is shifted from place to place. (It is underlined to make it stand out.)

(a) In the middle	(b) At the beginning	(c) At the end
College football, <u>although it has numerous fans</u>, lacks the wide appeal of professional football. One reason is that the professionals are so good. Another is that they get better publicity.	<u>Although it has numerous fans</u>, college football lacks the wide appeal of professional football. One reason is that the professionals are so good. Another is that they get better publicity.	College football lacks the wide appeal of professional football, <u>although it has numerous fans</u>. One reason is that the professionals are so good. Another is that they get better publicity.

In this case, the supporting clause probably gets too much emphasis in (a); in (c) it is just an aside that gets lost; and in (b) it seems to have just the right stress.

PUNCTUATION of supporting clauses is outlined in Chart 2, entries 1 to 3.

9. <u>If two sentences are related, signal the reader about the relationship.</u> (Chapter 3)

TO SIGNAL THE READER THAT THE NEXT IDEA		USE	EXAMPLE
(1)	remains true, despite what was said earlier,	yet; use nevertheless to be more formal.	I had already seen the movie. Yet I stayed up to see it again.
(2)	is in contrast to the one before,	but or yet; use however to be more formal.	I had already seen the movie. But I wanted to see it again.
(3)	is a result of a previous one,	use therefore, thus, or consequently to be more formal.	We expected him to win. Therefore, we were shocked when he didn't.
(4)	is an additional fact,	and; use furthermore or moreover to be more formal.	I expected a good raise. And I got one!

When you use linking words, you can keep the two sentences separate, as above, or you can combine them to show a clear relationship. See Chart 2, entries 4 and 5, to review punctuation.

There are two more ways to combine two sentences:

		USE	EXAMPLE
(1)	Without a linking word,	a semicolon between the two sentences.	He was expected to take the course; he was also expected to get an A.
(2)	To dramatize that the second sentence explains the first,	a colon between the two sentences, and capitalize the first word of the explanation.	I expect him to criticize: He's my husband.

You can also use the colon to dramatize an explanation even when it isn't a separate sentence. In that case, though, you don't capitalize the first word. For example,

I have only one critic: my husband.

10. Make the sentences in a paragraph sound like a unit. (Chapter 3)

There are several devices you can use. One is to add some standard phrases or words called transitions that act as a bridge between two ideas. Here are some examples:

TO INTRODUCE AN EXAMPLE	TO ADD ANOTHER ASPECT	TO POINT OUT A CONTRAST	TO INDICATE A RESULT	TO INDICATE A TIME
For example, for instance, to illustrate, as an example, as an illustration	Besides, again, next, in the second place, similarly, in addition, finally, also, first, and furthermore, moreover,	Otherwise, in contrast, on the other hand, instead, meanwhile, still, despite this, just the same, but, however, yet, nevertheless,	In conclusion, to sum up, in other words, as a result, accordingly, in short, obviously, clearly, thus, consequently, therefore, so	At the same time, nowadays, up to now, so far, from then on, until then

Transitions are usually set off by commas because they aren't essential information.

A second way to link the sentences in a paragraph is to substitute a pronoun for a noun that was repeated unnecessarily. You may also purposely repeat key words or vary the patterns and the lengths of the sentences

All of these devices were used to improve the passage below. Read it as it was originally, in (a), and then as it was revised, in (b).

(a) Americans seem to like a convention, but no more than Americans seem to like a contest. A seventy-five-year-old top winner addressed the jingle and slogan makers at their annual convention in Florida. Her name is Lena Zavender. She said anyone can do it. They just have to try hard enough. She has won $113,000 over the last twenty years. She won a $75,000 house and a house trailer. She has won enough to earn herself a reputation as Jackpot Jane.

(b) Americans seem to like a convention, but no more than Americans seem to like a contest. A seventy-five-year-old top winner addressed the jingle and slogan makers at their annual convention in Florida. Her name is Lena Zavender. She said anyone can do it. They just have to try hard enough. She has won $113,000 over the last twenty years. She won a $75,000 house and a house trailer. She has won enough to earn herself a reputation as Jackpot Jane.

11. <u>Tighten up sentences by simplifying clauses or phrases.</u> (Chapter 4)

In good writing, every word should count. So, if you can say something in fewer words, you are probably saying it better.

IF	THEN	EXAMPLE
(1) a clause starts with who is, which is or sometimes that is,	drop the first two words; if the other words could be dropped without changing the meaning, set them off by commas; if not, don't set them off.	(a) Burstein who is the new president of Rutgers is also a lawyer. (b) The book that is on the table belongs to the library.
(2) a supporting clause introduces the main clause,	drop the subject of the supporting clause, but be sure the subject is the first word of the main clause.	After I had analyzed the subject, I discovered she was right.

IF	THEN	EXAMPLE
(3) a word is so obvious it can be dropped,	drop it, and put a comma in its place.	(a) He was born in Keene, ~~in~~ New Hampshire, on July 4, ~~in~~ 1901. (b) This bowl is made of earthenware; that one, ~~is made of~~ plastic.
(4) a long expression is used to show ownership,	add 's to any singular noun; add ' to a plural noun that ends in s; add 's to a special plural that doesn't end in s; use special forms without ' for pronouns.	(a) John's car (b) The boys' cars (c) The men's cars (d) My car, her car, its feet, our car, their cars

12. Give all special descriptions the proper emphasis. (Chapter 4)

Special descriptions are just another way to develop an idea. If the special description is not a sentence, how you treat it depends on the emphasis you think it deserves.

IF	THEN	EXAMPLE
(1) it makes the meaning more specific,	don't set it off.	He said that the play Sleuth was very good.
(2) it is just the usual extra information that could be dropped,	set it off by commas.	I saw one play this year, Sleuth.
(3) it is extra information that you want to emphasize,	set it off by dashes. Dashes cancel all punctuation except ? or !.	I saw one play—Sleuth—this year.

(4) it is extra information that you want to de-emphasize,	set if off by parentheses. No punctuation goes before the (; and no punctuation goes before the) except ? or !.	(a) I saw one play (Sleuth) this year. (b) I saw one play (Sleuth), but I saw many movies.

A special description may also be a complete sentence. In that case, you couldn't use commas to set it off. But there are other treatments, again depending on the emphasis you want.

IF	THEN	EXAMPLE
(1) it is a side remark that really isn't part of the main thread of the paragraph,	set if off by itself in parentheses; start with a capital and end with a period.	He showed me the photographs. (He is a good photographer.) They were all of his wife, who looked like a very interesting character.
(2) it is an explanation that you don't want to emphasize,	set if off by parentheses within the sentences; don't start with a capital or end with a period; don't use punctuation before a (; use nothing except ? or ! before a).	He showed me the photographs (they were all of his wife), and I could see that he was good.
(3) it is an explanation that you want to emphasize,	set it off by dashes; dashes cancel all other punctuation except ? or !.	He showed me the photographs—he's really good!—and I asked him to take some of my nephew.

(See also Chart 2, entries 1 and 8.)

13. Simplify long descriptive phrases or clauses by clustering a few key words. (Chapter 5)

Two- or three-word descriptions often carry a lot more punch than the longer phrase or clause, and certainly they lead to word economy, as in the following examples:

	ORIGINAL	REVISION
(1)	He wrote an article that was long and poorly organized.	He wrote a long, poorly organized article.
(2)	The professor wanted a paper that would be four or five pages.	The professor wanted a four- or five-page paper.

(Entry 11 on Chart 2 reviews punctuation for two- and three-word descriptions.)

14. Emphasize the relationship between a set of sentences by presenting them as a list. (Chapter 6)

A list screams a relationship between ideas because all the items are expressed in a consistent form.

In comparing (a) and (b), you'll agree that the treatment in (b) emphasizes the thread binding these items together—strangely enough, by keeping them apart. As you can see, the words in both samples are identical.

(a) There are only a limited number of reasons why people send their children to private schools. They feel that private schools offer better academic training. They simply want to flaunt their wealth. They're looking for social contacts for themselves. They're avoiding the social issues of public-school education.

(b) There are only a limited number of reasons why people send their children to private schools:

(1) They feel that private schools offer better academic training.
(2) They simply want to flaunt their own wealth.
(3) They're looking for social contacts for themselves.
(4) They're avoiding the social issues of public-school education.

Chart 2, entries 12 to 15, summarizes the various ways of treating lists. Be sure the list is consistent, whatever form you choose.

15. Check to see that subject, verb, and possessive pronoun agree. (Chapter 7)

You will probably write agreeing subject, verb, and possessive unless you become so involved in the writing that you forget about agreement. But watch for these common pitfalls.

IF	THEN	EXAMPLE
(1) a distracting phrase or clause intervenes between the subject one and the verb,	ignore the interven-ing phrase, and use a singular verb and possessive.	One of their three children is an artist.
(2) a pronoun like everyone is the subject,	use a singular verb and possessive.	Everyone knows his own mind.
(3) the word number is the subject,	(a) if the subject is a number, use a plural verb.	(a) A number of students are going.
	(b) if the subject is the number, use a singular verb.	(b) The number of protesters has decreased.
(4) a collective noun is the subject,	(a) use a singular verb and possessive if the noun repre-sents a single unit.	(a) The jury is unanimous in its decision.
	(b) use a plural verb and possessive if the noun repre-sents a plural .	(b) The class are divided in their ideas.

(See also Chart 2, entries 16 to 19.)

16. Check to see that you are consistent in time and point of view. (Chapter 8)

Inconsistencies in time or viewpoint are very common, especially in first drafts. To prevent confusion, you should read through your drafts once just to check consistency. When you have chosen a time or viewpoint, make sure you do not shift abruptly without reason.

	VIEWPOINT	USE	EXAMPLE
(1)	the writer's,	use I.	I read the book.
(2)	the reader's,	use you.	You read the book.
(3)	impersonal,	use a noun or pronoun.	(a) The students read the book. (b) They read the book.
(4)	common to writer and reader,	use we.	We realize the sad state of affairs.

	TIME	USE	EXAMPLE
(1)	for something that already happened,	use the past tense.	He won the election.
(2)	for something that is happening now or happens habitually,	use the present tense.	(a) He is voting Republican this year. (b) He always votes Republican.
(3)	for something that is going to happen,	use the future tense.	He will vote this year.

17. If you use the word "only" or "just," make sure it carries the meaning you want. (Chapter 8)

Where you put little words like only and just can affect the meaning of the entire sentence.

EXAMPLE	MEANS
1. Only children go to these parties.	no one else but children goes to these parties.
2. Children only go to these parties.	they go, but that's all they do.
3. Children go only to these parties.	they don't go to any other parties.

In general, you should try to put a word like only or just as close as possible to the word it describes.

18. Check the passive sentences to see if any should be made active. (Chapter 8)

In an active sentence the doer of all the action is also the subject of the verb. But in a passive sentence, the real doer may not even be mentioned. The verb has a subject, but this subject is actually the one who receives the action—not the one who does it. This kind of passive is often appropriate—sometimes more appropriate than its active counterpart would be.

Here are two occasions when you would probably choose the passive:

	IF	USE PASSIVE	NOT ACTIVE
(1)	the real doer of the action is obvious,	His contribution is appreciated.	His country appreciates his contribution.
(2)	the real doer of the action is not important,	He was driven to the station.	The taxi driver drives him to the station.

In the first sentence in the table on the previous page we would know from the context who was doing the appreciating. In the second, we're not concerned about who took him to the station; our concern is only that he got there. (However, if something happened on the way to the station that involved the taxi driver, the active form would be preferable.)

As a further example, (a) below has mostly passive sentences, whereas (b) has mostly actives. Note the effect of passives here—either because the real doer of the action is unimportant or because he is so obvious he doesn't need to be mentioned.

(a)

(1) The Soviet practice of giving free but unwanted psychiatric treatment to imprisoned writers is well known. (2) But the list of outrageous Soviet prison sentences is almost as long as the sentence. (3) One was given to Valentyn Merez after a secret trial in the Ukraine. (4) And Mersey Kalik, the film-maker, was expelled from his union for having applied for a visa to Israel.

(b)

We all know the Soviet practice of giving free but unwanted psychiatric treatment to imprisoned writers. (2) But the list of outrageous Soviet prison sentences is almost as long as the sentence. (3) Valentyn Merez got one after a secret trial in the Ukraine. (4) And his union expelled Mersey Kalik, the film-maker, for applying for a visa to Israel.

Whichever passage you prefer, you'll probably agree that the passives at least aren't objectionable.

But passives can be very awkward. Usually the clue to an awkward passive is that the real doer of the action is introduced by the word <u>by</u> and <u>follows</u> the verb; the doer is not the subject of the verb.

Compare these two versions below of essentially the same passage: (c) has mostly passive sentences; (d) has all active sentences.

(c)

(1) <u>A number</u> of writers <u>have been imprisoned by Mexico</u> since July 1968, with no formal charges and no indication of a trial date. (2) Novelist <u>José Revueltas is</u> one—a man in his sixties and in extremely poor health. (3) <u>A letter was written by playwright Arthur Miller</u> inquiring about him. (4) <u>But Mr. Miller was advised by</u> the then <u>President Diaz</u> to mind his own business. (5) Yet about the same time <u>a meeting was held by Diaz and LBJ</u> to congratulate one another on the great relations between their two countries.

(d)

(1) <u>Mexico has imprisoned</u> a number of writers since July 1968, with no formal charges and no indication of a trial date. (2) Novelist <u>José Revueltas is</u> one—a man in his sixties and in extremely poor health.

(3) Playwright Arthur Miller wrote a letter inquiring about him. (4) But the then President Diaz advised Mr. Miller to mind his own business. (5) Yet about the same time Diaz and LBJ met to congratulate one another on the great relations between their two countries.

You'll probably agree that (d), the direct approach, sounds much stronger. And notice that it is shorter.

19. Make sure you haven't used any unnecessary words. (Chapter 9)

Even when you have presented your ideas in a logical sequence and have checked to see that you have not repeated any of them in unnecessary sentences, excess words can still clog up your sentences and obscure your meaning. Here are two clues to useless words that you can look out for:

CLUE	IF	THEN	EXAMPLE
(1) The word there	(a) it is the only subject of the sentence,	(a) keep it.	(a) There are two solutions
	(b) it is not the main subject of the sentence,	(b) drop it and the is or are with it, and revise the sentence.	(b) ~~There is no solution~~ you can't give a solution.
(2) The word it used as the subject of a verb	(a) it represents the real subject, which has already been mentioned,	(a) keep it.	(a) I dropped biology. It bored me.
	(b) it is just a hedge to hide the real subject,	(b) revise the sentence without the it.	(b) ~~It is probable that~~ the Padres probably will lose again.

Wordy expressions are harder to spot, but they crop up in everybody's writing. Look out for these particularly:

COMMON WORDY EXPRESSIONS	POSSIBLE REDUCTIONS
(1) owing to the fact that	(1) because, since
(2) the fact that he could not be found	(2) his disappearance
(3) she is a person who	(3) she
(4) used for study purposes	(4) used for study
(5) in the vicinity of	(5) near
(6) call to your attention	(6) remind you
(7) in regard to	(7) about, for
(8) in a defensive manner	(8) defensively
(9) question as to whether	(9) whether, question whether

Another kind of waste is an expression that at least partly repeats another word or expression in the same sentence. Here are some common offenders and their treatments:

REPETITIOUS EXPRESSIONS	EXAMPLES
(1) evident (or visible) to the eye	His defects were not visible ~~to the eye~~.
(2) continue to remain	Relations ~~continue to~~ remain friendly. (OR delete <u>to remain</u>, whichever is appropriate.)
(3) such as . . . etc.	He wore warm clothing, such as heavy sweaters *and* long, heavy socks. ~~etc.~~
(4) large in size	The rooms are large. ~~in size~~
(5) more preferable	Action verbs are ~~more~~ preferable.
(6) personally I	~~Personally~~ I like the mountains.

(7)	while at the same time	He took French ~~while~~ at the same time he took Spanish. (OR delete <u>at the same time</u>.)
(8)	repeats over again	History repeats. ~~over again.~~
(9)	shape or form	We carry boxes in every shape. ~~or form.~~ (OR delete <u>shape.</u>)
(10)	each and every	Each ~~and every~~ voter must decide for himself. (OR delete <u>each</u>.)

20. <u>Check to see that you have been as positive and definite as possible</u>. (Chapter 10)

Good writing is vigorous. Here are a few ways to make your writing stronger:

	IF YOU SEE	THEN	EXAMPLE
(1)	a general noun,	change it to a specific noun.	He reads *The New York Times* ~~the newspaper~~ every day.
(2)	a general verb plus a phrase or adverb,	change it to a specific verb.	He *slaved* ~~worked like a slave~~ on that report.
(3)	a general verb plus a noun,	change it to a specific verb.	He *questioned* ~~raised the question~~ whether hot pants were appropriate for the office.
(4)	(a) the word <u>not</u>, unless it is used to show a contrast,	(a) try to find a substitute that will avoid <u>not</u>.	(a) He *disobeyed* ~~did not obey~~ his own principles.
	(b) the word <u>not</u> used for showing a contrast,	(b) keep it.	(b) He needs love, not discipline.

IF YOU SEE	THEN	EXAMPLE
(5) a hedge like rather or pretty	try to use something more specific.	He was ~~pretty unhappy~~ disappointed about the outcome.

Still another way to achieve vigor in your writing is to drop the clichés. They're so comfortable and familiar that they no longer attract attention. Here are a few common ones you can learn to avoid:

(1) after all is said and done
(2) a good time was had by all
(3) age before beauty
(4) the best-laid plans of mice and men
(5) a sight for sore eyes
(6) I saw my whole life pass before my eyes
(7) circumstances over which I have no control
(8) all good things must come to an end
(9) a fate worse than death
(10) it isn't the heat, it's the humidity
(11) members of the opposite sex
(12) by and large
(13) along these lines
(14) it goes without saying
(15) do your thing
(16) freaks out
(17) as luck would have it
(18) grew like Topsy
(19) good luck in all your endeavors
(20) his better half

No list could cover all clichés, of course. The clue is this: If a group of words comes to mind easily, it is probably a cliché.

You should also try to avoid big, fancy words (usually they come from Latin) when plain ones will do. If they don't add a new dimension besides the extra letters, they're just pretentious space-wasters. Here are a few you can avoid, with alternatives:

FANCY WORD	USE INSTEAD
(1) utilize	use
(2) possess	has
(3) attain	reach
(4) informed	told
(5) desire	want

Compare the two versions of the following passage: (a) is general, vague, and pretentious. Notice how much more vigorous version (b) sounds:

(a)

All of us who are now adults had our instruction with history books that didn't make much mention of the role of black Americans. We were not taught that 3,000 blacks risked their lives fighting in the Revolutionary War. We were not taught that 200,000 blacks served as Union soldiers during the war almost a hundred years later, or that blacks provided a number of able seamen to the New England whalers of the nineteenth century.

(b)

We adults studied history books that overlooked the role of black Americans. We read nothing about the 3,000 blacks who fought in the Revolutionary War. We learned nothing about the 200,000 black Union soldiers during the Civil War, or the many black seamen with the New England whalers in the nineteenth century.

21. Check to see that you have handled the details consistently and accurately. (Chapter 11)

Now for the details, the odds and ends. First, you should make certain that you haven't made any spelling errors. A good speller is often the one who takes the time to check the spelling of a word. If you're uncertain about a spelling, look it up in the dictionary.

A second detail to check is capitalization. The general rule is to capitalize a word if it is a particular name (or a part of a particular name). But use a lower-case (small) letter at the beginning of a word that is just a general reference to a special name. As an example, you would capitalize Bayer's in Bayer's aspirin because Bayer's is a particular name of a drug. But you would not capitalize aspirin because it is just a general reference to a drug. Consult Chart 3 for specific examples.

Two other kinds of special situations are the title of a publication and the use of quotation marks with other punctuation. Entries 27 and 28 in Chart 2 outline these situations.

The last kind of detail to check is a number: Should you spell it out or use a figure? There are many sets of rules or conventions that you can adopt. The one recommended here is easy and useful for most writing (except technical writing). The general rule is to spell out any whole number under 100 and to use the figure for 100 or over. You can consult Chart 4 for exceptions.

Once you've completed your changes, go through the manuscript one more time to make sure it reads smoothly. Then type up the final copy. But don't forget the important last step: proofreading. Proofreading means that you check the final copy to see that all revisions were included and any typing errors corrected.

And there you have it: the final manuscript.

CHART 1: COPYEDITING SYMBOLS

ERROR	SYMBOL	MEANING	EXAMPLE
1. SENTENCE SHOULD HAVE BEEN INDENTED TO BEGIN A NEW PARAGRAPH.	¶	A new paragraph starts here.	¶ This sentence should have started a new paragraph, but it didn't. ¶ So, I put a paragraph symbol there.
2. SENTENCE SHOULD NOT HAVE BEEN INDENTED BECAUSE IT DOES NOT BEGIN A NEW PARAGRAPH.		This sentence should not start a new paragraph.	The next sentence should not have started a new paragraph. So, I inserted a "run-together" symbol.
3. WORDS (OR A SENTENCE) ARE OUT OF ORDER.		Transfer the words to the place indicated by the arrow.	He a new bike won.
4. LETTERS OR WORDS NEXT TO ONE ANOTHER ARE IN A REVERSE ORDER.		Rearrange the letters or words.	We can nveer be sure.
5. WORDS, LETTERS, OR PUNCTUATION MARKS NEED TO BE TAKEN OUT.		Take out.	This, this iss my motto.
6. SOMETHING NEEDS TO BE ADDED.	^	Insert.	This ^is my motto.

CHART 1 : COPYEDITING SYMBOLS (Continued)

ERROR	SYMBOL	MEANING	EXAMPLE
7. A LOWER-CASE LETTER SHOULD BE A CAPITAL.	≡	Capitalize.	Today is mike's birthday.
8. A CAPITAL LETTER SHOULD BE A LOWER-CASE LETTER.	/	Make a capital letter a lower-case (small) letter.	Today Is Mike's birthday.
9. AN ABBRE-VIATION OR A FIGURE SHOULD BE SPELLED OUT.	○	Spell out.	The margin is 2 in.
10. TOO MUCH SPACE IS AL-LOWED BETWEEN LETTERS OR WORDS.	⁀‿	Close up the space.	That is the problem over all.
11. NOT ENOUGH SPACE IS AL-LOWED BETWEEN LETTERS OR WORDS.	# or ⌐	Add space.	Thatis theproblem these days.
12. A LETTER OR A WORD SHOULD BE IN ITALIC TYPE.	___	Use italic type.	Mary McCarthy wrote The Groves of Academe.
13. A LETTER OR A WORD SHOULD BE IN BOLDFACE TYPE.	~~~	Use boldface type.	Remember this principle!

CHART 1: COPYEDITING SYMBOLS (Continued)

ERROR	SYMBOL	MEANING	EXAMPLE
14. SOMETHING WAS DELETED BY MISTAKE.	stet	matter that was previously canceled should be retained.	stet ~~You should never say this.~~ . . . . .
15. MATTER WAS NOT INDENTED AS IT SHOULD HAVE BEEN.	] [	matter is to be indented.	]This matter is [to be indented.

CHART 2: SITUATIONS AND THEIR TREATMENTS

SITUATION	IF	THEN	EXAMPLE
1. ANY SUPPORTING CLAUSE OR PHRASE THAT INTRODUCES A MAIN CLAUSE	(a) it is a clause or any phrase except an essential one,	(a) set it off by a comma.	(a) After he warned us, he left.
	(b) it is a short, essential phrase,	(b) don't set it off by a comma.	(b) In the fall the leaves turn.
2. ANY SUPPORTING CLAUSE OR PHRASE THAT INTERRUPTS OR FOLLOWS A MAIN CLAUSE	(a) it interrupts the sentence flow or is not essential,	(a) set it off by a comma(s).	(a) The law, as I found out, isn't clear on it. The law isn't clear on it, as I found out.
	(b) it follows the main clause and is essential,	(b) don't set it off by a comma.	(b) I cried when I saw him. We drove to the airport.
3. A SPECIAL SUPPORTING CLAUSE THAT DESCRIBES A PERSON OR THING IN THE MAIN CLAUSE	(a) it is extra information,	(a) set it off by comma(s); for a person use <u>who</u> (as subject) or <u>whom</u>; for a thing use <u>which</u>.	(a) Mr. Smith, who is only fifty, retired. Mr. Smith, whom we just met, retired. My check, which was late, finally came.
	(b) it is essential information,	(b) don't set it off by comma(s); use <u>that</u> for everything; for a person also use <u>who</u> (as a subject) or <u>whom</u>.	(b) He is the boy who (that) won. He is the boy whom (that) we met. This is the book that we read.

CHART 2: SITUATIONS AND THEIR TREATMENTS (Continued)

SITUATION	IF	THEN	EXAMPLE
4. ADVERB	(a) it links two main clauses,	(a) put a comma after it only if it has four or more letters. (Don't put a comma after <u>and</u>, <u>so</u>, <u>but</u>, <u>or</u>, <u>nor</u>, <u>yet</u>.)	(a) I like English, but I like math more. I like English; however, I like math more.
	(b) it is not a linking adverb,	(b) set it off by comma(s) only if the reader should pause to emphasize it.	(b) Sometimes I like to watch TV. Sometimes, I like to watch TV.
5. TWO MAIN CLAUSES JOINED	(a) no linking adverb is used, to indicate a close relationship,	(a) put a semicolon between the two main clauses.	(a) I worked late many nights; I hated it.
	(b) a short linking adverb) (<u>and</u>, <u>but</u>, <u>yet</u>) is used to be informal,	(b) put a comma between the two main clauses.	(b) He wore a coat, but he was cold.
	(c) a four-letter adverb (or longer) is used for variety or for emphasis,	(c) put a semicolon between the two main clauses.	(c) He wore a coat; however, he was cold.
	(d) at least one main clause has a phrase or supporting clause set off by commas,	(d) put a semicolon between the two main clauses no matter what the linking adverb is.	(d) Even though he wore a coat, he was cold; but he stayed on the post.

CHART 2: SITUATIONS AND THEIR TREATMENTS (Continued)

SITUATION	IF	THEN	EXAMPLE
5. TWO MAIN CLAUSES JOINED (Continued)	(e) the second clause is an explanation of the first, for a dramatic effect,	(e) put a colon after the first clause and capitalize the first word of the second. (If the explanation is not a clause, don't capitalize the first word.)	(e) He won three letters: He is a talented athlete. (He won two letters: in track and in fencing.)
6. A SET OF UNLINKED SENTENCES		(a) sentences may be linked by linking adverbs and other transitions. (b) a pronoun is substituted for a noun if the reference is clear. (c) a word or phrase purposely is repeated for emphasis. (d) the patterns and lengths of the sentences are varied.	(a-d) After a lifetime of exposure to many pesticides, human beings may have accumulated enough to suffer genetic effects. After the deposit of so much mercury in human beings' waterways, swordfish have unsafe concentrations. Among other excessive deposits in foods have been the additions of artificial preservatives and flavors.

CHART 2: SITUATIONS AND THEIR TREATMENTS (Continued)

SITUATION	IF	THEN	EXAMPLE
7. A SPECIAL DESCRIPTION: NOT A SENTENCE	(a) it narrows the meaning and makes it more specific,	(a) don't set it off.	(a) The book <u>Rebecca</u> was also a movie.
	(b) it is the usual nice-to-know, extra information,	(b) set it off by commas.	(b) His first book, a novel, was a success.
	(c) it is extra information that should be emphasized,	(c) set it off by dashes, which cancel all punctuation except <u>?</u> or <u>!</u>.	(c) His first book--a novel? --was a success. This was his first book--a novel--but it was a great success.
	(d) it is extra information that should be de-emphasized,	(d) set it off by parentheses. No punctuation goes before the opening parenthesis. No punctuation goes before the closing parenthesis except <u>?</u> or <u>!</u>.	(d) His first book (a novel!) was a success. This was his first book (a novel), and it was a great success.

CHART 2: SITUATIONS AND THEIR TREATMENTS (Continued)

SITUATION	IF	THEN	EXAMPLE
8. A SPECIAL DESCRIPTION: A SENTENCE	(a) it is set off by itself,	(a) enclose in parentheses. (It begins with a capital and ends with a period.)	(a) The photo was great. (It was of his father.)
	(b) it is within another sentence and it needs to be emphasized,	(b) same as 7c.	(b) He is tall—is he over 6 feet?—and he's fat.
	(c) it is within another sentence and needs to be de-emphasized,	(c) same as 7d.	(c) He is tall (he's over 6 feet), and he's fat.
9. A SPECIAL DESCRIPTION: EXPRESSES OWNERSHIP	(a) a noun is the owner,	(a) add 's to all singular nouns, even one that ends in s. Add ' alone to all plural nouns ending in s. Add 's to plural nouns not ending in s.	(a) Mary's bell Tess's bell the girls' bell the children's bell
	(b) a pronoun is the owner,	(b) use the special form without an apostrophe: my, our, your, his, her, their, its, or whose,	(b) This is its home now.
10. A SPECIAL DESCRIPTION: OBVIOUS WORDS LEFT OUT	(a) a word or words are obvious between city and state or between day and year,	(a) drop the obvious word, or words, and insert a comma instead.	(a) I was born in Newark ~~in the state of~~, Ohio, on June 8 ~~in~~, 1932.

CHART 2: SITUATIONS AND THEIR TREATMENTS (Continued)

SITUATION	IF	THEN	EXAMPLE
10. A SPECIAL DESCRIPTION: OBVIOUS WORDS LEFT OUT (Continued)	(b) other words are obvious or are repeated from a similar situation,	(b) same as 10a.	(b) This bowl is ~~made of~~ pewter; that bowl, ~~is made of~~ silver.
11. A TWO-WORD DESCRIPTION	(a) a descriptive word is an -ly adverb,	(a) no punctuation is necessary.	(a) He is a politically active student.
	(b) two descriptive words or units separately describe different characteristics of the noun (you can't reverse them),	(b) same as 11a.	(b) He has two new pens. He has two red wool sweaters.
	(c) a descriptive word describes another descriptive word plus a noun acting as a unit (you can't reverse the descriptive words),	(c) same as 11a.	(c) They bought a new beach house. They bought a new frame beach house.
	(d) two descriptive words or units act together to describe the noun as if they were really one word,	(d) join the descriptive words by a hyphen. (With two descriptions alike except for the beginning word, shorten the first to the beginning word plus hyphen, if hyphen is necessary.)	(d) He makes short-range plans. He makes many short-range plans. (English is either a two-~~credit course~~ or ~~a~~ three-credit course.)

CHART 2: SITUATIONS AND THEIR TREATMENTS (Continued)

SITUATION	IF	THEN	EXAMPLE
11. A TWO-WORD DESCRIPTION (Continued)	(e) two descriptive words or units separately describe the noun, but both describe the same characteristic (you can insert <u>and</u> between them and you <u>can</u> reverse them).	(e) put a comma between them to mark where the <u>and</u> was dropped.	(e) It was a dull, dreary day. We spent three dull, dreary days there.
12. AN INTRODUCTION TO ANY COMPLETE LIST	(a) it is not a sentence,	(a) don't put any punctuation after it.	(a) His grades were A, B, and D.
	(b) an expression (<u>as follows</u> or <u>the following</u>) is added, to make a sentence,	(b) put a colon after it.	(b) His grades were as follows: A, B, and D.
	(c) it was already a sentence without <u>as follows</u> or <u>the following</u>,	(c) put a colon after it and a comma before <u>as follows</u>.	(c) His grades were fair, as follows: B, C, and D. He got the following grades: B, C, and D.

CHART 2: SITUATIONS AND THEIR TREATMENTS (Continued)

SITUATION	IF	THEN	EXAMPLE
13. A REGULAR, COMPLETE LIST	(a) no item has a comma and none is a sentence,	(a) use any introduction. Put a comma after each item except the last.	(a) He needs a hat, a coat, and shoes.
	(b) at least one item has a comma but none is a sentence,	(b) use any introduction. Put a semicolon after each item except the last.	(b) The train stopped at Hartford, Conn.: Springfield, Mass.; and. Pittsfield, Mass.
	(c) each item is a sentence,	(c) use introduction of form 12b or 12c. Put a semicolon after each part except the last. Capitalize first word of first item.	(c) He claims this: She was bound; she was gagged; and she was robbed.
14. AN OUTLINE LIST	(a) no item is a sentence,	(a) use any introduction. Number or letter each item; capitalize the first word of the first item; and separate items by commas or semicolons. Add <u>and</u> to next-to-last item (or <u>or</u> in a list of choices).	(a) He expects the following grades: (1) An A in French, (2) an F in math, and (3) a C in history.

CHART 2: SITUATIONS AND THEIR TREATMENTS (Continued)

SITUATION	IF	THEN	EXAMPLE
14. AN OUTLINE LIST (Continued)	(b) each item is a sentence or more than one sentence,	(b) do the same as in (a), but end with semicolons or periods if items are single sentences; end only with periods if items are more than one sentence. (Don't add <u>and/or</u> to next-to-last item if periods are used.)	(b) He told me this: (1) I want to be a senator; or (2) I want to be a governor.
15. AN INCOMPLETE LIST	(a) the introduction is a sentence followed by <u>such as</u> or <u>including</u>,	(a) put a comma (not a colon) before <u>such as</u> or <u>including</u>, but not after.	(a) His grades were excellent, including three A's.
	(b) introduction in a sentence followed by <u>as an example</u>, for example, etc.,	(b) put a comma (not a colon) before and after the expression with <u>example</u>.	(b) His grades were excellent, for example, three A's.
	(c) the main verb in the introduction is the verb <u>include</u>,	(c) handle the same as a regular, complete list.	(c) His grades include the following: 2 A's and 3 B's.

CHART 2: SITUATIONS AND THEIR TREATMENTS (Continued)

SITUATION	IF	THEN	EXAMPLE
16. THE WORD ONE IS THE SUBJECT		(a) the verb is singular, despite any intervening words. (The verb in an intervening supporting clause whose subject is who or that must be plural when who or that represents a plural.)	(a) One of the new students who are auditing the course is really a graduate.
17. A PRONOUN LIKE EVERYONE IS THE SUBJECT	anyone, everybody, each, none, anything, no one, everything, nothing, nobody, somebody, or someone is used,	the verb and possessive pronoun are singular.	Everyone has his own plans.
18. THE WORD NUMBER IS THE SUBJECT	(a) it is used with a,	(a) the verb and possessive pronoun are plural.	(a) A number of men are making their own plans.
	(b) it is used with the,	(b) the verb and possessive pronoun are singular.	(b) The number of men making its plans is growing.

CHART 2: SITUATIONS AND THEIR TREATMENTS (Continued)

SITUATION	IF	THEN	EXAMPLE
19. A COLLECTIVE NOUN LIKE TEAM IS THE SUBJECT	(a) it represents a single unit,	(a) the verb and possessive pronoun are singular.	(a) The group has voted its own interests.
	(b) it represents separate individuals,	(b) the verb and possessive pronoun are plural .	(b) The class are divided in their views.
20. A SHIFT IN VIEWPOINT OR IN TIME	(a) it is a shift in viewpoint,	(a) keep to one viewpoint unless there is reason to change. The subject is a pronoun for a personal viewpoint: you, the reader's; I, the writer's; we, the writer's and reader's. The subject is a noun (or pronoun replacement) for an impersonal viewpoint describing the topic.	(a) You expect to see a change. I expect to see a change. We expect to see a change. The change (it) will be apparent.
	(b) it is a shift in time,	(b) keep the verb to one time: the past tense for something that has happened; the present for something that	(b) I expect this to happen. You expect this to happen. We will expect you at once.

CHART 2: SITUATIONS AND THEIR TREATMENTS (Continued)

SITUATION	IF	THEN	EXAMPLE
20. A SHIFT IN VIEWPOINT OR IN TIME (Continued)		is happening; and the future for something that will happen.	
21. THE WORD <u>ONLY</u> OR <u>JUST</u>		put it as close as possible to the word you want it to limit.	She was the only daughter. (This means he didn't have any other daughters.) She just bought a car. (This means she bought a car a short time ago.)
22. A PASSIVE SENTENCE	(a) the real doer of the action is not mentioned, either because it is obvious or relatively unimportant,	(a) maintain the passive. (Change to active only if passive switches emphasis away from the doer too abruptly.)	(a) He was greeted warmly. He was escorted to his seat. (If emphasis was shifted too abruptly: Mary escorted him to his seat.)
	(b) the real doer of the action is mentioned after the verb and is introduced by the word <u>by</u>,	(b) make it active: Start with the real doer of the action.	(b) ~~He was bitten by~~ a rabid dog, bit him.
23. THE WORD <u>THERE</u>	(a) <u>there</u> is the subject,	(a) <u>there</u> is a suitable subject unless it is overused.	(a) There are actually two choices.

CHART 2: SITUATIONS AND THEIR TREATMENTS (Continued)

SITUATION	IF	THEN	EXAMPLE
23. THE WORD <u>THERE</u> (Continued)	(b) the sentence already has a subject, concealed by <u>there is</u> or <u>are</u>,	(b) take out the useless <u>there</u> and revise as necessary.	(b) ~~There are~~ too many students *are enrolled* in this course.
24. THE WORD <u>IT</u> AS THE SUBJECT	(a) the <u>it</u> represents something,	(a) don't change it if it's clear.	(a) This candy isn't good. It is too sweet.
	(b) the <u>it</u> doesn't represent anything,	(b) take out the <u>it</u> and recast the sentence as necessary: Decide how definite you want to be.	(b) ~~It is necessary for~~ a pitcher ~~to~~ *must* conserve his energy. ~~It is believed~~ grades in school are *believed to be* punishing. *The teachers* ~~It is~~ believe~~d~~ that grades in school are punishing.
25. THE WORD <u>NOT</u>	(a) you want to emphasize the negative or the contrast between a positive and a negative,	(a) keep <u>not.</u>	(a) He is not guilty. He is thirty, not forty.

CHART 2: SITUATIONS AND THEIR TREATMENTS (Continued)

SITUATION	IF	THEN	EXAMPLE
25. THE WORD NOT (Continued)	(b) there is no special reason to emphasize the negative,	(b) replace with a word with the same meaning that does not require not.	(b) Your boss did not obey the rules.
26. A HEDGE LIKE RATHER OR PRETTY	other examples: a little, a bit, very, awfully,	if possible, replace the hedge and the word it affects with a more specific word; or delete the hedge to be more definite.	Your boss is pretty upset. The children are rather restless.
27. THE TITLE OF ANY PUBLICATION	(a) it is the first or last word and any word in the middle with the exception of these in 27b,	(a) capitalize.	(a) In Cold Blood; The Holy Roman Empire
A. Capitalization	(b) it is a word in the middle and is an article, a linking adverb like and, but, or, nor, or the to in the infinitive;	(b) don't capitalize.	(b) Gone with the Wind; Ends and Means; or She Stoops to Conquer
B. Punctuation	(a) it is a book, movie, newspaper, magazine, opera (or is long enough to be a book),	(a) underline (italicize) it.	(a) Paradise Lost

CHART 2: SITUATIONS AND THEIR TREATMENTS (Continued)

SITUATION	IF	THEN	EXAMPLE
27. THE TITLE OF ANY PUBLICATION (Continued)	(b) it is only part of a book or is not long enough to be a book by itself,	(b) put quote marks around it.	(b) the T.V. show "Bonanza"
28. OTHER PUNCTUATION AT THE END OF A QUOTATION	(a) the quotation ends in a comma or a period,	(a) put the comma or period INSIDE the closing quote mark.	(a) I saw the show "Bonanza." I read the poem "Trees," and I loved it.
	(b) the quotation ends with a colon or a semicolon,	(b) put the colon or semicolon OUTSIDE the closing quote mark.	(b) He said, "I do not choose to run"; however, nobody believed him. "I do not choose to run": Calvin Coolidge.
	(c) the whole sentence is a question or an exclamation,	(c) the ? or ! goes OUTSIDE the closing quote.	(c) Who said, "I do not choose to run"? That's "Trees"!
	(d) the quotation is a question or an exclamation,	(d) the ? or ! goes INSIDE the closing quote.	(d) He said, "Why not!" He asked, "Why not?"
	(e) a quotation is within a quotation,	(e) use single quotes around a quotation within a quotation.	(e) I asked, "Did you like 'Trees'"?

CHART 2: SITUATIONS AND THEIR TREATMENTS (Continued)

SITUATION	IF	THEN	EXAMPLE
29. OTHERS			

CHART 3: CAPITALIZATION

GENERAL RULE: CAPITALIZE any word that is a special name, or a part of that name. But DON'T CAPITALIZE a word that is just a general reference to the special name.

SITUATION	IF	CAP	NO CAP	EXAMPLE
1. BUILDING STREET, OR OTHER PUBLIC PLACE	(a) it is actually a part of the name,	✓		(a) University Place the Plaza Hotel
	(b) it is a general term or not actually a part of the name,		✓	(b) Go back to the hotel.
2. TRADE NAME	(a) it is a trade name,	✓		(a) Kleenex
	(b) it is a general name for the product,		✓	(b) tissue
3. HIGH SCHOOL OR COLLEGE CLASS OR CLASS MEMBER			✓	(a) the freshman class
			✓	(b) a freshman
4. DAY OF THE WEEK, MONTH, OR SEASON	(a) it is a day of the week or a month,	✓		(a) Tuesday January
	(b) it is a season,		✓	(b) spring, fall, summer, winter
5. HOLIDAY		✓		Christmas Eve
6. FAMILY MEMBER	(a) it refers to a particular person, and is either a part of the name or is used instead of the name,	✓		(a) I'll ask Mother Uncle Jim

CHART 3: CAPITALIZATION (Continued)

SITUATION	IF	CAP	NO CAP	EXAMPLE
6. FAMILY MEMBER	(b) it is a general reference, or not actually a part of the name,		✓	(b) I'll ask my mother.
7. INSTITUTION, COMPANY, CLUB, OR OTHER ORGANIZATION	(a) it is a part of the name,	✓		(a) the League of Women Voters
	(b) it is a general reference to the name,		✓	(b) the league, the upper house of Congress
8. OFFICIAL TITLE	(a) it precedes the name and is a part of it,	✓		(a) Doctor Jones
	(b) it is not a part of the name,		✓	(b) Tom Jones, a doctor a doctor, Dr. Fry
9. GEOGRAPHICAL PLACE	(a) it is actually a part of the name,	✓		(a) the Sahara Desert,
	(b) it is not a part of the name, or it is a direction,		✓	(b) the California desert go north, go east
10. LANGUAGE OR RACE OR CULTURAL GROUP	(a) it is a special language or any special group distinguished by language, race, or religion,	✓		(a) Frenchman, English, Negro, Catholic
	(b) it is a group distinguished by color, size, or local usage,		✓	(b) white man, black man, redneck, midget

CHART 4: NUMBERS

GENERAL RULE: SPELL OUT any whole number that is less than 100; USE THE FIGURE for 100 and any higher whole number--also for numbers like scores.

EXCEPTION	IF	THEN	EXAMPLE
1. NUMBER BEGINNING THE SENTENCE	it is any size,	always spell it out.	Two hundred ten men and 105 women graduated.
2. ROUND NUMBER	(a) it is an even hundred or an even thousand,	(a) spell it out.	(a) He graded fifteen-hundred papers.
	(b) it is a million or a billion, and not money,	(b) use a figure, but spell out million or billion.	(b) It happened 2 billion years ago.
	(c) it is a large sum of money (million or billion),	(c) use a figure and a dollar sign, but spell out million or billion.	(c) They owed $2 million.
3. DATE		use the figures.	I was born January 4, 1955.
4. PART OF A BOOK		use the figures.	Figure 14 is in Chapter 4, page 98.
5. FRACTION OR DECIMAL FRACTION OR PERCENTAGE		use the figures.	He grew 1/2 inch. It grew by 80 percent.
6. NUMBERS IN THE SAME CATEGORY		Follow the general rule, but spell out an initial number; otherwise use figures for all if one is 100 or more.	About ten years ago one company had 120 employees; now that company has only 50 employees.

Index